WALLACE STEVENS' EXPERIMENTAL LANGUAGE: THE LION IN THE LUTE

WALLACE STEVENS' EXPERIMENTAL LANGUAGE: THE LION IN THE LUTE

Beverly Maeder

St. Martin's Press
New York

WALLACE STEVENS' EXPERIMENTAL LANGUAGE

Copyright © Beverly Maeder, 1999. All rights reserved. Printed in the United States of America. No part of this book may be used or reproduced in any manner whatsoever without written permission except in the case of brief quotations embodied in critical articles or reviews. For information, address St. Martin's Press, 175 Fifth Avenue, New York, N.Y. 10010.

ISBN 0-312-21334-4 (cloth)

Library of Congress Cataloging-in-Publication Data

Maeder, Beverly, 1944–
   Wallace Stevens' experimental language : the lion in the lute /
Beverly Maeder.
     p. cm.
  Includes bibliographical references and index.
  ISBN 0-312-21334-4 (cloth)
  1. Stevens, Wallace, 1879–1955—Criticism and interpretation.
  2. Experimental poetry, American—History and criticism.
  3. Stevens, Wallace, 1879–1955—Language. I. Title.
PS3537.T4753Z6776   1999
811'.52—dc21   99-12847
                                     CIP

Design by Binghamton Valley Composition

First edition: September, 1999
10 9 8 7 6 5 4 3 2 1

CONTENTS

ACKNOWLEDGMENTS

THE ROOTS OF THIS BOOK REACH BACK FAR BEFORE I EVER DREAMED THERE was such a writer as Stevens. The reading of Stevens that follows is based on the sense—even the sensation—that Stevens' poems and prose are written in a language that at first sight seems opaque even to the native speaker of English like myself. This is something we tend to forget as we read and come to create hypothetical landscapes and narratives from Stevens' poems. This book could not have been written without the conviction that it is possible to enter into an understanding of such a work while resisting the temptation of totally domesticating it. It means accepting both the enrichment of the encounter and the difference that makes the poetry other. This conviction may be linked to my own pleasure in the possibilities of encounter that exist more generally across languages and cultures and among academic disciplines. I am thankful to a number of teachers who fostered this sense, among them, in chronological order, my teachers of French literature at Brown, Harvard, and Lausanne who instilled in me the love of the difficult and the "other," Patrick Hanan who taught me that Quintilian could be respectfully used to elucidate twentieth-century Chinese literature, and James Schroeter and Manfred Gsteiger who encouraged me to read eclectically.

At various phases of my work on Stevens, Peter Halter, Robert Rehder, and Helen Vendler, in their different voices, provided models of intellectual vitality and rigor. Each gave generously of his or her time, offering invaluable encouragement and support as well as concrete suggestions, and asking tough questions. Numerous colleagues sparked new reflections or read parts in progress, among them Jay Blair, Romy Berger, Luc Erne, Neil Forsyth, Toni O'Brien Johnson, Ian Kirby, Roelof Overmeer, Raymond Peitrequin, Peter Trudgill, Margaret Tudeau, and Boris Vejdovsky. Friends in other fields also helped me to tread paths outside the usual boundaries of literary studies. I mention only François Félix, Françoise Prebandier, Ann Arvin, Louise Yuhas, and Erik Maeder. Finally, my students helped me keep an ever fresh view of Stevens' poetry, not only by bringing new eyes and new readings to it but by communicating their enthusiasm. I would like to thank them all.

I am pleased to acknowledge the support of the University of Lausanne for arranging spaces during which I could work on this book and the Swiss National Science Foundation for awarding me an indispensable grant for research and travel.

I am grateful to the staff of the Literary Manuscripts section of the Huntington Library for the wonderful conditions they provided there. Thanks go to Ute Bargmann and Sue Hodson in particular. In addition, the staff of the Special Collections and Archives at the University of Massachusetts at Amherst, the staff of the United Nations Library in Geneva, and Robert J. Bertholf of the Poetry and Rare Books Collection at the State University of New York at Buffalo all receive grateful acknowledgment here. For the most recent phase, my deepest thanks go to Maura Burnett, who provided the first enthusiastic and encouraging editorial support, and Amy Reading, who gave invaluable assistance and met not only routine but emergency situations with particular competence.

Finally, I would like to thank Thor and Daphne for just being who they are, the way they are, and Erik for sustenance of mind and heart.

ABBREVIATIONS AND NOTE ON SOURCES

CP   *The Collected Poems of Wallace Stevens* (New York: Knopf, 1954)

Letters   *Letters of Wallace Stevens*, ed. Holly Stevens (New York: Knopf, 1966)

NA   *The Necessary Angel: Essays on Reality and the Imagination* (New York: Knopf, 1951)

OP   *Opus Posthumous*, ed. Milton J. Bates. Revised, enlarged, and corrected edition (New York: Knopf, 1989)

Palm   *The Palm at the End of the Mind: Selected Poems and a Play*, ed. Holly Stevens (New York: Knopf, 1972)

The Collected Poems of Wallace Stevens (CP) has been used as the source for all the poems collected in it.

In block quotations from certain long poems like "Thirteen Ways of Looking at a Blackbird" and "The Man with the Blue Guitar," the inclusion of a roman numeral at the head of a quotation indicates that the stanza or section is quoted in full.

INTRODUCTION

All poetry is experimental poetry.

—*Adagia* (*OP* 87)

Readers of Wallace Stevens have for years been struck by the way his poetry invites probing behind its metaphorical surfaces to call up the poet's ideas about our place in the world and about the role of language in our sense of being. The poet's lectures, collected in *The Necessary Angel: Essays on Reality and the Imagination*, have also seemed to legitimize such a search in the sense that Stevens depicts poetry and philosophy as pursuing the same reality through different means. Calling philosophy "the official view of being" that uses "reason" to "approach truth," he goes on to call poetry "an unofficial view of being" and to argue that poetry may even be superior to philosophy because the poet "finds a sanction for life in poetry that satisfies the imagination" (*NA* 40–41, 43). Thus, although Wallace Stevens did not use the terms epistemology or ontology, his readers have done so, untrained though most of us are in the rigors of philosophical argumentation. And critics schooled in what we call the humanist tradition of criticism have sought access to the philosophical "meaning" of Stevens' poetry through the academic disciplines that have passed down to us a selection of the writings of Plato or Aristotle, Kant, Nietzsche, Heidegger, and Derrida, to mention a few.

In the mid-sixties, when ten years had passed since Stevens' death and his *Letters* were being edited by his daughter, this sensitivity produced the first great wave of works on Stevens. It reflected Stevens' own stated concerns about expanding our sense of "reality." Many took up Stevens' own dualistic framework—"reality" and "imagination"—to apply them to the poetry itself. Thus J. Hillis Miller devoted a chapter of his *Poets of Reality*[1] to Stevens and accorded him the highest honor of being considered the only American modernist poet, along with Williams, to have created a new relationship between human consciousness and "reality." Miller's emphasis on consciousness or the mind takes into account an analysis of modern man finding himself alone in the universe, divested of divine support. If not all critics shared Miller's phenomenological focus on the mind, the question of the subject-object dichotomy in a secularized world was nonetheless foremost in the discourse of many of the principal writers on Stevens.[2]

Poetry then was seen by critics, as it was by Stevens himself, to enact a reaching out to a new world in which the transcendent order was reduced to a myth that no longer had relevance. The self therefore had a heightened responsibility in establishing its place in the given order—or disorder—of the outside world. The poet's poetry, it was felt, attempted to create new collective meanings by integrating the subject into this new world and binding the whole together, through language, to create a fiction of being.[3] Miller would see this task as unachievable, except insofar as the late poems, he says, "affirm themselves neither as imagination nor as reality but as both together."[4] Riddel would be persuaded of the reconciliation of tensions existing between self and world through poetry and would say about his book on Stevens, though guardedly: "My thesis, if I may claim one, is that Stevens' total work constitutes metaphysically the act of creating oneself (always, of course, within naturalistic possibility) and living (figuratively, but in a very real sense, actually) in poetry."[5]

Such preponderantly humanistic views of the function of poetry and of the attendant "meaningfulness" of language have continued to inform innumerable studies that display otherwise widely divergent orientations. At the risk of tremendous reduction, the great variety of existent approaches can be suggested by mentioning a few of them. Bloom's reading has put Freudian and kabbalistic thinking to bear upon the poet's struggle with his poetic forefathers and the rhetoricity of his own discourse.[6] Benamou searched in alchemical treatises a way of illuminating Stevens' holistic tendency.[7] Lentricchia and Leggett's literary historical approaches have shown the affinities or influences linking Stevens' ideas with those of William James or Charles Mauron and Henri Focillon.[8] Vendler's reading has elucidated parallels between Stevens and Keats, for instance, to draw a message out of the evolution of Stevens' style.[9] Gelpi and Perloff have inferred Stevens' conceptual stance in the contrastive light of poems by other modernists like William Carlos Williams and Ezra Pound.[10] A reflection on gender has been used by Nyquist to open up new perspectives on the expression of desire in Stevens' poetry.[11] Halliday's study of the way other people are acknowledged in the poems shows Stevens' persona to be deficient in intimacy.[12] Illuminating as such studies are, they seem to gravitate around the search for finding at least a kernel of stateable "meaning" in the poems. This kernel may be of many orders: that Stevens shows he "has evaded confronting the true center of being" in "The Motive for Metaphor";[13] that the supposed solipsism of "Tea at the Palaz of Hoon" is sterile; or that the "demand that the reader reanalyze" made in "The Snow Man" "is inseparable from the realization that [a pure] perception is forever unavailable," for instance.[14] Underlying these studies both old and new are assumptions about language that resemble those that many critics attribute to Stevens himself—that the prime task of language is to represent thought, perception, or imagination or, more subtly, something about poetry itself; that language is the human subject's way of making sense of the world and his or her complex relation to it. Yet the resistance Stevens' poetry presents to our understanding impels us to look at that part of language that stands before any stable translation and that has to do with the necessities of English itself.

Language-oriented "deconstructionist" discussions of poetry have pondered what happens to the function of language when it is seen to have lost its ground. Riddel, one of the first to adopt a deconstructionist view of literature, considered that modern poets and critics alike were placed in a dilemma in inheriting a "language of Being or presence." This conception of language, writes Riddel, stands "at the authoritative center of our thinking, and the varieties of dualism emanating from it compose the manifold of what was up to Nietzsche an unbroken western tradition."[15] If language then comes to be seen as fundamentally groundless and self-undermining, it is condemned to sign its own de-centeredness or its inability ever to name the absence that replaces the center. In criticism it seems to me that American versions of deconstructionist perspectives like Derrida's[16] (and even some parts of Derrida's work itself[17]) sometimes "fall" into the development of a "theory" that indeed cannot overcome this dilemma, for the theory still relies on a reality principle that is no longer a theological but an ontological one, by focusing as it does on the loss of a "center."[18]

All readers recognize that Stevens' language is ambiguous and multi-layered. The pleasure of exegetical sleuthing is unlimited for anyone who wants to pick apart grammatical constructions, mine etymologies, or exploit the secondary denotations of words given in the *Oxford English Dictionary* (as Stevens reportedly did). This pleasure, however, comes laden with a danger, a danger like the one Derrida identified in "White Mythology" as seeking in semantic depth an originary, historical, hard-and-fast reality behind the word. But as R. P. Blackmur intimated decades ago,[19] Stevens' poetry provides two kinds of pleasure, of which the search for a solid semantic basis may be only one. Along with the more austere pleasure of trying to root out sayable cognitive meanings, Stevens' work provides in large measure the more sensuous and nonconceptual pleasure of the direct apprehension of patterns, which we can call aesthetic pleasure. Observing this lends credence to a statement like the following, made by Stevens in a letter to one of his commentators in 1952: "My object is to write esthetically valid poetry. I am not so much concerned with philosophic validity."[20] Thus it may be possible to adopt an extra-ontological approach in which the philosophically oriented rhetoric of subject-object and language-object dualism is banished or at least attenuated.[21]

The patterns formed by the words and the grammar of Stevens' poetry then become an inexhaustible field for another kind of exploration. A number of critics have explored the aesthetic dimension of Stevens' poetry through its rhetorical structures, its figures of speech (metaphor, simile, etc.) and tropic patterns (anaphora, praeteritio, etc.). Like the work of the New Critics in the 1940s and 1950s, their studies focus less on ideas than on the materiality of the poems themselves, while remaining confident in the ability of language to construct a world view that is adequate to one's sense of it. To the extent that they can be grouped together, the works of Bloom, Vendler, and Cook,[22] for instance, all do this while reminding us of the poetic heritage Stevens is building on, be it Whitman and Emerson, Keats and the Romantics, or Dante, among others. As early as 1965, among the essays collected in *The Act of the Mind*, Helen Vendler and Mac Hammond[23] provided us with precious insights about Stevens' grammatical forms. Among the numerous textual surface features they noticed are the mitigations of modals (*might*, *may*), the "timeless, unqualified nature of infinitives," the frequent use of *as if*,[24] grammatical shifts when a word is repeated.[25] In those days, such features were read by Vendler as signs of what happens in "the poet's mind"; for Hammond they remained a repertory of what he called "metapoetry." These seminal essays showed the difference that exists between taking statements made in poems as stable entities and noticing how "qualified" Stevens has made them, how resistant to definition they are. Yet most close readers have subordinated their insights to defining Stevens' thought, mind, or even desires—whether in the mode of humanist criticism centered on notions of the "self," or deconstructive criticism centered on finding an implicit theory of language in Stevens' poems. Even Rosu's recent work, which approaches Stevens' language as something other than representational, cannot avoid seeing ideas or cognition as somehow, though not represented, "enacted" in the sound patterns it produces.[26]

Thus, although critics have taken into account various linguistic tactics that prevent Stevens' poems from coalescing into stable statements, few have focused on the material body of the poems' trajectories or taken a hard look at the non- or extra-ontological implications of his particular uses of English lexis and syntax. Yet if Stevens is an "introspective voyager," he is also a voyager through a landscape of language, an artist who pays attention to its minutest details before choosing and adjusting the elements of his composition. These details are not only the denotative and connotative possibilities of the English vocabulary, although the semantic foundation of the signifier-signified bond is richly modulated through Stevens' metaphors, from inherited metaphors like the sun to new ones like the pineapple. Nor are they only suggestive words, like the title of "Somnambulisma" (CP 304), or resonant combinations of common words, like the "reader leaning late" in "The House Was Quiet and the World Was Calm" (CP 359). But often the signs of Stevens' work are integrated into a surface texture—the material body of language—that prevents a stable apprehension of hypothetical landscapes, narratives, arguments, or "ideas." What is more, Stevens explores the linguistic terrain through visibly foregrounding the functional possibilities of English—the articles the and a, prepositions, prefixes, and the verb to be—and disrupting reference among succeeding statements. While creating a referential opacity, Stevens' linear surfaces also bare the artifice of their own construction. It is the surface texture of Stevens' English that will be propelled into the foreground in the present book.

The chapters that follow therefore recognize the representational function of language—explored in various ways by phenomenological, rhetorical, deconstructionist, and historical critics—while emphasizing the ongoing linguistic adjustments made by the poems' speakers. Part I of this book attempts to modulate the traditional approach to Stevens' poems. It deals with the readjustments Stevens makes in relation to metaphor. We see that in the lyrics of *Harmonium* Stevens struggles with inherited theological and ontological metaphors, protesting against them or inverting their hierarchy. In a few poems in *Parts of a World*, on the other hand, the struggle "against" is superseded by one of Stevens' most exhilarating forms of exploration, the disruptive movement of appositional metaphors. Part II forages into linguistics to examine another kind of disruption, one effected by the seemingly banal and rigid use of the copula with *to be*. Here an extended reading of "Thirteen Ways of Looking at a Blackbird" serves as a prime example of the creative "artifice" that is made possible through copular relations. Through Stevens' baring of the functional core of language, English becomes a place for extra-ontological (as well as ontological) speculation. Part III is more patently exploratory. It examines "The Man with the Blue Guitar," a poem I consider to exemplify Stevens' ambivalent use of metaphor and his foregrounding of the functional core of English in the most daring way. The poem first gives a voice to an audience that is nostalgic for the outdated dream dealt with in Stevens' earlier poetry, the dream of a stable space of knowing and being that is speakable in language. The audience's demands provide a foil for the performer, who counterbalances this paradigm, not so much by contradicting it as by developing strategies that emphasize the instability of reference in language. Chapter 5 looks at tactics such as the way the performer encrypts topical events in the poem so as to reveal their linguistic precarity. Chapter 6 draws an inference from the music metaphor to demonstrate how the poem becomes an exercise in temporal, perishable ongoingness through its insistent making and unmaking of its own surface patterns.

Although it is undeniable that there is a general development in Stevens' poetry from visual to philosophical themes, for instance, the poet's experimentation with metaphor, syntax, and ongoingness does not follow a straight line. Rather, there is a movement back and forth among different approaches that are already present in the early poetry. The Epilogue of my book, then, reminds us that even in the poems of old age, which define the poet's own death as their horizon, the poetic texture exploits the lessons learned in the earlier poetry and continues to look forward in language, rather than backward toward causality.

This book does not trace the development of Stevens' strategies through his career but looks in depth at a few examples of his most radical and original experiments. Thus the sequence of chapters does not follow the chronology of Stevens' poems except insofar as the first poems discussed are from *Harmonium*, "The Man with the Blue Guitar" occupies Part III, and the last poems discussed are from *The Rock*. Rather, the chapters follow a methodological itinerary from a consideration of the referential value of metaphor, to a consideration of the extra-ontological possibilities of language; from concepts used in literature and philosophy, to those utilized in linguistics, and finally to some borrowed from the aesthetics of music; from an approach that responds to half a century of Stevens criticism, to a more free and experimental one; from the narrow field of Anglo-American literature, to a broader field of language in which English is one language among many and literature is an art form in some ways analogous to music. The itinerary followed thus might be said to move, in the words of "The Man with the Blue Guitar," from "the lion locked in stone" to "the lion in the lute."

Part I

1

❧

WORMY METAPHORS AND POEMS OF AGAINSTNESS

The twilight overfull
Of wormy metaphors.

—"Delightful Evening" (CP 162)

Metaphors and the Relation of Resemblance

Both Stevens' poetry and early commentaries on it were haunted by the shades of Wordsworth and Coleridge and the English poets who followed them. Stevens inherited a world conceived of in terms of interrelations between "imagination" and "reality." In such a world, the subject-self is seen as an agent of imaginative powers and of "speculative inquiry" confronted with the object-world that is "perceived immediately."[1] At the same time, the inherited object-world is also imbued with transcendent powers to which both literature and religion pay homage. The world with man in it can be seen as a harmonious and uplifting whole, such as the one Emerson evokes in "Nature" when he writes: "The stars awaken a certain reverence, because though always present, they are always inaccessible; but all natural objects make a kindred impression when the mind is open to their influence."[2] Similarly, in the world represented in Wordsworth's poetry, nature is the force that is "universally active" and reveals herself in the phenomena that the poet depicts.[3] God is the other force.

Stevens can be seen as sharing a modern discomfort toward inherited understanding of these forces. J. Hillis Miller was one of the first to review this discomfort systematically in turn-of-the-century Anglophone poets. In his early phenomenological study, *Poets of Reality,* he postulates that (as concerns his roster of major poets) by the later nineteenth century God had disappeared not only from the human subject's heart but from the object-world of nature. Miller, relying on Stevens' own prose writings in part, relates Stevens' "version of the death of the gods" to this transformed world view and goes so far as to say that the "vanishing of the gods . . . is the basis of all Stevens' thought and poetry."[4] By the 1950s when Stevens wrote "Metaphor as Degeneration" (CP 444–445) and "The River of Rivers in Connecticut" (CP 533), the "transcendent realm, above and beyond what men can see," Miller contends, is replaced by that which is "within things as they are, revealed in the glistening of the steeple at Farmington, in the flowing of time, in the presence of things in the moment, in the interior fons of man."[5]

In the course of his poetic career, Stevens reiterated, though with decreasing frequency, the idea that not only had the transcendent order disappeared from our visible world but the figures through which it had been represented were now outworn. Typically, as late as 1940, in "Asides of the Oboe," he enumerates three of them as "That obsolete fiction of the wide river in / An empty land; the gods that Boucher killed; / And the metal heroes that time granulates—" (CP 250). Thus he not only reconfirms the obsolescence of the divine order and the model it provided for erecting human heroes; he also unmasks those hierarchical constructs as having depended on, even having lived on, figures and forms elaborated by artists, such figures and forms as those represented metonymically here by fiction, painting, and bronze sculpture. Throughout his life, Stevens had an acute sense that history, as Vico remarked, is a history of the "progressive mental states" of humankind, and he extended his perception of these "mental states" to include the figures that are their outward expression. This is illustrated in the lecture "The Noble Rider and the Sound of Words," for instance, in which he discusses Plato's figure of the soul as a charioteer driving his winged horses across heaven. Plato's figure, Stevens claims, has become "antiquated and rustic," but not only because "the soul no longer exists." It is "antiquated and rustic" because the grounding of this figure in imagination rather than in reality no longer speaks to us.[6] We can only "understand" but not "participate in it" (NA 3–4) because the process of selecting and creating the figure no longer corresponds to ours.

The primary figure for Stevens was metaphor. Metaphor, by whatever name, has made possible much of our most moving poetry, from lyrics composed during the time of disorder between the Tang and Song dynasties in China, to Shakespearean sonnets six centuries later, to the poems of Wallace Stevens. Traditionally, Western writers have considered metaphor as a trope of resemblance.[7] The common denominator of resemblance merits attention because of its prevalence from Aristotle to Stevens and because of its capacity to bind together tropes such as metaphor, simile, personification, and prosopopoeia.[8] Before considering the properly linguistic issues attached to metaphor, I would like in this chapter to examine how Stevens tried to reconcile his skepticism toward traditional tropes with the presupposition that the resemblance between referents is the basis for the poet's work of metaphor.

Chapter 22 of Aristotle's *Poetics* has been translated diversely as saying that good metaphor is "the token of genius" because it "means an eye for resemblances," or that it implies "an intuitive perception of the similarity in dissimilars."[9] The presence of "dissimilars" implies that part of the task involved in metaphor-making depends on the metaphor-maker's ability to discriminate:[10] we find analogies in our environment by sifting the similar from the dissimilar. Aristotle's injunction that a good metaphor implies "an intuitive perception of the similarity in dissimilars" was marked in pencil by Stevens in the edition of the *Poetics* he probably read before he wrote his essay on "resemblance" (*NA* 71–82) in 1946 as part of "Three Academic Pieces."[11] In separating the "similar" from the "dissimilar," or "resemblance" from "difference," we implicitly refer to categories upon which resemblance and difference (inclusion and exclusion) can be founded. Thus in nature, a young girl's lips "resemble" cherries in respect to the category of color, and her youth "resembles" the spring of the year in respect to its freshness and promise. Resemblance here is a strategy for grouping objects or ideas within an implicit frame of reference, for assembling certain qualities or properties and not others, for sorting them according to certain criteria and not others.

Along with this sorting function, resemblance enables relations to be made. Suzanne Juhasz usefully stresses that metaphor is a transfer in which each term is significant but in which it is the total relationship that is primordial.[12] Thus metaphorical resemblance brings together separate realms within one sphere. Stevens also shared assumptions held by his contemporaries Williams and Pound that the power of metaphor as a "language form" is to "indicate relations that are at the core of [their] poetic concerns," and that metaphor can bridge the "gap" they were so aware of between subject and object, inner and outer.[13] On the highest level of empirical generality, the perception or conception of analogies allows us to establish patterns in our picture of the world according to selected—but often tacit—criteria. In Western narrative and poetry, figurations of divine and natural ontology have established structural bonds that integrate otherwise disparate things into a pattern. Such figurations, from Acheron and apple to Zeus and zodiac, bind our ordinary understanding of human life and speech to a supposed ground of meaning. The scheme of difference and resemblance becomes the tacit, a priori foundation for producing further metaphors of a divinely ordained order that situates man in nature with heaven above.

The poem "Delightful Evening" schematically illustrates this definition of metaphor and its effects. Herr Doktor takes on a meditative pose, grieving before a landscape that does not satisfy him, although it satisfies the speaker. With the "twilight overfull / Of wormy metaphors," the word "twilight" fits the little evening scene represented in the poem. But by punning on the signifier "light" and creating a spurious relationship between the obviously ironic "delight" and the two lights of "twilight," the poet sees to it that both delight and twilight are contaminated by disappointment. "Twilight" can be taken as a metaphor or metaphorical vehicle indicating a time of sterile maturity, a moment of dulled consciousness, the decline of a civilization. It can also be a *Götterdämmerung*, the twilight of the gods who are no longer believed in. The "wormy metaphors" (like the "rotted names" in "The Man with the Blue Guitar") attach a metaphorical adjective to the word "metaphors" to connote something like "meaningless words" or "invalid fictions." Thus "twilight," the first metaphorical substitution, brings into a relation of resemblance the world of the represented evening and a crisis of (perhaps metaphysical) consciousness. It links two realms, an inhuman with a human one, such as the cycle of day and evening with the pursuit of philosophical questions or a metaphysical ground. At the same time, the "wormy metaphors" self-referentially speak of the desperate ambition of finding a language with which to express relations. Read allegorically, then, "Delightful Evening" affirms the centrality of the trope of metaphor in maintaining a life-sustaining concept of a larger order of things, while at the same time it claims that concept to be bankrupt.

Stevens gives us other clues about the difficulties the disappearance of this order creates for using traditional metaphors in poetry. One specific difficulty is clearly articulated toward the end of his career when he returned to the theme in "The Course of a Particular" (*Palm* 367). In this lyric the leaves, which in an older day were emblematic of divinely imbued nature, do "not transcend themselves." They speak in a cry neither of "divine attention," nor of "puffed-out heroes," nor of human beings. They thus cry "without meaning more / Than they are in the final finding of the ear in the thing / Itself." This signifies that nature's sounds "mean" no more than the mere perception of them in the ear; more punningly, it also "means" that the cry "means" no more/no longer. The temporal dimension of the "course" lasts until the difference between the perceiver and the natural world translates as a feeling of indifference. "The Course of a Particular," a late poem (1951) that Stevens excluded from his *Collected Poems* in 1954, is an adieu to a hypothesis of natural and human vacuousness that had been ambiguously entertained in the early lyric "The Snow Man" (1921).

The contraction of meaning in "The Course of a Particular" is due to a change not in the leaves but in humankind. Lacking "fantasia," Stevens seems to be saying, modern observers may even lack the basic faculty Coleridge called "fancy," which Stevens interpreted as "an exercise of selection from among objects already supplied by association, a selection made for purposes which are not then and therein being shaped but have been already fixed" (*NA* 10–11).[14] The vestiges of an old schema of resemblance or analogy only reveal the separateness of each part. What is lacking here is a *source* of metaphorical activity—that is, the subject's imagination or interpretive skill to create new resemblances. For in a realist conception of the world like Stevens', metaphors in stories and poems should be understood on the representational level as an active production of the human eye, mind, imagination, not as a mere deciphering of signs or signatures that are given.[15] In "Three Academic Pieces" he says most clearly, "Resemblance in metaphor is an activity of the imagination," and it should not derive from mere "imitation" or "identity manqué" (*NA* 73) but be the fruit of a creative vision. Thus Stevens himself, at least until the early 1940s, saw the "act of satisfying the desire for resemblance" as the central activity of poetry. The linguistic means of "enhanc[ing] the sense of reality" (*NA* 77) was the domain of metaphor in its broadest sense.

Two of the great challenges for Stevens throughout much of his career were, in this context, first, to work against and undo old metaphorical equivalences, and second, to devise ways of using metaphorical resemblance to open up compositional potential and development. The younger Stevens wrote numerous short lyrics that grapple with the vestiges of those specific inherited metaphors that defined the place of human beings in the order of things natural and divine. Stevens' struggle is a struggle against the old "order" on which human purpose used to be founded, as has often been remarked. But it is one thing to brush away old notions of divinity with the comment, "And what's above is in the past / As sure as all the angels are" ("Evening without Angels," CP 136), or "She sang beyond the genius of the sea" ("The Idea of Order at Key West," CP 128). It is another thing to write liberated poetry in a *Götterdämmerung*, an "Evening without Angels" or a not so "Delightful Evening" that is a "Twilight overfull / Of wormy metaphors" (CP 162).

As a poet of "againstness" from *Harmonium* to *Parts of a World*, Stevens struggled furiously against the confinements of the hierarchical underpinnings of metaphysical order inherent in the play of old metaphorical resemblances. Metaphors of transcendent authority, both divine and natural, were worked into poems that show dependence on this authority to be chastising and inhibiting to the modern poet's freedom. It is my contention that Stevens was implicitly working less against the idea of divinity and its immanence in nature per se than against the hierarchical patterning the idea imposes on human imaginative and linguistic development. This can be seen as an important if largely unstated challenge to Stevens.

Metaphors of Divine Order

Figurations of both divine and natural order are continually present in the poetry of Stevens' contemporaries, even though the decline of traditional belief had made the place of a transcendent force in individual destiny problematic, and the metaphors for them had started to seem "antiquated and rustic" to many. But whereas T. S. Eliot would reintroduce Christian doctrine into his poetry (and convert to Anglicanism), Stevens would keep up a poetic (and public) stance that contested the hegemony of Christian doctrine and generally treated the issue with less frequency and less urgency as he evolved. It is for this reason that most of the poems in this section on metaphors of divine and natural order are drawn from the earlier poetry, primarily from *Harmonium* (1923), with only a few incursions into *Parts of a World* (1942) for comparison or contrast.

The ontological-theological order that Stevens inherited is authorized by a hierarchical system that appears in the poetry as restrictive and deceptive. A number of poems in *Harmonium* indeed approach the problem of worn-out religion through its most restrictive avenue—the eschatological component of Christianity, a perspective that implies not only a hierarchy of power but also a merging of God's power over and purpose for us with our mortal end. As Montaigne punningly complained, the emphasis in Christian doctrine on the rewards of heaven confuses the *bout* of life, its final end or moment, with the *but*, a life's goal or purpose.[16]

A good deal of the explicit "againstness" we find in Stevens' early poetry satirizes the primacy that metaphysical tenets give to heavenly reward over earthly satisfactions. The second poem in *Harmonium*, "Invective against Swans" (*CP* 4),[17] attacks the eschatological pole of the theological doctrine by pitting an ironized "soul" against the "ganders" in the first and final couplets.

> The soul, O ganders, flies beyond the parks
> And far beyond the discords of the wind.

and

> And the soul, O ganders, being lonely, flies
> Beyond your chilly chariots, to the skies.

It is the time of year when the sun's "descending" announces the temporary death of nature, and the title's swans[18] decline with the sun: debunked in the title, they are further degraded to the rank of "ganders," evoking both geese and human dullards. These park-bound creatures are confined by domestication and surrounded by art that has been desecrated by crows' "dirt." The scene that fills the middle of the poem (and the parks) is particularly lifeless. Its own center is a simile of the "listless testament / Of golden quirks and Paphian caricatures" that bequeaths the ganders' "white feathers to the moon" and gives its "bland motions to the air." Its particular vacuity comes into sharp relief when compared to the celebratory fullness Emerson attributes to the work of the north wind in "The Snow-Storm":

> Speeding, the myriad-handed, his wild work
> So fanciful, so savage, nought cares he

For number or proportion. Mockingly,
On coop or kennel he hangs Parian wreaths;
A swan-like form invests the hidden thorn . . .

In Stevens' poem, the swans or ganders provide the criteria for what the soul is not. Although the soul is said to transcend the parks' confines, there is no suggestion as to what the soul's supposed metaphysical superiority might be. Further, the negative metaphor produces an ironic reversal; for although the ganders, those degraded swans, metaphorically "resemble" the body trapped in a physical enclosure, they also resemble the soul in whiteness and ability to fly. Thus the invisible, metaphysical soul is contaminated by its metaphorical resemblance to the physical ganders or swans, even as it is said to escape the birds' degenerated environment. The soul's metaphysical heaven is ironically reduced, like the "lonely" soul itself, to a lone "flies"/"skies" rhyme in the final couplet.

The emptying of the transcendent in this poem might be conveniently characterized as what Stevens would later call "evasion by . . . metaphor" ("Credences of Summer," CP 373). The "soul," by negative resemblance, may also have become a "mere" metaphor with no ground. It becomes fit to be used only ironically, because the arbitrariness of the authorizing structure is unacceptable. This is what is revealed in "A High-Toned Old Christian Woman" (CP 59) in the injunction to "Take the moral law and make a nave of it / And from the nave build haunted heaven," and then "take / The opposing law" and build from it too. And although the speaker in "Christian Woman" proclaims the "supreme fiction" to be poetry as contrasted with the woman's "moral law," his satiric humor cannot mask the fact that his own problematic architecture springs from the metaphoric "nave" and "peristyle." Such poems are bereft of constructing other than negatively. As Kenneth Burke writes, any "'negative *idea* . . . also has about its edges the positive *image*' of what it negates."[19] When the poet protests absence in negative presence, even ironically, he is caught using the hierarchy of the system of values he debunks. Just as the parodic function of the "gander" and "swan" metaphor empties the word "soul" of eschatological transcendence in "Invective against Swans," Stevens' use of architectural contrast contaminates both sides of the resemblance.

In Stevens' metaphors of againstness the use of traditional word-signifiers and concept-signifieds confirms their dominant place in a structure. The composition of metaphors in "Of Heaven Considered as a

Tomb" (*CP* 56) uses "heaven" (rather than "soul") to signify our mortal fate, to satirize the polarizing force of the spiritual versus material hierarchy. The terms of the title signify both the transcendent vault of heaven and the earthly vault of sepulchre. The "tomb of heaven" is then placed ironically in its implicit hierarchy as the tomb that lies above. It is a source of anxiety because the "darkened ghosts of our old comedy" may be condemned to continuously seeking "whatever it is they seek," or else may be stopped by "the one abysmal night." These two views of eternity's time are wittily brought together in the spatial metaphor of the "icy Elysée" that combines the characteristics of Christian heaven's "topmost distances" and earth's "gusty cold" with a reversal of Elysian sunshine as night and the Elysian underworld as upper sphere.[20] Eleanor Cook has also pointed out the reversal of the "standard" starry-sky topos as it appears at the end of Coleridge's *Biographia Literaria*.[21] These inherited tropes remain merely reversals, dependent upon the "positive image" of what they question. The double metaphor of the dead as actors and death as darkness fails to do even this much. In the "darkened ghosts of our old comedy" and the "dark comedians" we hear Macbeth's "Life's but a walking shadow, a poor player / That struts and frets his hour upon the stage, / And then is heard no more" (*Macbeth*, 5.5.23–25). But we hear not even that here.

Patently satirical poems like "Invective against Swans" or "Of Heaven Considered As a Tomb" seem to invert the inherited hierarchy of values in order to play against the very hierarchicalness of the structure that had legitimized "wormy metaphors." In "Heaven Considered," the speaker is kept in a position of inferiority and impotence, shown by his recourse to "interpreters." The question, "What word have you . . .?" of the dead, besides familiarly meaning "Do you have any news?" also signals the gap between the word-world of the living and the inarticulate, possibly wordless world of the dead. This is confirmed when the interpreters are later enjoined merely to "Make hue" and "Halloo" to those who have gone to the heaven-tomb. Unlike the Interpreter in *Pilgrim's Progress*, whose capital role it is to explain allegories,[22] these interpreters are hollow men. The verticality of the scene and the hierarchization of word structures that represent it impede the formulation of new questions about life and death.

Even a more ambitious poem like "Sunday Morning" (*CP* 66–70),[23] though it rings with memorable language and sober reflection, belies an againstness that ironically inverts heaven's reward and earth's satisfactions, the top and bottom of the hierarchy, rather than devising a new structuring principle. The poem's several subject positions all confront the divine and spiritual with the earthly and bodily. As Eleanor Cook has observed, "The arguments are obvious and stale. But the implicit homiletics: that is another matter. It is in the area of rhetoric that Stevens does battle, not in the area of dialectic."[24] In particular, Cook detects Stevens' challenge to the language of Milton and the Bible in sections I, V, and VIII. From my perspective here, considering the intensity of the younger Stevens' attempt to integrate metaphors of resemblance into new patterns, sections I, III, V, VI, and VII are particularly interesting. Not by accident, they deal pointedly with questions of theological hierarchy.

Section I illustrates the drift from an appreciation of the here and now to an eschatological-oriented belief. "Complacencies of the peignoir, and late / Coffee and oranges in a sunny chair" first instigate a metonymical and spatial movement. The epicurean woman's whole being is drawn toward another realm, as her "dreaming feet" lead her to the "silent Palestine" of Christ's sacrifice. The final "Dominion of the blood and sepulchre," however, can also be seen as the transformation of the opening coffee and oranges and "sunny chair" induced by the resemblances of metaphor.[25] The woman's sensuous comfort thus finds its analogue in a theological symbol that also has its origins in a bodily life—the wine-and-bread celebration of the Last Supper and the Son's interment.

Picking up the strand of Christ's "blood" and humanity, section III inserts Christ's birth into a double structure. On the one hand, it contains three implied narratives of each of the three divine engenderings. On the other hand, it is a condensed "history" of the evolution of religions: from Jove's motherless "inhuman birth," to the virgin birth of Christ and its "commingling" of our blood, to the possibility of a totally human version.

> Shall our blood fail? Or shall it come to be
> The blood of paradise? And shall the earth
> Seem all of paradise that we shall know?
> The sky will be much friendlier then than now,
> A part of labor and a part of pain,
> And next in glory to enduring love,
> Not this dividing and indifferent blue. (III, 9–15)

On the surface one might say with Adelaide Kirby Morris that given this pattern, the woman "must then admit the possibility of evolution from 'the thought of heaven' to a divinity that 'must live within herself'" (CP 67) of section II.[26] Yet even Jove is measured by the "human" standard of the "king," the negation of "inhuman" and "no mother," and the pun in "Large-*mannered*" (reutilized in "The Man With the Blue Guitar" IV). The narrative of the evolution of religion depends on personification. In addition, the human "hinds" situate Jove hierarchically. They return to recognize the "commingling" (a seemingly nonhierarchical word) of human and divine that defines Christianity, and thus reinforce the hierarchy of earth and "virginal" blood below, and "star" and "heaven" above. The third stage projects an anthropomorphized paradise into the future, leaving "earth" and "sky" in an ambiguous relation.

The hierarchical bias of religious metaphors seems most confining, however, in the implied narrative of each divinity's engendering. These are clustered around the series of representations of human motherhood that ends by integrating "labor" and "pain" (of both working the land and giving birth) into the speaker's imagined "paradise." The vocabulary of this final vision is redolent with double registers that point to a metaphorical contamination of what Kirby calls the divine "within" by a concern with divine origin in the "sky" and "blue" (Mary's color) of heaven, and the "glory" of paradisal splendor. The semantic organization of the entire section keeps returning to the mutual imbrication of physical and divine, even as the section's statements tend to reject past versions of the birth of divine figures because of their vertical perspective. On the other hand, such verticality imbues the stanza's temporal logic. In the story of the expulsion from the earthly Garden of Eden, paradise is origin and first home, while in the promise of a return to God's presence, paradise is heaven but also end as purpose, not only Montaigne's *bout* but the *but* he disputed. The reverie of the eschatological "Dominion of blood and sacrifice" that closes section I foreshadows the absorption of the mothering metaphor of section III into a vision of end, in a final hope that the "sky will be much friendlier than now." The course of an individual human life, the fertile engendering by and of "our blood," is made subordinate to the eschatological "enduring love" to which it is compared but can no longer attain.

The palliative to "all our dreams / And our desires" is given by the adage "Death is the mother of beauty" in section V. This formulation is so hypnotizing that it imposes the "need for some imperishable bliss" even on maidens' love, the prelude to mothering. Death "makes the willow shiver in the sun," mingling the promise of death with the maidens' love here on earth. When the phrase "Death is the mother of beauty" is taken up again to close section VI, it introduces another conceptual difficulty: death is a "mystical" mother "Within whose burning bosom we devise / Our earthly mothers waiting, sleeplessly." Thus, although the section's image of paradise is an image of earth frozen in a stilled moment, the transcendent, not the earthly, is what preconditions the focus of our desires on the sensuous lives embodied in "Our earthly mothers waiting, sleeplessly." If the personification of death as a mother is a "bosom"/matrix for actual ("earthly") mothers, it creates a vertical tautology equating death as mother of transformed versions of earth with the earth as the engenderer of stilled figurations of (death's) paradise. Each seems the superfluous mimesis of the other. Paradise is earth malformed just as "Malformed, the world was paradise malformed" ("The Pure Good of Theory" III, CP 332).

   Neither do the dynamic relationships that follow in section VII seem to develop alternative metaphors or an alternative structure. Helen Vendler calls this section Stevens' "poem of the Götterdämmerung," a representation of "anachronistic primitivism" in which "prophecies of a new divinity are wistfully and even disbelievingly made."[27]

> Supple and turbulent, a ring of men
> Shall chant in orgy on a summer morn
> Their boisterous devotion to the sun,
> Not as a god, but as a god might be,
> Naked among them, like a savage source.
> Their chant shall be a chant of paradise,
> Out of their blood, returning to the sky; (VII, 1–7)

The archaism of the scene brings us back to our ancestral source as well as to a possible archetypal image of sun worship[28] (already latent in the "sunny chair" of section I). Although Harold Bloom praises this section for the "new order" created out of its "metaleptic reversals of the poem's prior figurations," an order in which followers of the Nietzschean god among man manifest both "origin and purpose,"[29] the "return" to the sky can also be read as a repetition of the impeding structure of hierarchical-ness found in Stevens' other religious metaphors. The chant denotes idolatry, the submissive worship of a "lord." Its figures are derivative of ancient myth and Judeo-Christian successors of it insofar as they enact stories of "blood," the blood of sacrifice in the chant "of paradise, / Out of their blood, returning to the sky," and the blood of reproductive trans-mission. Blood seems to be the "natural" but male metonymy of the sen-suality and sensuousness of maternal "desire/s" of sections II and VI. The section is an ingrown expression of the larger poem's central figures. But the chief impediment to creating a new structure, it seems to me, is the tautological end implied in this disguised eschatology. Indeed, "returning to the sky" closes the circle of the chant's being "of" paradise—a chant about but also from paradise. For the returning chant originates in par-adise as well as in the men's blood; it originates, in sum, in the metaphors men have constructed to form paradise.

Thus not only in minor poems but in this major work in *Harmo-nium* we find Stevens mining the old theological metaphors even as he tries to debunk them. This metaphor-making depends on "using religious forms to deny religious forms."[30] Stevens' figures rely on anthropomor-phism since earth provides the analogues for the divine order. Attempts in "Sunday Morning" to give form to a human-centered vision of sensu-ous pleasure end up relating them to engendering and dying and to God-centered, transcendent value. The religious metaphors tend to merge the implicit life-narrative into a circle or tautology. Jove and paradise in sec-tion II and the return of "men that perish" in the sun's "summer morn" are products of our collective metaphor-making ability or our ability to create ensembles of resemblances. The earth's pleasures are imbricated in rhetorical substitutions that never form any independent pattern but can only deplete the divine by taking an ironic view of the earth as model, as in section VI, or by conceding domination to a metaphor of transcen-dent power that closes the trope in on itself, as in VII.

To sum up, the family of metaphors centering on motherhood and unfolding to include earth-birth and paradise-death itself illustrates the repeated linkage of questions of origin with questions of end. Sections III, V, and VI exploit metaphors of motherhood, but since the coher-ence is built on earthly and human figurations in relation to heavenly value, and since the poem's initial female dreamer desires yet doubts the adequacy of the earth, the value of the very concepts of earthly and heavenly paradise are contaminated. The euphoric section VII, on the other hand, turns the speaker's metaphors back around heaven and summer, as though bound to a "source." On the rhetorical level, the rivalry between two hierarchies locks the figuration of death into tableaux that leave the hierarchies intact.

Stevens himself can be seen to summarize this experience in the words of a persona invented almost two decades after *Harmonium* in "Dezembrum" (*Parts of a World*, CP 218). The second stanza states his theme as an old obsession:

> Over and over again you have said,
> This great world, it divides itself in two,
> One part is man, the other god:
> Imagined man, the monkish mask, the face.

On this poem's night, however, not only can the speaker identify the "other" divine part solely as a projection, a mask created in man's image, but he cannot free himself from the need to refer to its authority. He can continue: "Tonight there are only the winter stars. / The sky is no longer a junk-shop." This provides a temporary banishment of the governing instance. As it will be put still later in "The Pure Good of Theory" III (CP 332), "To say the solar chariot is junk // Is not a variation but an end." In "Dezembrum" the multiple stars, not the lonely sun, become an acceptable projection of man, of men, "like a crowd of faces / Moving round the sky and singing / And laughing." Limpidly, simply, "an intenser love" is freed from the paralysis otherwise imposed by "angels" and "the dead," signs of man's dependence on a power situated at the top of an anthropomorphic hierarchy that defines man's end for him. The "imagination" has free play to please itself in its own humanity. Yet—there seems always to be a "yet" in these naysaying poems— substituting the stars/faces for the heavenly "junk-shop," or replacing one metaphor for another, fails to satisfy, just as the recognition of humanity's desire to find itself in God fails to satisfy in "Sunday Morning" III. The poem's "intenser love" and "desire" are enclosed in the "rigid room" of the poem's final stanza amidst failed metaphors of "toys" and "thing-a-ma-jigs." Such are the inhibitions the theological hierarchy places on the development of a new vocabulary and new metaphors, as remembered and commemorated here.

Metaphors of Natural Order

As "Sunday Morning" and "Dezembrum" illustrate, metaphors of divine order may be coupled in Stevens' early work with those of natural order. Nature includes both natural cycle, design, or order revealing and governing our destiny ("Sunday Morning" VII), and natural forces, vitality, or sympathy connecting us with the place we live in as well as with a divine presence ("Sunday Morning" III). The assumption of divine immanence in nature is part of the inheritance Stevens received from his romantic predecessors, whose poetic imprint on Stevens has been abundantly discussed.[31] Stevens struggled most intensely with metaphors of natural order, both singly and in connection with his revolt against representations of the divine in *Harmonium* (1923), while vestiges of their problematic status remain through *Parts of a World* (1942).

In Europe and America, the things of nature have provided a pool of references from which poets have drawn and continue to draw material for writing "significant landscapes." Although fractures had already appeared in the set of correspondences they provide,[32] it was only with modernist poetry that the bond and the means of expressing it had to be reconsidered. In Stevens' work, poems as diverse as "Nuances of a Theme by Williams" in *Harmonium* (CP 18) or "The Brave Man" (CP 138) and "Autumn Refrain" (CP 160) in *Ideas of Order* contest this bond; and nature, bereft of any authorizing kinship, is made something potentially stultifying, even dehumanizing.

"The Death of a Soldier" (CP 97) performs a series of moves that deny the pertinence of both divine and natural orders. It explicitly cancels divine purpose in having the fallen soldier fail to "become a three-days personage," a follower of a resurrected Christ. An initial advantage is given to resemblance with nature and the possibility that an impersonal natural order might integrate within itself the meaning of death. But Stevens foreshortens the Renaissance topos of autumn to equate it precisely with the end rather than with the prospective time of "yellow leaves" as in Shakespeare's Sonnet 73, for instance. Stevens' autumn fulfills the obliteration of the maidens straying "impassioned in the littering leaves" in "Sunday Morning" V. It is the end of a natural cycle that is only linear, with no possibility of starting up again. Moreover, Stevens' "Death of a Soldier" ravages the reprise of the metaphor with biting irony in the second half:

Death is absolute and without memorial,
As in a season of autumn,
When the wind stops,

When the wind stops and, over the heavens,
The clouds go, nevertheless,
In their direction.

The landscape described is what we see when clouds scud along in the upper atmosphere, hastened by the currents there, whereas at ground level all is calm. "When the wind stops, // When the wind stops," not only does breathing cease, but the spirit traditionally associated with wind and the breath of life no longer abides in our presence. As for the clouds, their direction is "theirs" alone, or perhaps ambiguously that of the distant "heavens." The clouds' movement and time continue without life. The pathos and kinship that underlie the use of the metaphors in the poem are blasted by the final stanza. If the clouds scud "over the heavens," not only is divinity eliminated from the landscape, but the nature in which the divinity had been immanent is indifferent. And being indifferent, it no longer offers consolation.[33] That it is no longer valid as a metaphor for human destiny is shown by the fact that Stevens breaks the relation of resemblance between natural force, divine order, and human life.

In a more experimental mode, "The Wind Shifts" (CP 83–84) redisposes the elements in the metaphor's hierarchy but fails to camouflage the impotence of old metaphors of nature. In it, man is not likened to nature, but nature's wind is compared to man; yet neither nature nor man makes much sense. Four successive attempts are made, with deadly insistence, to create a simile for "how the wind shifts." It strings out five comparisons with humans, balancing the variations with contraries like "eagerly" and "despairingly" and "proudly" and "angrily." As Jacqueline Vaught Brogan points out, Stevens' use of simile foregrounds the latent tension between two different processes that language effects—intimating the possibility of oneness or correspondence between two realms, and revealing the gap between them.[34] Indeed, here each human attitude is gratuitous and detached from the others. There is no coherent framework for man's similarity with the wind, unless randomness is itself the fundamental resemblance. Readers may feel that human volatility is indeed like the wind and that the metaphorical process by which we read the poem allows us to see the resemblance both ways. The relationship may even be tautological if we read the letter *w* as an upside-down *m* and find a pun on "wind" and human "mind." In any event, the poem closes on stultifying indifference:

> This is how the wind shifts:
> Like a human, heavy and heavy,
> Who does not care.

Stevens' terms here reveal not the idolatry or nostalgia for paradise of "Sunday Morning" but a nostalgia for comforting kinship with nature's cosmic order.

In Stevens' early deployment of metaphors of nature, the against-ness of the strategies he uses leaves an empty space that his speakers often despair of filling. If nature has lost its ability to speak, this dimin-ishes not only people's sense of human potency but also their perception of the linguistic and poetic forms that might be used to overcome the loss. This is one implication of a cluster of poems in *Harmonium* that in-cludes "The Doctor of Geneva" (CP 24), "Banal Sojourn" (CP 62–63), "The Man Whose Pharynx Was Bad" (CP 96) and "Anatomy of Monot-ony" (CP 107–108). In "The Man Whose Pharynx Was Bad," for in-stance, the speaker laments that "The time of year has grown indifferent," and links nature's lack to his own limiting conflation of "Mildew of summer and the deepening snow" in his "routine." "I am too dumbly in my being pent" might be said to double the void of his "being" (in "I am" and "being pent"). The "malady of the quotidian" is met with a hypothetical "Perhaps if winter," but it fails to generate "new orations of the cold" in the poet's words.

> One might in turn become less diffident,
> Out of such mildew plucking neater mould
> And spouting new orations of the cold.
> One might. One might. But time will not relent.

The "time" evolved in the last line, the mortality of the speaker's already "dumbly" benumbed "being," is merely an excuse for the inability of the man to produce his own legitimizing metaphors.

In his late lecture, "Imagination as Value" (1948), Stevens states the need to "somehow cleanse the imagination of taint of the romantic"

(*NA* 139).[35] Typically, Stevens never pins down or illustrates the "content" of his concept of the romantic. But we can savor its connotations from the basic contrast he makes between productive imagination and an ineffective romantic version of it. Calling the imagination "the liberty of the mind" and the romantic "a failure to make use of that liberty," Stevens describes what he sees as the failure of the romantic and sets up a complex four-term correlative analogy (one of the four forms of metaphor mentioned by Aristotle in chapter 21 of the *Poetics*): the romantic is to the imagination as sentimentality is to feeling. Implicitly, joining the beginning of the correlation to the end, we also have: the romantic is to the imagination as minor wish-fulfillments are to the liberty of the mind. Both "minor wish-fulfillments" and sentimentality are symptoms of an inhibiting force that it is necessary to resist in order to obtain that liberty of the mind that Stevens valued above all things, for, he says, "The imagination is the only genius. It is intrepid and eager" and can reach what the romantic never can—"abstraction" (*NA* 138–139).

Working against easy satisfactions in poetry certainly entails dislocating resemblances with nature, as well as disrupting the "complacencies of the peignoir" of a "Sunday Morning" on the theological side. Achieving a "liberty of the mind" cannot be accomplished simply by resisting representations of nature and their use as metaphor.[36] It requires the ability to pick apart the articulations of given analogies and their expression in metaphor, as in the quotation from "Imagination as Value," in which a new formal correlation is achieved. In this essay, Stevens says plainly, but also illustrates obliquely, how important it is to redistribute the roles. But as we have seen, the experiments of "The Death of a Soldier" and "The Wind Shifts" end up abolishing or attenuating the relevance of nature for the human subject without shaking off the inhibiting force of the "minor wish-fulfillments."

Other experiments grapple more resolutely with redefining the respective roles of nature and humans in the metaphors that establish their "resemblance." The process of redefinition entails the threat of encountering a void, as is plain in such much commented poems as "The Snow Man," which I will discuss later. At the very least, reworking the balance between the two sides can make the relation itself deeply ambiguous and destabilizing. "Six Significant Landscapes" (*CP* 73–75) illustrates the disquieting effects. The occasion of section I was Stevens' discovery that, as he wrote to his wife, "larkspur comes from China."[37] In this vignette the old man coheres with the natural scene. The typed atmosphere of

Oriental calm and harmony is derived from the old man's being humbly positioned to receive something from nature, a Western rather than Chinese expectation.

I

An old man sits
In the shadow of a pine tree
In China.
He sees larkspur,
Blue and white,
At the edge of the shadow,
Move *in the wind.*
His beard moves *in the wind.*
The pine tree moves *in the wind.*
Thus water flows
Over weeds. (Emphasis added.)

Stevens' prepositional foregrounding of locatives stresses that the man's position is doubly "in" the natural place ("In the shadow" and "In China"), and that within this place part of it ("larkspur") is "in" another element of it ("in the wind"). The protagonist's sight/consciousness includes the larkspur, described as being within the circumference of the shadow, but it then fades out in the double reiteration of "in the wind" in "His beard moves in the wind. / The pine tree moves in the wind." In the poem's development, the wind displaces the larkspur, but in the represented or referential scene, the wind includes the movement both of the larkspur seen by the man and of the beard and pine tree, which are part of the scene but not the seen. The prepositional "Over weeds" moves the closing lines beyond both the given landscape and the man's consciousness.

There is something more here than a parallel between human and natural process of the kind that pervades classical Chinese lyrics, and more than "romantic" sympathy between man and nature. Through a play on the spatial reference of "in the wind," the wind becomes a force by which the man and his small natural circle are governed despite his consciousness. The image of the wind infuses the scene with its only movement, establishing a kinetic resemblance among the man's beard and larkspur and pine tree. The water analogy reinforces it in the closing couplet. Wind and water are thus said to resemble each other, like wind on man and water over weeds. In this criss-crossing network, each element is given a place, while all are subordinated to nature embodied as ongoing process.

"Landscape" III, however, protests against the passivity of the man and the inclusive force of nature posited in section I. "I measure myself / Against a tall tree" challenges nature's intimidating law or standard. Countering Whitman, Stevens shapes his persona's bravura into a mere comparison, making him "much taller" than a tall tree, rather than an absolute, and his short lines (especially "Of the eye") tease the eye, we might say, of persona and reader. Nevertheless there is a degree of Whitmanian expansion of the ego in the grasping of "For I reach," "I reach." This third section helps reveal how rigidly the first "Landscape" is contained by its espalier of prepositions and by the positioning of the man within the circumference of the shadow. Section III's speaking "I" does not deny nature's power over human life or imagination but proposes his own self as rival force. Nevertheless, the "I"'s hubris is weakened by the final disturbance of the ants that "crawl / In and out of my shadow." This addendum can be read as an allegory for an interpretation that the speaker would like to repress, that nature's ants remind him of nature's liberty and of its own perennial existence and his death. In other words, nature indeed turns out to be—despite the speaker's attempts at evasion—not only an unavoidable model for human life but a reminder of human frailty and a sign of the speaker's own limits.

Something of a similar development takes place in "In the Clear Season of Grapes" (CP 110–111), for example, which affirms the pleasure derived from looking at the things of nature by first denying attachment in "A flip for the sun and moon, // If they mean no more than that" before reversing this denial:

> . . . But they do.
> And mountains and the sea do. And our lands.
> And the welter of frost and the fox cries do.
>
> Much more than that . . .

As in "Landscapes" III, a tendency toward allegory can be detected in the climax, which directly follows the excerpt just quoted:

> . . . Autumnal passages
> Are overhung by the shadows of the rocks
> And his nostrils blow out salt around each man.

The ominous imagery of a seasonal place being "overhung by the shadows" subdues the zest for landscape with a metaphor for the threat of death. A curious pronoun change introduces another complex metaphor when "his nostrils" displace an "I" that had jubilated in the natural world. If, as Joan Richardson claims, the "salt" "each man" exhales affirms his intimate link with and even creative role in the forming of the sea, then indeed the final "man" may be seen as contributing "to the making of his sea, his first home."[38] In such a resemblance, each man is related to the Creator and becomes a creative spirit in nature. But this also means that the breathing spirit of "his nostrils" is a creator of interpretations of nature. And here the very role of metaphor is thrown into relief in the appearance of the "autumnal passages" and "shadows of the rocks." Are they manifestations of an ungovernable force within? This might be suggested by the positioning of the possessive "his" *before* its "normal" antecedent, "each man." Do they arise unexpectedly from the speaker's interior debate? Or, as figments of the salt-imagination, are they marks of man's interpretive superiority? The things of nature do not, we see, speak themselves in the debate over what the "sun and moon" "mean." They must be brought forward by language. And this activity almost always includes the creation of authorizing metaphors.

The Movement Beyond

Stevens never entirely ceased to evoke the things of nature as possibly giving human beings a sense of belonging to a greater pattern. Oak leaves, hyacinth, grass, locust, thunder, bird-cry, river, sea, star, sun—these parts of his world continued to have illustrative and metaphoric potential for Stevens' poetry. From *Harmonium* (1923) through *Parts of a World* (1942), the relative importance of particular and general is gradually readjusted. The humble and particular facts of the landscape of farm or garden come to occupy less space, as the greater facts and forces—river, air, sun—occupy more. However, *Parts of a World* occasionally follows the pattern more frequently used in *Harmonium*, in which a sensible species or genus breeds a broader figure that also draws man into it. Thus, in "On an Old Horn" (CP 230), the colors of stones may be (by resemblance) or be part of (by synecdoche) the boomings of the bird that speaks the Logos, a speech in which man "proclaimed himself, was proclaimed;" and in "Contrary Theses (II)" (CP 270), the "locust-leaves" illustrate "the grand mechanics of earth and sky," the sum of which is the crucible for a speaker's encounter with "the abstract," "The premise from which all things were conclusions, / The noble, Alexandrine verve." We are thus reminded of Aristotle's consideration that the transference operated by metaphor can be based on "analogy" or, as we will see later, consist of a transfer "from genus to species, or species to genus, or from species to species."[39] More typically, however, the particulars that festoon *Parts of a World* are mere illustrations of a broader principle rather than the starting point or foundation of resemblance. What is fundamental is that as Stevens' experiments evolve and the poet's language acquires a new flexibility within the inherited assumptions and systems, there appear poems that attenuate the stratification of the terms involved.

The issue of how to relate the human to something greater without making one or the other subservient is an overriding concern in *Parts of a World*. Stevens uses numerous compositional combinations to cast doubt on the possibility of achieving satisfaction, either philosophically or artistically. "Les Plus Belles Pages" (CP 244–245) problematizes the man-nature relationship by segmenting, by alternating various incomplete versions of inclusion such as " . . . Nothing exists by itself. / The moonlight seemed to" and "Two people, three horses, an ox / And the sun, the waves together in the sea," and by denying "The moonlight and Aquinas seemed to" with "The automaton, in logic self-contained, / Existed by itself." In "Landscape with Boat" (CP 241–243), Stevens' speaker ends an account of the ascetic's long, self-defeating, reiterative speculation with his own speculation of what the ascetic *might* have been able to "suppose" but cannot—that is, the alternative stated in "'The thing I hum appears to be / The rhythm of this celestial pantomime.'" Another tactic used by Stevens is to represent the sacrifice of something essential, as in "Woman Looking at a Vase of Flowers" (CP 246–247), in which natural objects are integrated into a "profounder reconciling act" at the cost of "clairvoyance." Stevens' problem is only partially, as he writes in "Botanist on Alp (No. 1)" (CP 134), that "Marx has ruined Nature, / For the moment," or that the figures for transcendence have become, like Plato's figure for the soul, "antiquated and rustic" (NA 4). The question is how to recompose images of natural givens and human life within a new linguistic structure.

As we have seen, the implicit reaffirmation of the supremacy of a transcendent order often accompanies what I have called Stevens' metaphors of againstness. A few rare lyrics in Stevens' early work nonetheless escape againstness by using an initial metaphor for natural forces in a way that attenuates or even ignores the theologized view of a transcendent nature. They tend to exploit the metaphor of nature's fertility, allowing the engendering potential of the comparison, as it were, to become not only the theme but the very spring of poetic production. The contrasting solutions of "Nomad Exquisite" (1919, collected in *Harmonium*) and "Oak Leaves Are Hands" (1942, collected in *Parts of a World*) exemplify two such transfigurations.

In 14–line "Nomad Exquisite" (CP 95), a tropical scene fertilized by "the immense dew of Florida" is a metaphor for the life force. The natural model of fecundity expands to include passions, song, color, and movement and culminates with

> So, in me, come flinging
> Forms, flames, and the flakes of flames.

A state of receptivity in which the metaphoric act can take place is implied in the "hymn and hymn" brought forth in the "beholder" who beholds. In the "blessed mornings" of the scene and the "hymn and hymn" of a viewer's response, the religious denotations are secularized by the revolving of the "green" in "green sides / And gold sides of green sides" and the tropical exoticism of the scene the speaker compares his state to. The articulation of the "As . . . As . . . So" simile structures the three stanzas, foregrounding the resemblance between his receptivity and the self-reflexive development of the poem, culminating in the evanescent "So, in me, come flinging / Forms, flames, and flakes of flames." It . is eye is like the "eye of the young alligator," his "hymn" is the poem's final play of alliteration and assonance in "flakes of flames."

Nature as genetrix remains a valid model for poetic creation. "Nomad Exquisite," rather than becoming enclosed in a struggle with againstness, dilates an originary metaphor of authoritative fecundity before compressing a like joyousness into the speaker's description of his own poetic inspiration in the last two lines. Harold Bloom (one of the poem's rare commentators and an admirer of it) regrets that Stevens did not keep his earlier version of these last two lines: "So, in me come flinging / Fruits, forms, flowers, flakes, and fountains."[40] He reads Stevens as deleting these lines in order to "place the poem finally out of nature and into the Paterian Condition of Fire," though, he says, the flame is only a "hard or antithetical one, flaking off into the component tropes of the poem."[41] But surely Bloom is ignoring the recombinatory—and reimagining— activity of Stevens' published version. It seems more adequate to say that the poem escapes becoming "hard" or "gemlike" by concentrating on the double source of metaphor, the world of nature and the poet's eye and voice. The crossing of such activities as vegetable growth and animal or bodily movement with linguistic invention is suggested in a few other very early poems like "Earthy Anecdote" (CP 3), "Ploughing on Sunday" (CP 20) and "Life Is Motion" (CP 83). But "Nomad Exquisite" also foreshadows, through its title and development, that fruitful wandering of metaphor that I will look at in chapter 2—a structural movement of metaphor away from the denotative authority of the originary metaphor toward an ever-moving horizon in which the poet's language is revealed as an active shaper.

The carefree "Nomad Exquisite" is succeeded by some more doubtful offspring, including the somber, "Evasive and metamorphorid," Flora Lowzen in "Oak Leaves Are Hands" from Parts of a World (CP 272). Florida's "lightning colors" are replaced here by the "chromatic" figure of a nature goddess who is an avatar of both Flora and Mac Mort. She is said to have both "created" and "invigorated," out of mere "movement of few words," a palette of "Archaic and future happenings, / In glittering seven-colored changes."

Cook stresses that Flora recalls Circe and that the poem is positively sinister.[42] Vendler too, who usefully catalogues a rich selection of possible associations and word formations, sees Flora Lowzen as a "bridge" to Stevens' later poems in which we find female representations that are "of more sinister import, like Madame La Fleurie, the cannibal bearded mother."[43] On the other hand, we are reminded of Harmonium's "Domination of Black" (CP 8–9), in which the mournful peacock's cry is set against the proliferation of color deployed by the bird's tail, and the call of death contributes to the aesthetic pleasure the poem exudes. Vendler provides convincing evidence of the "Gothic excess" of the stilted and archaizing vocabulary of "Oak Leaves" as signs of Stevens' repudiation of the demented mode of Lady Lowzen.[44] Is Lady Lowzen a femme fatale, a "Belle dame sans merci"? Or is she the "mother to the original maternity of nature," as Frye has labeled her,[45] or a variegated Ur-mother to the mother of "Sunday Morning"? The import of the original nature metaphor is lost in the transfiguration of the title's oak leaf hands into an ambivalent fairylike creature the speaker is both attracted to and repelled by. I would stress that if it is difficult in this "riddle" poem, as Doggett calls it,[46] to decide on the attitude of the speaker, and if "Oak Leaves Are Hands" falls into decadence, it is because of the speaker's own language about the fatal yet invigorating lady, for the lady does not speak for herself.

What is interesting for us here is that the original resemblance between leaves and hands is merely an occasion for the poem. The speaker exploits the metaphor only haphazardly when the poem stumbles midway upon the simile of acorn "brood[ing] on former oaks" and Flora Lowzen's invigoration of "Archaic and future happenings." When Henry David Thoreau placed leaves and body parts in a long line of resemblances from the thawing sand and clay to "sappy leaves or vines" to forms that show how blood vessels are formed, he could conclude, "The Maker of this earth but patented a leaf."[47] In "Oak Leaves Are Hands" Stevens has eliminated his early againstness by eliminating any hint of a divine pattern or master trope attendant to the originating resemblance. The speaker revels in his own linguistic invention but seems to be mocking Flora's invalidity as metaphor and nature's ineptitude as artificer.

The title "On the Adequacy of Landscape" (CP 243–244) denotes the need to speculate on the "adequacy" of landscape in its two manifestations, as a natural given and as a constructed art form. It implies doubts about whether landscape is "adequate" to or, more etymologically, equal to the "desires" of the "people" evoked in the poem. In any case, the poem itself is not a landscape-picture but an exposition of attitudes about parts of the landscape. The desire for the landscape's cock and sun and the satisfactions achieved are evolved along a trajectory of undecidable syntactic relations that implode the metaphorical resemblances within the artwork.

The poem distinguishes between two opposing clusters: on the one hand, owl, night, and shrinking people who avoid the discursive brightness of "central things" that the owl offers;[48] on the other hand, cock, red sun, and "sharpest" people who turn toward cock and sun and who desire intensely. The first part of the poem deftly shifts the grammatical subjects of its unsymmetrical clauses from "owl" (stanza 1) to "the people" who "turned off" from the owl (stanza 2), then to another logically different "people" opposed to the first (stanza 4). The latter people are "sensible to pain" (whereas the former are said to have "empty hearts") and "turn toward" cocks and sun (stanza 4). An unusual "Nor" (stanza 3) marks this shift to the world of the cock and the "blood-red redness of the sun," then continues in stanza 4:

Beyond the keenest diamond day
Of *people* sensible to pain,
When cocks wake, clawing at their beds
To be again,

And *who*, for that, turn toward the cocks
And toward the start of day and trees
And light behind the body of night
And sun, as if *these*

Were what *they* are, the sharpest sun:
The sharpest self, the sensible range,
The extent of what *they* are, the strength
That *they* exchange,

So that *he that* suffers most desires
The red bird most and the strongest sky—
Not *the people* in the air that hear
The little owl fly. (Emphasis added.)

The cock in this half of "On the Adequacy of Landscape" is a natural sign "toward" which people turn in order to encounter both their own humanity (one possible referent for "what they are") and cosmic force ("the sharpest sun") (stanza 6). It is a centripetal object that exhibits the red physicality of blood and sun and, through its daily repetition of "clawing," displaces the owl and its cohorts' "being there" (stanza 1) with its urge to "be again" (stanza 4). It metamorphoses the man's/sun's forceful vitality. The cock's sympathizers are associated with the intensity of superlatives (six in all) that bind the cock, the sun, and human desire in a relation of resemblance—a relation that initiates the metaphorical move in stanzas 3 and 4. The parts of this tripartite relation would seem to be mutually fulfilling and not hierarchical. What allows for an exchange of "strength" (later attributed to "strongest sky") is grammatically elided or present only in the colon in stanza 6.

Neither cock nor sun can be identified as the origin of daily re-
birth. The sentence grows through ramifying subordinate clauses, evasive
pronouns, and juxtaposed nouns that in turn constitute ambiguous an-
tecedents. Neither logically nor syntactically can cock or "sharpest sun"
(stanza 6) be identified as a transcendent power "behind the body of
night / And sun" (stanza 5).[49] In contrast to a theologized version of the
figure, then, the sun is clearly not a First Cause, Prime Mover or lawgiver
who lords it over human beings. Although the sun functions generally as
a metaphor for human vitality, it does not weigh in the poem as a legit-
imizing authority with its implication of telos, despite its implications of
permanence in cyclicality. It might be said to cast off the old "romantic"
with its "minor wish-fulfillments" discussed by Stevens in "Imagination
as Value." The againstness of the people who avoid the world of the owl
is displaced by their acceptance of the intensity of pain and desire
through the syntactic disruption of chains of hierarchy among the ele-
ments of metaphor.

Parts of a World shows that Stevens continued to feel the weight
of the "antiquated" old metaphors at least into the early 1940s. He
continued to ruminate on the intellectual and artistic problem of how
to construct new patterns from hierarchical tropes. An advanced syn-
thesis of the problem is developed in "The Latest Freed Man" (CP
204–205), written in 1938. The poem meets the problem head-on,
recognizing the shackles of "the old descriptions" and their metaphors
of divinized nature while pressing againstness into the service of cre-
ative energy, although its disruption of hierarchy is not total, as we
shall see.

The narrative tells of casting off the old "truth" and its attendant
"doctrine of the landscape" in order to meet both things themselves and
the self among things.

> Tired of the old descriptions of the world,
> The latest freed man rose at six and sat
> On the edge of his bed. He said,
>   "I suppose there is
> A doctrine to this landscape. Yet, having just
> Escaped from the truth, the morning is color and mist,
> Which is enough: the moment's rain and sea,
> The moment's sun (the strong man vaguely seen),
> Overtaking the doctrine of this landscape . . ."

The narrativelike beginning encourages us to imagine this "latest freed man" in 1938 getting up at Stevens' habitual hour, sitting on the edge of his bed, looking at the early morning light wafting in through the window, then being struck once again with the sun's vigorous constancy and its ability to transform the night's darkness into a riot of color and shape. The final two lines mention objects Stevens saw every day in his room, including the portrait Stevens owned of his Parisian bookseller, Anatole Vidal, and what may be a play on a quotation from a letter by Vidal describing himself as someone who *"fait fi des joliesses banales"* (who scorns banal prettifying):[50]

> It was everything being more real, himself
> At the centre of reality, seeing it.
> It was everything bulging and blazing and big in itself,
> The blue of the rug, the portrait of Vidal,
> *Qui fait fi des joliesses banales*, the chairs.

Before writing this poem, Stevens had evoked a rising or contrasting sun and its power to metamorphose not only the external world but the poet's spirit in several works—in his early play, "Three Travelers Watch a Sunrise" (*OP* 149–177), the 1930 turning-point poem "The Sun This March" (*CP* 133–134), and such poems as "The Brave Man" (*CP* 138), "Botanist on Alp (No. 2)" (*CP* 135–136), "Gubbinal" (*CP* 85), and "Gubbinal"'s contrary, "A Fading of the Sun" (*CP* 139). "The Latest Freed Man" is one of a series of preparatory exercises for the final troping of sunrise and bird cry in "Not Ideas about the Thing but the Thing Itself" (*CP* 534). It is as though the daily fact of the sun's rising was both a permanent resource in Stevens' internalized mythology and, more simply, the central enabling condition for the pleasure of seeing that is represented in numerous poems.

"The Latest Freed Man" contrasts the mythology's supposed "doctrine" of the landscape with morning's sensuous presence in "color and mist," which, the man says, "is enough." The man's opening words echo "A very felicitous eve, / Herr Doktor, and that's enough" in "Delightful Evening" (*CP* 162), while retranscribing the "Doktor"'s "wormy metaphors" as the "doctrine" (ll. 4, 8, 10) of "doctors" (ll. 12, 19). Aquinas the "Angelic Doctor" and scholastic theology more generally are the synecdochal images that another mythical element, the sun, is said to be "overtaking." The allusion to Aquinas nonetheless anchors the central association of the sun with the ox (an emblem of Aquinas, as Cook reminds us[51]), and thus takes part in the movement of sensuous awakening. The metaphor of sun/human power loosely embraces: (1) freed man — being — without description = ox, which supersedes (2) doctors — truth or doctrine — description = ant of the self (the latter recalling the ants that deflate the hubris of the man whose shadow they crawl over in "Six Significant Landscapes"). The ox is an avatar of the sun that comes up "bull fire" in "Add This to Rhetoric" (CP 198), the catalyst that allows the man to become ox-like. His ox-like strength seems to resemble the sun's (ll. 20–22), while the sun is also personified as the "strong man" (l. 7). Thus the central tension or paradox of this poem is that the ox acts as a metaphor for the sun while "logically" it is a metalepsis for the freed man's awakening state, an effect substituted for the cause. How can the sun metaphor avoid reproducing mere againstness and the entrapment in hierarchical transcendence it implies?

The precondition for awakening is established by the man himself: he has just "Escaped from the truth" (l. 4). As Eleanor Cook says, the man's very activity implies a polemic against Saint John's sentence, "Ye shall know the truth and the truth shall make ye free," and the poem's stance is thus partially anti-Logos or anti-Word in the narrow religious sense.[52] To my mind, however, the poem's claim for "freedom from religious orthodoxy," as Cook puts it, is most interesting, first because the "doctrine" also figures a belief in a world order based on moribund religious and natural "truths" in a broader sense, and second, in our context, because it is the synecdoche signifying the struggle for linguistic freedom within transcendent metaphor.

The odds against attaining freedom from old doctrines can be seen in the fact that the man, as I have said, immediately fits the sun into a system that personifies it as "the strong man vaguely seen" (l. 7). This is a remnant of both anthropomorphic theology and the pathetic fallacy. Do the parentheses around this phrase show how inevitable and inescapable such a personification is, as Miller has argued for "Not Ideas about the Thing but the Thing Itself"?[53] One pitfall, then, in the search for "freedom" is the reinscription of an implied Prime Mover or Logos. Solipsism is another potential pitfall. The freed man voluntarily ignores any doctrine (ll. 4–6) before comparing the sun in the mist to "a man *without* a doctrine" (emphasis added), thus turning the sun into a metaphor for his *own* certitude and sense of being. There is a touch of the solipsistic circularity here that one finds parodied in "Tea at the Palaz of Hoon" (*CP* 65).

It is not really paradoxical that in this anti-Logos poem the authority of the natural metaphor is affirmed. The crucial fact of the poem is that the affirmation changes in both ontological and linguistic nature as it drifts from the credo, "'Of him [the sun] / And of his works I am sure'" (ll. 8–9) to the evasiveness of "To know that the change and that the ox-like struggle / Come from the strength that is the strength of the sun, / Whether it comes directly or from the sun" (ll. 20–23). More importantly, not only are the lines of causality obscured or even broken referentially on several occasions, but a repeated verbal strategy using one of Stevens' most favored lexemes, the verb *to be*, outshines the very sun and breaks down any potential schematic layering of resemblance. The most insistent strategy consists of modulations with an anaphoric "It was": "*It was how* the sun came shining into his room" (l. 14), and later "*It was how* he was free," "*It was how* his freedom came" (l. 23), "*It was being* without description, being an ox" (l. 24), "*It was* the importance of the trees outdoors" (l. 25), "*It was everything being* more real" (l. 28), and ending "*It was everything bulging and blazing*" to introduce the objects into the poem-room (l. 30) (emphases mine). "It" has no "real" or grammatical antecedent. "It was how" and "it was —ing" simply posit process that needs no legitimizing ground or cause. The resulting composition can be likened to the role of realistic representation in a Magritte painting, as in several paintings he titled *La Condition humaine:* a landscape, for example, is painted on the canvas in realistic shapes and shadings as a given; but a copy of the scene appears in a frame or on a window of the represented scene, showing that the painting does not derive its authority from a supposed original existing in nature. It is the artist that assumes both, with his angle of vision, his choice, his geometry.[54] In Stevens' poem the man sitting on the edge of his bed and the effect of the sun shining in are in a somewhat similar relation. The sun is a necessary but not a sufficient condition for awakening and loses its priority as creator. Stevens' "landscape" does not fit canonical rules for art but surmounts the yoke of control exercised by dead metaphors that had been taken as literal truth models to be copied in other forms both natural and artistic.

This is not a "*joliesse banale.*" Stevens' verbal play avoids describing "how" or what his sentences point to, until the last three-line sentence finally bursts forth with its specific "bulging and blazing" and its series of newly defamiliarizing yet vitalized signs. The reiterated structure exemplifies the impossibility of finding a single ground for explaining either some kinship between man and the things around him or the fullness of being that both the human and the inhuman and the given and the made exude in this poem. The metaphors avoid the subservience to semantic depth and its implied metaphysical Logos so favored by philosophy's etymological discourse, as Derrida shows us in "White Mythology."[55] Rather, they promote modulation within a nonhierarchical structure. Within the sequence of Stevens' poems, "Sunday Morning"'s "green freedom" is succeeded here by the final "blue of the rug."

The freedom contains the residues of againstness. As Cook says, "Modern art, we hear ad nauseam, 'frees' us from older conventions of art. It does and it does not, as Stevens' play in this poem tells us."[56] Cook does not tell us how "it does not," although she sees the evasiveness of claiming freedom "from." Indeed, "The Latest Freed Man" details how freedom "from" is claimed within a web of againstness, within a complex conceit of subordination and governance. The landscape of written signs culminates in a diversity and potency that are diffused referentially throughout the man's whole environment. While starting with the sun as a central metaphor, the poem's developing structure manages to surpass rather than merely contest the old verities that used to define man's life as a flawed emanation of divine or natural law, a mortal reflection of the immortal, a visible form of the invisible, or as a fleeting "particular" defeated by nature's cyclical time.

The enabling force of the signs in this poem goes beyond the concept of metaphor Stevens sketched later in "The Effects of Analogy." In this essay, he identifies poetry as being "the outcome of figures of speech," or "the outcome of the operation of our imagination on another through the instrumentality of the figures. To identify poetry and metaphor or metamorphosis is merely to abbreviate the last remark" (NA 117–118). I think that the metaphors of "The Latest Freed Man" induce the reader to free her or himself partially from the literalness of resemblance, just as they tell of the freed man momentarily freeing himself from doctrine and exploiting his own strength of being and seeing. The metaphorical pairings between sun-man, self-ox, sun-ox—with their ambiguous lines of causality—are initially reinforced but then give way to such new images as oak-leaves, rug, portrait, and chairs. The path the poem takes at the end seems to lead toward the metonymical logic of contiguity but with the twist that the list of new objects is potentially unlimited. These seemingly trivial objects, with their new prominence and their new signs, come into the landscape through the speaker's heightened "being," what Stevens' might have called his "imagination." They are enough.[57]

In terms of Stevens' work with metaphors of natural and divine order, "The Latest Freed Man" produces a formal movement opposite that of the much anthologized "Anecdote of the Jar" (CP 76). In "Anecdote of the Jar" things are said to be ordered around the jar, and they even resemble it in the play with the sign "round" in the poem, whereas in "The Latest Freed Man" the space (referential and formal) is not determined by the sun but seems to be gradually occupied by things as they take on life for the awakening man. In "Anecdote" the sign for the jar is present in all three stanzas, whereas in the "Freed Man" the sign for the sun disappears and leaves things on their own in the last third of the poem. Moreover "Anecdote" ends in a hierarchical gesture of "dominion" coupled with an exclusionary gesture in which the jar is said to "not give of bird or bush, / Like nothing else in Tennessee." "The Latest Freed Man," on the other hand, remains open to the inclusion of, but not dominion over, new objects. In 1938 it is Stevens' "latest" step beyond the initiatory "Nomad Exquisite" in developing the "metamorphosis" of initial rapprochements.

In the poems we have looked at, Stevens' metaphors are closely attached to the traditional troping move that personifies divine and natural forces and, in turn, defines man's dependent status in the scheme of these two orders. Stevens foregrounds resistance "against" their predetermined linguistic and conceptual forms, but in moments of greater freedom he explores rhetorical means of retaining some of the imagery of such traditional figures as the sun in "The Latest Freed Man," while resisting the imaginative hegemony of the hierarchical sun-man metaphor. That is, he is sometimes able to develop the material form of time-worn metaphors in new directions.

In Stevens' work with "wormy" metaphors—as in the other types of work that are the subject of the following chapters—the form Stevens' development takes evokes the necessary mediation between a poetic voice and a reader's eye and ear. It is only this form, become "thing," that can be scrutinized and examined. The potentialities it contains cannot exist without a human context (writer and reader), but the rapprochements established in a particularly dense way by metaphor may point to unsuspected relations that are a stimulus to new awareness. As readers we are able to sift apart (or "cribler," as in "The Motive for Metaphor") the characteristics of the linguistic/material reality itself from the characteristics of its psychological effect, a distinction that Stevens, as a man of his times, never makes in his own essays. The philosopher or linguist can never argue conclusively about the validity of considering resemblance as a common denominator for demarcating metaphor from other kinds of language. Neither can the literary critic ever persuade us definitively about it. The work of the poet, however, can present to our view chains of words that expand the ways resemblance works in metaphor. Considering metaphor as a trope of resemblance is useful because it allows us to discriminate between poetic structures in which the metaphors remain dead and turn in circles, and those in which the metaphors lead away from the confining assumption of an original ground.

2

WORLD AND WORD *AU PAYS DE LA MÉTAPHORE*

> Reality is a cliché
> From which we escape by metaphor
> It is only au pays de la métaphore
> Qu'on est poète.
>
> —*From Miscellaneous Notebooks* (OP 204)

Metaphor and Transfer

Stevens seemed to have an acute sense of the imaginative and conceptual constraints that made the world he had inherited cohere. His work with metaphor translates an effort to create an expanded word-world within which to integrate human life. The "cliché" of "reality" from his *Notebooks* is precisely this: it is the set of fixed relations and fixed significance we give to the so-called given world, such as the pathos the Romantics attributed to nature, as contrasted with the possibility of a vision cleansed of fixed meanings that we saw in "The Latest Freed Man." Metaphor is the material of a positive "escape," the linguistic means of renovation. My purpose here is not to distill a theory of metaphor, poetry, or even language from the traces Stevens left. Many critics have woven together phrases and sentences by Stevens as strands in a theory of metaphor that Stevens might have supported.[1] But I would not be the first to observe how imprecise Stevens himself is about defining metaphor and its effects,[2] and to add that as a guide for reading Stevens' poetry, his own views are partial (in both senses of the word) at best.

Throughout Stevens' career, however, we find poems themselves that explicitly raise the issue of linguistic expression. Their self-referentiality invites us to examine them not as examples of discourse about theory, but as examples of patterns of linguistic enactment. Sixteen poems even promote the word *metaphor* specifically, six of which are collected with other poems of "transport" (another translation of the Greek *metapherein*) in *Transport to Summer* (1947).

Aristotle, in addition to designating the per/conception of "resemblance" as a basis for metaphor, also opens the way for considering metaphor as a transfer. "Metaphor," he says, "consists in giving the thing a name that belongs to something else, the transference being either from genus to species, or from species to genus, or from species to species, or on grounds of analogy."[3] Aristotle's vocabulary stresses the need to "place" (*titein*) or "carry/bear" (*pherein*) a sign in or to a different referent in terms that translate roughly as "replace," "displace," "substitute," "transfer."[4] This word-focused description of metaphor applies to synecdoche (such as part for whole) as well as to relations of "resemblance." Aristotle seems to claim that there is a proper use of each word, without which it would not be known whether a transfer were taking place. Normalcy is a question of usage: one usage will be ordinary, another strange (1457b, 1458a, 1458b).[5] But within the broader linguistic framework, the idea of transfer can attach the epistemological task of creating resemblances within the given world to the task of constructing categories and then transferring words within and among them. Language can be seen as a symbol system in which there is considerable leeway for replacing one word by another without risk of chaos.

Although Aristotle's remarks on metaphor rest on a theory of art and language as a mirror of nature, and although the representational theory of art has continued to dominate writing of all sorts, in today's consciously post-Nietzschean and post-Saussurean intellectual climate, it is easier for us than it was for Stevens to conceive that language is not transparent but something added to reference by the user. Yet even Stevens suggests that metaphor in particular constructs new word-worlds, or as he claims in "The Noble Rider and the Sound of Words," "A poet's words are of things that did not exist without the words" (*NA* 32).

His poems being poems, not philosophical treatises, their arcs encompass rather than state the "existence" of metaphor and treat its mobility as potentially both efficient and problematic. The fact that Stevens uses the French *"pays de la métaphore"* to designate the poet's "country" can be read as an emblem of metaphor's double potential of expansion and estrangement.

There is a hint in some early poems that semantic transfer merely reveals the distancing potential of metaphor, that it produces the perverse effect of separating the writing subject from the object. Yet this cleavage can be masked by the freshness of the celebratory imagery representing the visible world. In "The Paltry Nude Starts on a Spring Voyage" (CP 5–6), for example, the pleasure of new images of the sea is attached to the metaphor of Venus on her shell, at the same time as the known-ness of Botticelli's Venus displaying her charms, figuring the beauty and hope of love and art, is jarred.[6] The very first words of the poem, "But not," mark a voluntary rupture with the familiar representation (itself, of course, metaphorical in Botticelli's work).

> But not on a shell, she starts,
> Archaic, for the sea.
> But on the first-found weed
> She scuds the glitters,
> Noiselessly, like one more wave.

The first stanza brings out the pleasure of fresh yet opportunistic discovery, in "the first found weed," which allows a concise metaphorical transfer in "She scuds the glitters." Yet the "paltry nude" is said to be "discontent," "Tired," and "Eager" and moves within a "circle of her traverse of the sea" (stanza 3), which proves to be a confining metaphor. For this is called "meagre play" (stanza 4), too confined for the "goldener nude / Of a later day," who, as the last stanza (5) says,

> Will go, like the centre of sea-green pomp,
> In an intenser calm,
> Scullion of fate,
> Across the spick torrent, ceaselessly,
> Upon her irretrievable way.

This second metaphorical figure evolves in a context in which the "sea" (signifier and signified) of stanzas 1 to 3 appears only as "sea-green pomp," a mere qualifier of a qualifier, added to the name of a pigment, and not even the pigment itself like the "whited green" used to paint

Vincentine in the "Apostrophe" to her (CP 52–53). The material "stuff"
is also superseded by words like "intenser" and "spick" and "pomp" and
"calm"—that is, qualities and states. The change in the representation is
not absolute but one of degree. The metaphorical space also becomes less
restricted as the first nude's "circle" is replaced by the hypothesis of that
of another ideal figure who is (presumably) "like the centre of sea-green
pomp," free of boundaries, in the movement of "her irretrievable way."
Reading this poem self-referentially, one can see it inaugurating a reshuf-
fling of natural objects and their qualities and a decomposition of an art
form that constructs our worlds: it moves away from its grounding in a
preexistent phenomenal world of natural elements and perceived objects
and its origin in an inherited metaphor, and it looks forward to a time
when the figures of poetry—its metaphors—will go beyond the already
imagined pleasure of moving as if in "the centre of a sea-green pomp."

Despite the energy of the framing stanzas, the poem casts doubt on
the effects of the metaphorical transformation it refers to and starts to
enact. Negatives and privative prefixes and suffixes strew the ways of
both nudes with difficulty. It almost seems questionable whether the "toil
of verse" will ever, as Wordsworth wrote, be rewarded by a song rising up
"Full-formed, like Venus rising from the sea."[7] The metaphorical misap-
propriation of "torrent" and "way" by the quotidian "spick" (of "spick
and span" = "new") and "irretrievable" make these elements of the
seascape surprisingly unfamiliar but not yet self-fulfilling. The poem's
end predicts a movement away from both dear objects and dear forms of
expression toward a future poetry that is unfettered and brave. The "scul-
lion of fate," a transfer within the Venus conceit, threatens to signify that
metaphoric work is indeed still "meagre play." The transfer of Stevens'
speaker's new signs onto Botticelli's old metaphor creates an estrange-
ment without the desired expansion of experience of the phenomenal
world.

A number of poems in Harmonium contribute to the vast search for
innovative forms in the visual and literary arts that took place in the years
between 1870 and the aftermath of the First World War. Painting styles as
wildly different as French Impressionism and Whistler's series of "Arrange-
ment[s]" and "Symphon[ies]," to say nothing of the de-compositions of
Cubism, showed the realist mode as creating a deceptive familiarity with
things, just as Botticelli's Venus could be seen as a familiar and "direct"
representation of a metaphorical figure. Similarly, a number of Stevens'
experiments unmask the nostalgic delusion of finding any simple way of

replacing metaphor and its inherited obfuscations with another language.

A few of his earliest published poems, for instance, reply to the assumptions of innovative artistic and poetic movements like fin-de-siècle aestheticism (as in "Disillusionment of Ten O'Clock," *CP* 66) and Imagism. Most interesting for us is his attack on Imagism's advocacy of seemingly direct, autonomous verbal images and its assumption that language can perform an innocent mediation with thing or emotion. The bridge crossing in "Metaphors of a Magnifico" and humanity's "light" in "Nuances on a Theme by Williams" are specific metaphors for the mediation performed by language. They are even metaphors for the world-making work of metaphor, represented as an incapacitating absence in "Metaphors of a Magnifico" and as an imprisoning presence in "Nuances." They come as close as any poems Stevens ever wrote to representing what poetry should avoid.

"Metaphors of a Magnifico" (*CP* 19) problematizes the seemingly simple process of converting fact or event into statement. Through the permutations of three bridge crossings, the observation of twenty men entering a village is transformed from a collective to a singular experience. It thus seems to hone in on the crucial place of any "one man"'s action and consciousness in making bridge crossing an experience. Yet if, most cruelly in this time of war (the boots are mentioned in the fifth section), the difference between twenty and one must exist, the existence of one or of twenty marchers seems to be a matter of indifference to the speaker: the number is merely exemplary of a scene repeated scores of times in villages across Europe. The speaker seems to be casting around for a single propositional truth. A philosopher would ask: Is there a truth requirement? The poem seems to ask: What truthful statement can be made about "Twenty men crossing a bridge, / Into a village" besides reducing it as the speaker does here? Stevens' oeuvre reminds us that the process of reduction is not necessarily sterile. In the late poem, "Thinking of a Relation between the Images in Metaphors" (*CP* 356–357), for instance, the reduction of a group of wood-doves to a single dove ends with the hypothesis of an epiphanic moment in "the one ear of the fisherman." The "single man / In whose breast, the dove, alighting, would grow still" may be a place of union of inner and outer worlds. The "disclosure" the poem states as its own purpose is the result of variations and verbal transfers that finally distill even opposites into union. In "Metaphors of the Magnifico," on the contrary, the drive for statement in the middle of the poem interferes with its own realization by refusing to use *metaphora* or word transfers: "Twenty men crossing a bridge / Into a village" becomes frozen into a "real" tautological equivalence ("Twenty men . . . / Are / Twenty men") and thus existentially meaningless.[8]

It is clear that the mediation of linguistic assertion is at a dead end in "Metaphors of a Magnifico." A new "song" would presumably "transfer" other words into the speaker's direct assertions and thus infuse his language with content. But we infer that what is called "old song / That will not declare itself" may be too worn out to prevent the poem's collapse, like the "too many waltzes" in "Mozart, 1935" (CP 131) that deaden perception as well as art. Within the body of the poem the speaker finally tries a third tactic—the simple denotation of the objects of perception, the Imagistic approach with which the poem ends.

> The boots of the men clump
> On the boards of the bridge.
> The first white wall of the village
> Rises through fruit-trees.
> Of what was it I was thinking?
> So the meaning escapes.
>
> The first white wall of the village . . .
> The fruit-trees . . . (Ellipses in original.)

The narrative thread thus rehearses the speaking magnifico's attempts to build up a sequence of simple denotation. His assumption here seems to be that he should be able to take the sights and sounds he observes and the effects they have on his mind—"thinking"—and give them adequate expression. This would be the plane on which "meaning" would then come to be. But allegorically speaking, the "white wall" that "Rises" remains blank. And on the level of the word-world that might be written, the Imagistic positioning of the names of things perceived fails to create prolific transfers. The final attempt to both name and position comes to naught in the closing couplet, where no predicates can be found to fix the role of the grammatical subjects—which therefore remain incomplete. In the logic of the poem, such grammatical subjects can hardly be said to refer to anything outward or inward that "exists."

As a poem of its occasion, the failure of expression poignantly conveys the hopelessness of the war situation, the unspeakableness of what

can be observed, thought, and felt. The attempt to articulate proposi-
tional truth catalyzes the speaker's estrangement. The poem's final, un-
completed trace epitomizes the gulf on a philosophical level between
perceiving the phenomenal world and making statements about it. To
speak metaphorically, the poem cannot repress its own failure to "cross"
the "bridge" from sensibilia to "meaning." Neither statement/definition,
nor worn-out songs/poems, nor denoting/naming are sufficient means of
expression. None of the magnifico's verbal tactics can fulfill the role for-
merly attributed to metaphor, in which the oblique reference and inclu-
sionary gesture produced by transfer had the potential to multiply the
given represented in language.

"Nuances of a Theme by Williams" (*CP* 18) denounces the delu-
sion that by stripping statement down to a minimum a poet can provide a
viable alternative to metaphor. He uses William Carlos Williams' Imagis-
tic poem "El Hombre" as a foil, first quoting the four lines of Williams'
apostrophe to the "ancient star," then amending it. Williams' basic refer-
ence is a comparison between the isolation of the Morning Star, which is
gradually outshone by the sun that ignores its presence, and the solitude
of the human subject, the *hombre*/man, darkened already (like the French
ombre, shadow) by the title and counting for little in the universe.

Although Williams claimed that Stevens "liked" his poem,[9]
Stevens' emendation reveals the poem's foible: in apostrophizing the
star, Williams' speaker recognizes the apostrophized star as other
("strange") but also implicitly appropriates it. As Gelpi points out,
Stevens refutes Williams' (Imagist-related) practice with his own Imagis-
tic insistence on stripping the object of all metaphor.[10] Indeed in Stevens'
first counterstanza, the speaker exhorts the star not only to "Shine alone"
but to mirror neither his "face nor any inner part" nor anything else; that
is, he exhorts it to resist and be itself, independent of the poet-observer's
anthropomorphizing designs and needs. Stevens' second counterstanza
ridicules the misuse of the natural object by "humanity."

> Lend no part to any humanity that suffuses
> you in its own light.
> Be not chimera of morning,
> Half-man, half-star.
> Be not an intelligence,
> Like a widow's bird
> Or an old horse.

By inverting the old hierarchy of nature's law, Williams' pattern has "suf-fuse[d]" (read: "sub-fused") the old image under/into human need, reduc-ing it to the pitiful "widow's bird" and "old horse," which are also destined to receive human projections. The reader of Keats' "Bright star, would I were stedfast as thou art" is reminded that Keats used the star as a model for the "still stedfast, still unchangeable" lover. But Keats' speaker, though personifying the star, lauded the star's "lone splendor" as something that is not to be mimed or shared. On the contrary, Keats' poem respects the star's integrity. Stevens accuses Williams' monstrous "Half-man, half-star," on the other hand, of being mere "chimera," de-prived of its own, particular qualities. Williams' betrayal is not precisely solipsistic because it does not question the status of the star's existence. The irony Stevens' speaker sees in Williams' poem is that although the star is said to "give" courage to the speaker, it is actually the human being, the *hombre* of Williams' title, that gives his own feeling of solitude to the star. In this sense, Stevens' poem debunks the fiction of pathos and the hierarchical againstness of Williams' move. The rhetorical paradox of Stevens' poem is that, as Weston has noticed, Stevens' speaker is bound to celebrate the separateness of the star only with rejected metaphors,[11] metaphors used against themselves.

Thus Stevens' poetic act reveals concomitantly the epistemologi-cal question of how we perceive and conceive the outside world and the disingenuousness of Williams' apostrophe. Stevens' riposte pounds out the metaphoricity that Williams' language ostensibly hides. But the poem itself offers no alternative to the metaphorical transfers Stevens' speaker amplifies.

Metaphor and the Object World

One of Stevens' recurrent subjects from *Harmonium* through *Transport to Summer* to *The Auroras of Autumn* (1950) is the conceptual and artistic aim of using metaphorical transfer to distill something else out of sense perception—thought, increased awareness, a parallel pleasure. Caught between an appreciation of the direct pleasure provided by the objects of sight (and to some extent hearing) and a suspicion of the primacy of the structures of the mind that Kant hypothesized, Stevens at his most self-conscious seemed aware that language was neither the equivalent of a thing nor the direct expression of the mind. Poems like "Metaphors of a Magnifico" and "Nuances of a Theme by Williams" can be read as poems that show dead-end uses of language, two ways of wrongly claiming to be free of metaphor, among the modernist experiments.

Stevens' work with language's use in representation navigates between two opposing ideas, that metaphorical language epitomizes the most alienating potentialities of language—its ability as sign to reveal our difference from the world and the separation of our minds from the things they contemplate—and that metaphor is a sign of the involvement required of the maker and thus a tool for incorporating the human subject and objects of sense in the same creative space. Numerous poems thematize the epistemological slant on the mediation between subject and world through language. Two late examples, "Crude Foyer" (1943) and "Bouquet of Roses in Sunlight" (1947), are particularly instructive in the ways they couch "crude" ideas about sensibilia and metaphor in sophisticated forms.

"Crude Foyer" (CP 305) is built on a metaphor that brings together several meanings of the word "foyer." "Foyer" as (entrance) hall in English combines with a less extended sense deriving from its Latin etymology in *focus* = "fire," the French *foyer* meaning "hearth," then "home." The "foyer" not only shares the connotations of theater and home but initiates the motif of knowledge as seeing, through the "foyer of the spirit" being placed "in a landscape / Of the mind" (rather than "in the wind" as in "Six Significant Landscapes" I). The French *foyer* is thus also exploited in its optical sense, which reminds us that English adopted the Latin word *focus* for this optical meaning. The poem enacts epistemological doubt about the validity of empiricist notions of the privileged relation between sight and knowledge and the (post-)Kantian assumption of the primacy of the structures of the mind. It is a self-problematizing reflection on the origin and content of knowledge.

The poem advances in one of Stevens' hallmark styles, by syntactic increments. To an initial definition, "Thought is false happiness," a putative subordinate clause is hung in apposition. It is never completed, however, but branches out, the second branch ramifying three times, the third ramification producing at least three small branches itself, or perhaps four. (The function of the final subordinating "that" suggests other branchings besides the one I have numbered [iv] on the basis of grammatical parallels.)

Thought is false happiness: the idea
[1] That merely by thinking one can,
Or may, penetrate, not may,
But can, that one is sure to be able—

[2] That there lies at the end of thought
A foyer of the spirit in a landscape
Of the mind, [a] in which we sit
And wear humanity's bleak crown;

[b] In which we read the critique of paradise
And say it is the work
Of a comedian, this critique;
[c] In which we sit and breathe

An innocence of an absolute,
False happiness, since we know [i] that we use
Only the eye as faculty, [ii] that the mind
Is the eye, and [iii] that this landscape of the mind

Is a landscape only of the eye; [iv] and that
We are ignorant men incapable
Of the least, minor, vital metaphor, content,
At last, there, when it turns out to be here.

The poem begins by refusing the satisfactions of rationalism, the idea that "merely by thinking" we can know. At first "thought" is defined as the means by which the subject can "penetrate" (stanza 1). It is the object of this verb that is not given but is continually withheld by the grammatical ramifications of the second, parallel, subordinate clause that begins in stanza 2. Moreover, the defining "Thought is false happiness" is mirrored by the suggestion that "False happiness" (c) may itself be an illusion because it is projected beyond the scope of thought by the continued deferral of the object. Neither is the Kantian or post-Kantian principle of taking the structures of the mind as determining the structures of knowledge a viable basis for "thought," since the place of such considerations (the reiterated "in which" of stanzas 2 and 3) is where we "wear humanity's bleak crown."

On the level of epistemology, the poem is a retrospective glance at "Tattoo" but also "Tea at the Palaz of Hoon" (both from *Harmonium*) and their playful flirtations with empiricism and solipsism respectively.

"Crude Foyer" focuses on the receiver's end of sight, the "eye as faculty," whereas "Tattoo" (CP 81) focuses first on the "light" of the object world which "crawls under your eyelids / And spreads its webs there—." There the eyes are reattached to the "surface of the water" and the "edges of the snow," the light's own terrain, thus creating a circular pattern. The skeleton of the ambiguous "Crude Foyer," on the other hand, tends to connect knowledge to sense perception and to make knowledge a natural consequence of mere empirical sense data. "Tea at the Palaz of Hoon" (CP 65) takes the reverse tack. It makes of its bombastic speaker a self-created, declining sun-god, whose outer and inner worlds circle in "the compass" of the sea that he himself is. His rhetorical questions are partially answered by the circular auditory image of "And my ears made the blowing hymns they heard." Overall, the poem privileges the self as creator and is partially solipsistic. In "Crude Foyer," reduction rather than circularity is produced by metaphorical transfer. Landscape is reduced to the "landscape of the mind" and finally to the "landscape only of the eye"— paralleled (by the "that" of iv) with our ignorance.

This knowledge about knowing is a metaknowledge encapsulated in an alienating syntax of metaphors. It is not clear whether the imagery of the outer landscape should be applied to patterns of knowing. Nor is it clear whether the eye decodes the outer landscape in relation to the patterns of external nature (as in "Tattoo"), in relation to its own patterns, or in relation to the patterns of the mind (as in the solipsism of "Hoon"). The placing of "only" before eye (stanza 4), moreover, belittles its import, whatever it may be, even though it may determine everything that is in the mind. Notice too how the "of" has the vagueness of the French *de*. Does "only of the eye" imply belonging to the eye, or made by the eye—the eye as innocent receiver, or the eye as determining the form of what is received? In the context of this vagueness, the *over*-resemblance established by the reiterated "Is" obfuscates life-giving distinction between landscape, mind, and eye.

The speaker's "content" self-defeat illustrates the self-erasures produced by transfers of the signifiers that "carry" the foyer metaphor. What the poem says "turns out" (iv, last line) punningly represents a turning in, toward the eye, an eye whose focus is similarly not directed toward an outside "landscape" but toward an inside intimate space "at the end of thought" (stanza 2). This "end," within the self-referential space of the poem, is the end of the poem's "here." As Rosu notes, "Crude Foyer" depends on Platonism while it also reveals the limitations of "seeing" the world [the "eye" in the represented landscape, she says] as philosophy claims to.[12] The ingrown relations among the metaphors heighten our sense that the "foyer" is our very impoverished, or at least frustrating, epistemological "home." Seeing with the mind's eye is a dead metaphor, a "crude foyer"—as a place for seeing/focusing, and as a place for articulating a transfer of signifier from one noun position to another within the poem's syntax. The deployment of the metaphors in this case lacks a focus (*foyer*) because (using my own metaphors now) it lacks discrimination between background and foreground. The metaphor's culmination (end of stanza 4 and beginning of stanza 5) both confirms and denies what the penultimate line states about metaphor—that we are "ignorant men incapable / Of the least, minor, vital metaphor." Surely the poem uses at least "the least minor" metaphor, but the epithet of "vital metaphor" gives the poem a kind of self-irony.

Being a poem, "Crude Foyer" does not offer an analytic argument with logical discrimination between causes and effects. The poem's texture brings to the surface one problem that underlies the modern poetic use of metaphors by stating the desire for "vital metaphor." The modern writer may be concerned about the origin and status of individual experience, while doubting that science or philosophy can ever provide satisfactory versions of this experience. At the same time, the claim of a universal truth accessible by romantic subjectivity can no longer be the "subject" of poetry. Yet a skeptical epistemology, this poem says, has yet to find creative expression in the metaphors of poetry when it is the very object of poetic discourse.

"Crude Foyer" gives a glimpse of why it is hard for metaphor to make the distinctions necessary to the kind of question epistemology raises: metaphor involves semantic transfer that moves across boundaries, such as the eye to the mind and vice versa. This is one of the implications of Aristotle's comment that metaphor can be the transfer of a word "from genus to species, or from species to genus, or from species to species, or on grounds of analogy" (see above and *Poetics* 1457b). The linguistic transfer operated by poetic metaphor may, contrary to philosophical argument, abolish the difference between qualities, or it may blur the sequential line of cause and effect, as "Crude Foyer" blurs the inner-outer distinctions of subject-object and metaphor-mimesis, while retaining traditional dualistic referents. Indeed Stevens' poetic oeuvre retains this dichotomy right up to the end, with variants, as when in "Not Ideas About the Thing But the Thing Itself" (*CP* 534), the poem that closes the *Collected Poems*, the ear is substituted for the eye in "a scrawny cry from *outside* / Seemed like sound in his *mind*" (emphasis added).

The submissive tone of "Crude Foyer," however, seems to chafe at the reduction of "there" to "here" that ironically signs the impossibility of kinship. Or perhaps it is metaphor itself that can be seen as causing estrangement by crossing boundaries in a movement that takes the human subject away from the world. Stevens' poems seem to address both of these possibilities. Often the tension in a poem involves the perception that they both exist at once and that poetry is not the place to separate them.

The threat of distancing through metaphor is also perceptible in a poem contemporary with "Crude Foyer," "Bouquet of Roses in Sunlight" (CP 430–431), which seems, on one level of reading, to take a polarized position that places metaphor at odds with sense perception and its direct pleasures. It opens with a hypothesis, in "Say that," that the object world is so full of the "crude effect" of color that it cannot be "changed by metaphor." The first two stanzas are a variant of "Woman Looking at a Vase of Flowers" (CP 246), where things are not abstract but "close" and give direct pleasure, or "Debris of Life and Mind" (CP 338), where for a moment a "bright red woman" remains mute because "when the sky is blue, things sing themselves." The colors of the roses in "Bouquet" are "too much as they are / To be anything else" and would satisfy, perhaps, the desires of the audience in "The Man with the Blue Guitar" for "things as they are." They are sufficient to love and to delight in. They are self-sufficient, with no need for words.

The following five stanzas of "Bouquet" (stanzas 3 to 7) relativize the relationship between perceiver, object, and metaphor. Our "sense" of the world is in a dialectical relationship with it, and as our experience heightens it, it brings about a change in the world that is greater than the change produced by metaphor. The poem seems to say that only nonverbal experience can close the gap between world and human subject. Although human subjectivity dominates the scene, in "exceed[ing]" outside "changes of light," our "sense" does not deform but apprehends or touches directly, whereas, implicitly, metaphor does not.

> And yet this effect is a consequence of the way
> We feel and, therefore, is not real, except
> In our *sense* of it, our *sense* of the fertilest red,

Of yellow as first color and of white,
In which the *sense* lies still, as a man lies,
Enormous, in a completing of his truth.

Our *sense* of things changes and they change,
Not as in *metaphor*, but as in our *sense*
Of them. So *sense* exceeds all *metaphor*.

It exceeds the heavy changes of light.
It is like a flow of *meanings* with no speech
And of as many *meanings* as of men.

We are two that use these roses as we are,
In seeing them. This is what makes them seem
So far beyond the rhetorician's touch. (Emphasis added.)

    Here the word "metaphor" seems to denote a radical form of language that would obstruct the subject's relating to the bouquet. It is invested with stable associations even as it is attributed with creating change through the imagination. In terms of the opposition that is so firmly ingrained in Stevens' obsessive vocabulary, the poem seems to opt for the changes of reality over those of the imagination ("real" and "imaginings" in stanza 2).[13] Yet in Stevens' descriptions of his "imagination-reality complex," the poetic work of the imagination is never sharply distinguished from the task of writing itself and always includes the "escape by metaphor" of our epigraph. Thus when the word "metaphor" acts as a fixed motif in an otherwise semantically fluctuating "Bouquet," it threatens to divorce the poem from the poet's ability to give life, as Stevens said, to "the supreme fictions without which we are unable to conceive of" the world (*NA* 31).

    Although "Bouquet of Roses" proposes that there is a way to be in the pleasure of the senses without metaphor, yet it undermines the possibility of excluding metaphor. To take two examples, it implies that when in whiteness or in man, "the sense lies still, as a man lies, / Enormous, in a completing of his truth" (stanza 4), this completion would be corrupted by the effect of metaphor. But might not the simile become a pun on "lie" as untruth, pointing to its own enormity or outrageousness? Secondly, if metaphor could cause the source of pleasure "to be changed" (stanza 2), it would disturb the fit between the "as they are" (stanza 1) of the colors and the "as we are" (stanza 7) of the speaking subject, which frame the poem. But the language of philosophical authority that constitutes the poem's macrostructure ("consequence," "therefore," "So") lacks the logical force these words denote, as in the compressed pseudosyllogism:[14]

> Our sense of things changes and they change,
> Not as in metaphor, but as in our sense
> Of them. So sense exceeds all metaphor.

Moreover, the last stanza retreats from certitude about metaphor's weakness with a quasi-chiasmic "seeing them . . . them seem":

> We are two that use these roses as we are,
> In seeing them. This is what makes them seem
> So far beyond the rhetorician's touch.

The paradoxical twist is that if things are not beyond the changes of our sense(s), neither can they be beyond metaphor; they only "seem" to be. And the affirmed meanings of the poem are undermined to mean something else about metaphor.

The varying transfers of the word "sense(s)" in "Bouquet" bind together different signifieds, or, it might be said, are slipped into different situations where they accrete connotations belonging to other words in the poem like "we feel" (stanza 2), "his truth" (stanza 4), and "meanings" (stanza 6). This is "speech" while being "like a flow of meanings with no speech." It is as changing as the "changes of light" (stanza 6) and as "Our sense of things changes and they change" (stanza 5). Things necessarily change in words, and here the words act like ever-varying metaphors, in which an effect of transfer provokes resemblances and differences of connotation among the identical ("sense" and "senses") and the different ("feel," "truth," "meanings") words. The poem's semantic meaning is rather more like what Stevens says in "The Effects of Analogy," that what the poet "writes about is his sense of our world" (*NA* 119). It is related to our existence because it is not just a conglomerate of "meanings" but "a flow of meanings," going forward—as in the French *sens* = "meaning" or "direction"—and made individually applicable in "as many meanings as of men." There is also more than a hint of "sense" as signifying "meaning" that is added by people when they react to words, a concept Stevens encountered in I. A. Richards' *Coleridge on the Imagination*

(1934): "As a rule a part of the meaning is put into the word and the rest is left to our response to this meaning."[15] In "Bouquet of Roses" there is a "sense" that the reader's shifting reaction is a reaction to something shifting, a movement of the speaker's mind, some would say, carried on by the rhythmic reprise of words and phrases. But the reader's response also interacts with the work of metaphor, augmenting each perception through a cumulative process.

The poem seems to ask, then: What happens when sense perception and feeling encounter metaphorical language? Given that language is something other, other than both external world and self, and that metaphor is usually considered as a form that also substitutes one form of itself for another, can its methods compensate for the gap it signifies? The "roses" in this poem illustrate the confluence of separation and a compensation for it. They gather to themselves a panoply of names. They impose their existence by a refusal to be captured in the basic categories established by English as red or yellow but are worded as "the fertilest red" and "yellow as first color." This is one way colors not only "seem" but *are* "beyond the rhetorician's touch," by obliging language to bend itself to their particularities, by obliging it to enter into the activity of metaphorical transfer and admit to the artificiality of the color categories our vocabulary has established.[16] The inevitability of metaphorical transfer in language is clinched by the finalizing metaphor of "the rhetorician's touch" itself.

In sum, what the poem affirms and what it does are opposed. A paraphrase of the poem's statements affirms that there is a subjective plane of sharable or shared experience in which metaphor is illegitimate because the kind of change it produces would be purely external. Metaphor is opposed to meaning that is human, whereas the objects of sense perception are not because they give life to feeling and feeling to life. Metaphor would be the touch that separates us from our "meanings," from applications to each individual's life. But what the poem's metaphorical work does is to apprehend indirectly yet respect the integrity of the things perceived. The shifting words for colors, the slippage and transformation of the word "sense(s)," the metaphor of "the rhetorician's touch," and the other similes and metaphors all point to the very intervention of metaphorical language as what allows us to "use" (in the last stanza)—and be consciously active in using—the objects we observe. The objects have two lives: one in observation, one in representation. This second life, however, is deflected from the referent by metaphorical language to produce a new word-world that is not a mere accumulation of those definitions.

It is strange for a poetic voice to formulate suspicions about metaphor competing with things and our feeling for them. It speaks of a hypothetical ebb of confidence in the language of poetry, at best a naive demarcation of what metaphor is, at worst a doubt about the ability of the metaphors we produce to be a buttress against alienation. Even Stevens' late poems in *Transport to Summer* (1947) give hints of a nostalgia for a time when feeling seemed unadulterated by rhetoric, even if the rhetoric itself experiments with overcoming this longing and partially succeeds.

Constructive Metaphor

Wallace Stevens' poems perform basic research in the area of poetic language. By saying that they perform "research," I mean that they experiment with the process of metaphorical substitutions. They do the work of exploring how the language might allow not resolution but escape from the narrow world of the quandary about epistemology, to a further horizon. Nonetheless, there remains the question of how the poet is going to construct word-worlds and project a further horizon with the pieces of semantic landscape he has. How will he arrange the linguistic material of his metaphors (as opposed to denoting their referents) in a way that might still connect them to some basic observation about the world experienced outside of language?

Among the more pointed poems that thematize a polarized opposition between the order of nature on the one hand and the order of art and rhetoric on the other is "Add This to Rhetoric" (1938) (CP 198–199). Its introductory formula sets both the theme and the strategy of the poem, the alternance of art and nature: "It is posed and it is posed. / But in nature it merely grows." Such formulaic sentences are woven among more irregularly phrased examples of artistic media, beginning with the stones that "pose in the falling light" of sculpture, and including intricate overlappings of painting and poetry or other writing. The posed example of sculpture is dismissed with "Shucks . . . ," just as the word landscape with its "clouds, / Grisaille, impearled, profound" sputters out with "Pfft . . . " (Ellipses in original.) The second section of the poem confirms the impression that if nature "merely grows," this is a positive virtue compared to the ephemeral narcissism of art's (mostly self-referential) poses. Even the word "pose" mirrors itself in several different poses as passive, active, and reflexive verb, before finishing as a static noun.

Stevens' speaker denigrates the evanescence of the artist's work, which ends as a "fringed eye in a crypt." Nature's cyclicality outdistances art's linear course; nature's future light survives art's material substance. Nature's perennial life as a standard measure is exemplified, even incarnated, not surprisingly, as the sun.

> To-morrow when the sun,
> For all your images,
> Comes up as the sun, bull fire,
> Your images will have left
> No shadow of themselves.

The sun will remain the sun in its resurgent vitality, whereas the painter's picture (described in the following eight lines) will merely be "worn out" like the painter's dead model with her arm that "falls down." Art's poses contain their mortal meaning.

Yet the sun is not just the sun. Simple equivalence or identity (the outer shape of tautology) will not suffice. There is no escaping the blatantly metaphorical and generally rhetorical nature of (the art of) language. The evidence: even as the speaker castigates art's artificial limitations, he also evokes the sun, in his own language, as the rhetorical "bull fire." This indeed "adds" human "sense" to the word "sun," much in the way metaphorical connotation is developed in other poems written in 1938, such as the intensification of perception produced by the "ox" and "strength of the sun" in "The Latest Freed Man" or the looser metaphorical force of lion, ox, and dog that contest the "misery" of having nothing "at heart" in "Poetry Is a Destructive Force" (CP 192–193). Bloom, who sees "Add This to Rhetoric" as a "footnote" to "The Poems of Our Climate," says that both poems "have the Emersonian insight that everything that is not natural is rhetorical, which means that only the Not-Me, including the body, is free of rhetoric, while the soul itself 'lies in flawed words and stubborn sounds' [the final words of 'The Poems of Our Climate']."[17] From my perspective, although Stevens may have held some belief that corresponds to Bloom's description, the poem seems to demonstrate the fruitlessness of such a binary opposition when perception includes rhetoric, as in the poem's description of the "moon without a shape"—shaped by the word *shape*—that is said to stand "above" the framed painter's model. This, moreover, is suggested by "The sense creates the pose" that inaugurates the poem's closing formulae. If the term "bull fire" is an expression of the inevitable "humanity" of everything we notice (like the apostrophe to the star in "Nuances on a Theme by Williams"), this poem adds the inextricableness of perception and shape-giving to the simpler expression of the power of words in "Variations on a Summer Day" XIV, for example, which declaims: "Words add to the senses," and illustrates with pleasure-enhancing word-examples of "dazzle / Of mica" or "Arachne integument of dead trees" words that "Are," it is said, "the eye grown larger, more intense" (CP 234). As in the later "Bouquet of Roses in Sunlight," "sense" in "Add This to Rhetoric" is sense perception, feeling, thought, meaning, and the direction they and the poem's words take. Rhetoric is our natural condition and not something "added."

Contrary to the speaker of "Bouquet of Roses in Sunlight," this speaker does not merely denigrate the distractions of metaphor but makes a constructive contribution to clarifying the subtle if elusive distinction between "the figure" and "An evading metaphor" at its close.

> The sense creates the pose.
> In this it moves and speaks.
> This is the figure and not
> An evading metaphor.
>
> Add this. It is to add.

These final assertions evade paraphrase by keeping the specific antecedents of the pronouns *this* (three times) and *it* (twice) difficult to pin down. Is it the "pose" created by "sense" that is transferred grammatically onto "This" and thence displaced through "the figure" onto the final "Add this"? Or is it "the sense" and not "An evading metaphor" that is actually "the figure" (the figure, perhaps, of the poet's concept)? And there are other possibilities. At the end of the poem's path, the rhetorical foundations of experience are finally neither mourned nor celebrated. The assertion that "in nature it merely grows" comes to imply not that nature grows spontaneously without artifice but that growing is less than posing when posing involves awareness of one's own contribution, of one's adding. The rhetoric of "*the* figure" is the essential condition for recognizing our engagement in language so that poetry might move us and speak to us. "*An* evading metaphor" (emphasis added), on the other hand, is a transfer that "goes away" (*ex-vadere*) from us or separates us from our experience, like the dead-ended depictions the poem parodies. Some kind of "pose" is necessary. Moreover, the forceful performative— "Add this"—is more than a rhetorical reordering of the title: it indicates that it is possible, even necessary, to "add to" the dead-ended rhetoric of the artistic examples that precede. The poem that begins as a critique of the nullifying effects of most art ends as an expression of a hopeful approach to rhetoric and a brief enactment of the possibility of new metaphorical movement.

The construction of "Add This to Rhetoric" traces a short zigzag of steps. These steps are of the kind that Suzanne Juhasz defines as "an abstract statement paralleled by a metaphoric statement that embodies that idea," and that she calls Stevens' "characteristic form for the presentation of metaphor."[18] It is prevalent in *Ideas of Order, Parts of a World,* and *Transport to Summer* (including "Notes toward a Supreme Fiction"). The abstract generalization-metaphor pattern includes the "romantic" and the "heavy historical sail" in "Sailing after Lunch" (CP 120), the "truth" and the "grapes" in "On the Road Home" (CP 203), the "version of the thing" and "the fragrance of the woman" in "The Pure Good of Theory" (CP 332). And in "Connoisseur of Chaos" (CP 215–216), section I proposes a schematized variant of the principle:

> A. A violent order is disorder; and
> B. A great disorder is an order. These
> Two things are one. (Pages of illustrations.)

The poem does not merely "illustrate" a simple abstract to concrete or principle to metaphorical structure, however. Rather, like "Add This to Rhetoric," it alternates or zigzags from pole to pole, abolishing the logical separateness of the two levels. Alternating structure also informs the long postwar poem, "Someone Puts a Pineapple Together" (NA 83–87), in which discursive statements containing the lowest common denominator of the underlying idea are interspersed with a joyous catalogue of images. The self-referential subject of the poem, which literally "puts . . . together" a pineapple poem, puts forth verbal signs such as the "profusion of metaphor," "the metaphor that murders metaphor," the "truth" and "false metaphors." Toward the end it collects itself into a "form," which it says "is the pineapple on the table or else // An object the sum of its complications, seen / And unseen . . ." The pineapple poem is both object itself and created enfoldings ("complications" < *plicare* = "to fold"), object of transferred senses and transferred signs. This "world," the poem continues, is where "the total artifice reveals itself // As the total reality. . ." (NA 87).

The strategy of "Someone Puts a Pineapple Together," like that of "The Latest Freed Man" and "Add This to Rhetoric," shows that the hope for metaphor is not to find new words, new illustrations, or new transfers; rather it lies in the changes that take place between a poem's point of departure and its point of arrival, the path a poem takes. It becomes a metaphor for the poem itself. The path of the poem's exposition and illustration of metaphor culminates its expansion in the words "total artifice," which connote an intense awareness of the observer establishing relations and refracting and recomposing them in poetry. The question is how to expand the poem's course beyond an "evading metaphor" and move toward "the figure" of the whole as process.

Such poems about metaphor and rhetoric help us on our way to extracting from the very metaphors and structures of these poems a promise that the "total artifice" of the word-world gives value to the artifice of world-making. Another pineapple poem, "Poem Written at Morning" (CP 219), figures this self-referentially again: the title's "Poem" foregrounds the work's made quality, while its "Written at Morning" situates using rhetoric at the time of day that Stevens' mythology invests with expectations (which may be fulfilled or disappointed) of new experiences and fresh awareness. The opening stanza echoes "Dezembrum" (CP 218), the poem that precedes it in *Collected Poems*; but whereas the world that "divides itself in two" is split between man and gods in "Dezembrum," in this pineapple poem, as in "The Latest Freed Man," experience is divided between the visible things of the day and the mythologizing ("Poussiniana") we bring to it (as "The Paltry Nude" also implies). More generally, the double meaning and pun on "is" ("It is this or that / And it is not"), and the choice between categories "this" and "that" open the poem to multiple possibilities but with an awareness of the confines of word choice and the artifice that goes into their selection.

Typically for Stevens, the import of each of the four general statements about the way we experience the sensible world expands as the poem develops and changes.

A sunny day's complete Poussiniana
Divide it from itself. It is this or that
And it is not.
            By metaphor you paint
A thing. Thus, the pineapple was a leather fruit,
A fruit for pewter, thorned and palmed and blue,
To be served by men of ice.
                    The senses paint
By metaphor. The juice was fragranter
Than wettest cinnamon. It was cribled pears
Dripping in a morning sap.
                    The truth must be
That you do not see, you experience, you feel,
That the buxom eye brings merely its element
To the total thing, a shapeless giant forced
Upward.
            Green were the curls upon that head.

The conceit of painting places a double emphasis on the act of seeing on the one hand and on the transforming process of poetic art—based on the metaphors of synesthesia—on the other. While referring to sense perception, artistic activity produces what Stevens would call a "proliferation of resemblances" that "extends the object" ("Three Academic Pieces," NA 78). This activity leads to the reduction to "The truth" in stanza 4, which itself further expands seeing to experiencing and feeling, to culminate in the speaker's new "total thing" that displaces "A thing" painted by metaphor in the second stanza. Transfers and substitutions thus effect an expansion that allows the final green curls of the head to arise out of the preceding verbal trajectory.[19] They have no raison d'être without it.

    Both the linguistic details and the trajectory of the poem belie the adequacy of reading the poem merely for its epistemological significance. The "buxom eye," for example, cannot be taken simply as a synecdoche for sight. By resemblance, the eye is also a metaphor for the agent of painting, which is a synecdoche for all signmakers including the writers of poems. It is through the self-conscious virtuosity of the poem's words beyond simple resemblance as established by metaphor that its word-world exceeds the words' message. It is through transfer among species and genera of word sound and word formation, for instance. Thus in the second stanza it is not only the transfer of a visual and then tactile image that creates the "leather fruit, / A fruit for pewter," but the transfer of sounds and grammatical forms among words. The approximate internal rhyme of "fruit" and "pewter" is diminished in "blue" where the fruitfulness has already been overlapped by the concatenation of past participles, "thorned" and "palmed" (which will be taken up more humanly in "served"). This is a visually and auditively exciting pineapple, a highly crafted, if overdomesticated one. Both signifieds and signifiers become overfull. English no longer suffices. The pears are "cribled"? This too is domesticated, of course, by the English past suffix, yet is still foreign: the French *cribler* (to grade fruit according to size; or to riddle with holes) has no English cognate in the *Oxford English Dictionary*. The pears are high quality; the language is *recherché*. This is Stevens at his most epicurean.

The metaphoric activity of the painting/senses conceit has already produced layers of transfer among both signifieds and signifiers when, finally, in the fourth stanza we find "the total thing" added to by the eye-painting-language. One of the avatars of "a shapeless giant forced / Upward" can now be epitomized: "Green were the curls upon that head." Not only has the pineapple become part of the whole, a synecdoche for "the total thing," but metaphorical scrutiny of the thing referred to and the representation of it in the poem has cast it into a new doubly metaphorical role for each day's "total thing" as "a shapeless giant." The transformations effected by a series of signs are a stunning example of Aristotle's criterion that metaphor be the transfer of a word from one thing to another. As the pineapple's "thorned and palmed and blue" qualities are transformed into or displaced by "Green . . . curls," and as "fruit" becomes "head," the description appears as a process of changing the words (adjectives and nouns) used to signify things that are part of the whole. The shapeless giant that stands for the visible presences of the day need not be shapeless when there are such words available to give it shape and when heteroclite names allow the signified to remain implied while expanding the signifiers beyond pictorial representation.

To my mind, this new assertion of the power of metaphorical description invites us to look both *through* the words to the allegory of art suggested by the poem and *at* the words to the working of this art. The fruit first seems distanced by painterly transformation and hyperbolized by synesthetic description; the final transformation comes nearer to our own human image in a past day's morning mirror. It is produced by using the series of transfers to culminate in allegorically *adding* the human to the day. It suggests each day's human possibilities rising "Upward" to be worked on by language. It is evidence that the transfer of words promotes previously unknown or forgotten words and undreamed of associations and can indeed "create things that did not exist without the words" (NA 32).[20] The words are free, not bound by an explanatory construct or standard of authority. It is not "The poem of the mind in the act of finding / What will suffice," advocated by that more philosophical and didactic voice in "Of Modern Poetry" (CP 239–240). "Poem Written at Morning" shows optimism about the future of poetry and metaphoric activity as a liberated and liberating one. In the manner of "The Latest Freed Man," but without againstness, it claims fresh excitement in daily scenes. It produces signs that rejoice in the difference between commonly understood perception and creative perception, and between denotative representation ("pineapple") and inventive metaphor. The joy in the poem comes from the process of taking steps from resemblance into difference, so as to promote the constructive artifice of poetic enlargement.

Extravagant Metaphor

Experimenting with metaphorical patterning beyond the dream of the traditional Logos is one of the main strategies used for gaining poetic, thus linguistic, freedom in Stevens' universe. For if we can agree to say to the poet, "Take the place / Of parents, lewdest of ancestors. / We are conceived in your conceits" ("Prelude to Objects," CP 195), we can also recognize that part of the poet's task implied here is to construct new metaphors ("conceits") that will allow the development of new concepts ("conceits") within a new family or system.[21] Stevens had possibilities that his predecessors did not have, and he forged his own form of metaphorical construction in the atmosphere of modernist experimentation with all aspects of poetic form. Stevens' work with metaphor is revolutionary in demonstrating linguistic and intellectual "extravagance," Thoreau's term for intellectual and spiritual wandering beyond the usual boundaries; for Stevens created new patterns from the trope of metaphor, patterns that use word transfer based on resemblance as a point of departure from which precisely to depart.

Recognition of the revolutionary nature of this task is written into one of Stevens' poems on metaphor that looks back on his early work with metaphor. This is the much commented "The Motive for Metaphor" (*CP* 288), written in 1943. It is a poem of deepened recognition in which loss and gain are not easily balanced. It has been interpreted as representing Stevens scrutinizing his former self, a "you" addressee, whom he loads with either reproach or approval for having liked the between-ness indicated in the first three of the poem's five stanzas.[22] In my view, the poem taints the former self by associating it with the "half dead" natural objects of the between seasons, spring and autumn. The first three stanzas pile up attenuations, incompletions and mutilations, "half colors," "melting clouds," a "cripple" wind, the latter being a much diminished version of Shelley's West Wind, "breath of Autumn's being, / . . . from whose unseen presence the leaves dead / Are driven." As in "Add This to Rhetoric," the moon of the second stanza is a signal of nonrealization, blighted by ephemerality, but more particularly by a failure of definition, its remaining "obscure." These images denote approximations, not "changes." The phrase "words without meaning" also indicates failure and directs the reader to reading "brighter" and "melting" and "never quite" as signs of a lack of sharp edges, a lack of sharp beginnings and ends. What is represented here is made to cower before the closing metaphor of the "vital, arrogant, fatal, dominant X," which is not "half dead" but contains the opposition of life and death within it.

The muffled quality denoted in the first three stanzas finds a formal echo in the grammatical ambiguity that follows. The second half of the poem, beginning in the middle of stanza 3, defines the you in "an obscure world" thus:

Where you yourself were never quite yourself
And did not want nor have to be,

Desiring the exhilarations of changes:
The motive for metaphor, shrinking from
The weight of primary noon,
The ABC of being,

The ruddy temper, the hammer
Of red and blue, the hard sound—
Steel against intimation—the sharp flash,
The vital, arrogant, fatal, dominant X.

The junctures between the third and fourth stanzas and between lines 1 and 2 of the fourth stanza present a major difficulty of grammatical reading. David Walker reconstructs the grammar as: you did not quite want to be yourself, yet you (or: and you merely) desired the exhilarations of changes. Then in apposition: the exhilarations of changes find analogies in metaphor, and desire for them caused you to shrink from primary noon.[23] This is probably the only reading that makes the relationship between the two groups of stanzas (1–3 and 4–5) coherent. Patricia Parker shows that a "dominant" reading would place the "ABC of being" in apposition to the "weight of primary noon" and therefore opposed to/"shrinking from" the "motive for metaphor," but that a syntactic alternative would make the "ABC of being" stand in apposition to the "motive for metaphor" itself.[24] The syntax, however, is frankly incomplete and it is impossible to grant final authority to any one grammatical analysis. This in itself should make us wary of deciphering a single paraphrasable message or deducing Stevens' "definition" of metaphor from it.[25] Insofar as the poem is a statement *about* metaphor by Stevens, it seems to challenge old, vigorless depictions of landscapes—the "clouds," "bird," and "moon" of "the melting clouds, / the single bird, the obscure moon"—with daringly unstable metaphors. By strewing the grammar with obstacles to analytic comprehension, Stevens directs our attention toward the way the ambiguous "motive for metaphor" is materialized in the poem.

His experiment begins with this grammatical ellipsis at the point of transition. Because the syntax fails to establish a relation of coordination or subordination, we must look to the juxtaposition established by the colon to detect another kind of grammatical parallel. And we find one in the morphological parallel between "Desiring" and "shrinking from." They appear in chiasmus, prefiguring the final X, where they come together.

> Desiring the exhilarations of changes:
> The motive for metaphor, shrinking from
> The weight of primary noon

These are the two sides of the "motive," a tendency toward and a retreat from: desire for what is lacking, and shrinking from what should be but is not known. The first three stanzas illustrate, from this point of view, the effects of a safely metaphorized autumn "wind" whose banalized harm is to repeat "words without meaning." Spring and autumn, as we have seen, are contaminated as both signifieds and signifiers, as seasons during which words fail to express life or define self and world. They prevent coupling and understanding. But the "evasion" of the wind metaphor lies less in its own metaphoricity than in the chain of attenuations it produces in the signifiers of the second and third stanzas, ultimately even curbing the desire of a self who "did not want nor have to be" itself. This can be one meaning of the rupture between stanzas 3 and 4: the "you" was cut off from active desire, desire that needs to be stated here in order to produce a new chain of evocations and prevent further evasions of knowledge.

So what was shrunk from is finally stated, even created, in a series of heterogeneous names or disparate terms in stanzas 4 and 5, each of which constitutes a new transfer and displaces the other. They are not interrupted with general, abstract statements as in "Poem Written at Morning." This naming makes what had been avoidable now unavoidable, even if it is *stated* on the retreat side of the "motive" ("shrinking from / The weight of primary noon"). The initial element in the known that the self had withheld itself from can be stated as: "primary noon." In Lockean empiricist theory, primary qualities like solidity, extension, and mobility produce ideas in us that resemble their cause, so that their action confirms both the adequacy of our perception and the fundamental kinship of the objects of sense perception with the perceiving mind. In this perspective, the primary quality of "the weight of primary noon" can suggest the clearest and most obvious direct knowledge we can have, in opposition to the thrice repeated "obscure moon" of stanzas 2 and 3. But as a sign for what had been avoided, once it is finally stated it initiates an engagement that sets off incursions into the unknown—materializing "the exhilarations of changes."

It is indeed at this crucial disjuncture that new metaphorical motifs are generated. They call up signs of empirical qualities, the alphabet, the smithy, the soul, *recalling*, willfully or not, among other predecessors, Locke's *Essay on Human Understanding* (primary and secondary qualities), Browning's *The Ring and the Book* ("the ABC of fact"), Blake's "The Tyger" (the forge), Wordsworth's "Ode: Intimations of Immortality" and Marianne Moore's "The Past Is the Present."[26] But it is a process of allusion that completely transforms the sources and involves them in a chain of substitutions in which allusions are uprooted. In the second part of the poem, as the appositions roll forward, the movement of the sound of these metaphors creates a gathering momentum: the disjunction of line ending and grammatical unit ("the hammer / Of red and blue"), the lines ending in spondees ("hard sound," "sharp flash"), the pulsing swells of the last line, "The vital, arrogant, fatal, dominant X." These are what move the metaphors beyond their sources and beyond the cyclical known-ness of the seasons of the year and into unpredictable engagements (partially on an allegorical level), for the new forging of a new "steel" against, possibly, an "intimation" of the immortality of the soul.

The organization of the metaphors in the last two stanzas at first seems to point to a center, a place of essence, Vulcan's forge,[27] contained between "ABC" and "X." However, the "X" is also the beginning of an unstated, unfinished series XYZ. Retrospectively, the metaphors produced between "ABC" and "X" do not stand for all that could exist between alpha and omega. In refusing to circumscribe a complete definition of fixed center, the poem loosens metaphor from any essence or, cognitively, from any originary instance that would explain it. By this I mean not only that the poem departs from and beyond the theological and natural metaphors of our human destiny, but also that the meaning of the poem becomes free from Locke, Shelley, Blake, Browning, Wordsworth, and Marianne Moore as plausible predecessors. For instance, it may well be that the represented "stance," which Bloom insists on, is similar to one that Shelley represents in "To Night,"[28] but the metaphorical act Stevens sets into motion frees itself from occasion. It is not legitimized by an inherited structure in which its occasion must be inscribed. The incursions into the desired but feared movement of the metaphorical series radicalize palimpsest, to ban imitation and affirm the speaker's own originality.

The fearless temper of this movement, the "arrogant" mood of its maker projected self-reflexively into the forge, leads it to "claim for itself" (the etymological sense of the Latin *arrogare*) the complement to the "vital I" (of "Poems of Our Climate," CP 193) and the completion of the "vital metaphor" (of "Crude Foyer"): its "fatal" crossing out. It is possible to read its future as closed by the "dominant X," cut by its axe,[29] crossed out. The inventive engagement required by metaphor carries this risk: that by naming—and more particularly, by inventing new relations through the transfer of names—the poem comes to signify the namer's own mortality.[30] It is one result of the responsibility evoked in "Description without Place" V (CP, 344), which writes of "the difference we make in what we see // And our memorials of that difference."

This is the risk of the adventure but also the creative product of the speaker's involvement. Extravagant metaphor is freer in a forward-looking way. Its direction is aleatory, its destiny more mixed. It entails that the user accept joyfully the "sharp flash" (the sine qua non of dark shadow) of destiny as part of the exhilaration. "The Motive for Metaphor" puts into practice something that "Add This to Rhetoric" advocates: a material movement of metaphor that seems to derive its energy from the potential dangers of its own meaning. Language is given power to take the user with it.

In such poems we reach the furthest reaches of an implicit epistemology that demonstrates that the world cannot be held in place, inspected, expressed. The extreme motility of the word-worlds Stevens presents to the reader in such a poem exhibits more of the potential of the risks and pleasures of language than it does of any grounding in a universal truth. Despite Stevens' own theorizing, there is little trace of any clinging to a representative theory of language—even one so broad in scope as that of Shelley, for whom the "one" the poet gives voice to subsumes the infinite variety not only of human "motives and actions" but even of English grammar with its indication of "the moods of time, and the difference of persons and the distinction of place."[31] Earlier we saw Stevens distance himself from two of the comforting certitudes of such a theory of representation: that there exists a universal and unchangeable order implicitly originating in one authoritative source, and that the words of poetry are a privileged means for synthesizing the "value" of things and giving access to the transcendent, immutable order. In Stevens' poetry, we see now, the poet engages himself courageously in the potential of language to produce the changeable, and some of his experiments in change discredit the idea that the destiny of metaphor is to express something above or outside itself.

In addition to transforming the old theological and natural law metaphors that we find most obsessively rejected in Stevens' early poems, primarily in *Harmonium*, we can thus see that Stevens, like some of his contemporaries, Pound, Eliot, Williams, and Amy Lowell, questioned the very basis of poetic language, not merely with a view to deflating the old metaphors, but with a view to inventing new linguistic structures that might free the poet from the old ones. One new means of invention lay in activating the power of metaphor in order to lead it away from its originary models and the biographical occasion of writing.

Stevens punctuated his career with these experiments in

constructing metaphors that insist on the artifice of their word-worlds or develop an "extravagant" movement in an aleatory direction. The poem is, however, the responsibility of the poet. He literally shows it forth, signs his name. Whether it is "dear, gorgeous nonsense," like Plato's metaphor for the soul in the *Phaedrus*, or a poem that propels the fictive speaker and reader into the depths of their own problem of existential responsibility, like "The Motive for Metaphor," it is the poet's responsibility to assume it. The "meaning" (l. 4), then, of such a poem is not the truth function its propositions can fulfill but the effect of the changes it precipitates: a confrontation with the use of linguistic power. This power is not just epistemological here, even if the question of metaphor implicates the mind-world relationship. In such poems we meet the paradox that both old, inherited conceits and liberated, mobile metaphors often end up signifying death. The first are imprisoned within a given, commonly accepted system; the second develop beyond it. The effect of mobile, extravagant metaphor is inscribed in the double risk of poetry, in the sense that it seems to evolve partially beyond human intention, by activating sequences that depart from old conceits; but it epitomizes the power of language for engaging with life and divulging the contingency of infinite potential upon finite form. On the human level, it confronts the writing Stevens with the condition of his own mortality and the reader with his or hers.

Part II

3

&

THE MATERIAL OF "BEING"

A poem is a pheasant disappearing in the brush.

—*Adagia* (OP 198)

"Imagination" and the Material of Language

As we have seen, early commentators of Stevens eagerly latched onto the terms in which Stevens himself conceived the crucible of artistic creation: the "imagination" working on "actual reality." The terms "imagined" and "actual" or "real" (like the term "romantic") undoubtedly enabled Stevens to find a focus for his ideas on the process of artistic creation, especially in his lectures and essays. While Stevens at first conceived of the imagination as a characteristic of many forms of the irrational (as in his confused usages of the word in "The Irrational Element in Poetry," 1936), he later saw it as a personal power or faculty that increases one's consciousness of the world and creates a new "reality" (as in "Effects of Analogy," 1948).[1] Yet they entrapped him to some degree within the confines of dualistic concepts that were at best fuzzy, grand categories.

This phenomenological slant on the "imagination" places Stevens in apposition to Wordsworth and Coleridge (and Freud), who concentrated on delimiting a notion of the imagination as a creative faculty, deriving it post facto from the traces it leaves rather than suggesting what material forms it might produce in art. This is true even of Wordsworth's suggestion that the material form of poetry should be the "language really used by [common] men." Yet even as Wordsworth justifies his own use of "plainer" language in his *Lyrical Ballads,* he insists that the poet must also "throw over" the incidents of common life "a certain colouring of the imagination," as well as reveal through those incidents "the primary laws of our nature," one of which is the way "we associate ideas in a state of excitement."[2] Thus Wordsworth returns to the artist's mind as the crucible in which transformations take place, as though the material sign's only validity lay in its power to reveal the interworking of perceptions and laws in the poet's imagination. His reflections on poetry are themselves reflected back on his own poetic mind.

Likewise, the Stevens of *The Necessary Angel* is usually less interested in art as a product than he is in human consciousness itself, which is where he sees the process of making and unmaking taking place. Unlike Wordsworth's "Preface," however, Stevens' prose reflections on the nature of poetry are not so much prismatic mirrors that send back the image of his imagination as they are exercises in evasiveness. It is interesting to read how he exploits the vagaries and versatility of his terms. In "The Noble Rider and the Sound of Words" (1941), for example, the key term "imagination" is linked with "nobility" in such a way as to allow the author to define the imagination first as adhering to what is unreal, then as adhering to what is real. The argumentative leap is performed by defining two senses of the word "escapism." The pejorative sense applies to the poet who "is not attached to reality"; the creative sense concerns the poet capable of "resisting or evading the pressure of reality" (*NA* 30–31). Thus, even as Stevens writes about the potentially concrete phenomenon of analogy, his language seems to splinter into overlapping fragments that avoid defining the material of poetry. "We are thinking [of analogy] as likeness, as resemblance between parallels and yet parallels that are parallels only in the imagination, and we are thinking of it in its relation to poetry" ("Effects of Analogy," *NA* 110), he writes later; but he never defines the precise direction-degree-nature-form of the "relation" that would give analogy an existence. It might be said that even in the discursive mode of a lecture, he avoids the entrapments of philosophical or logical precision through a virtuoso performance of poetic modulation.

Thus Stevens is usually unwilling to tackle what the poet has "made" of the world and prefers to examine the existential aspect of the poet's imaginative activity, focusing on "the life that is lived in the scene it composes" ("The Noble Rider and the Sound of Words," *NA* 25).

Stevens' concept of the imagination is only tangentially an aesthetic one; it is primarily a construct of epistemology. In this, Stevens keeps alive his nineteenth-century heritage, perpetuating, moreover, an expressive theory of art in which the material forms of art are considered valuable for the emotion, imagination, or consciousness they reveal in either "correlative" or disguised form. Thus Stevens and Wordsworth seize on the activity of a particular poet's mind, a mind that is exemplary of the highest laws of the universe.[3] It forages inward to examine the itinerary of the self, as in Wordsworth's tracing of "What passed within me"—in his "own heart" and "youthful mind"[4]—or it introspectively reflects on what Stevens called "the act of the mind" ("Of Modern Poetry," CP 240).

However, Stevens—although his essays emphasize the creative potential of the individual "imagination" or insight that makes works of value possible—hints that what one reads in a work of art cannot be reduced to a reflection of the poet's (innate) genius or (consciously developing) mind. He writes unabashedly, for example, that the poet is not the final interpreter of his own work, and that the reader may place himself above the writer's intentions (*Letters* #396). And although this statement may still leave room for phenomenological criticism, which probes behind conscious intention to the workings of the mind so dear to Stevens, it also invites readers to probe their own understanding of the language they share with the writer. It prompts us to look at how a common linguistic culture, incarnated in a work, may supersede the individual artistic "imagination" as a basis for our appreciating a work of art. Stevens himself even casts glances in the direction of grammatical analysis—when he writes of the "choice of the commodious adjective" in "An Ordinary Evening in New Haven" (CP 475) or the "amorist Adjective aflame" in "The Man with the Blue Guitar" (CP 172); when he combines the sexual and grammatico-logical associations of *copulare* in "Winter and spring, cold copulars, embrace" in "Notes toward a Supreme Fiction" (CP 392); or when he puts the definite article on stage by ending "The Man on the Dump" with "The the" (CP 203).[5] But on a more subtle level, much of Stevens' earlier and middle poetry—up through the early 1940s—impels us in this direction through the ostentatiousness of his play with the artifices of English syntax and vocabulary.

I would like to shift ground, then, away from the poet's perceptions and imaginative activity, toward the materiality of the work. The work's material is a common linguistic culture, a language that gives form to a life that comes to us without form, a language art that creates patterns from our surplus in a context in which the forms that are readily available have become mere formulae for received ideas. Shifting ground to examine the allure of what is on the surface rather than what is behind, what is visible rather than what is invisible, stands in contrast to a "romantic" view of the sort Shelley voiced when he emphasized that "language and gesture, together with plastic or pictorial imitation, become the image of the combined [emotional] effect of [surrounding] objects, and of [even the savage's] apprehension of them."[6] By stressing the contingencies of language itself, we can look at a work that creates a situation that is necessarily different from the expression of any previously experienced "life" and consider it as a new situation with its own parameters. We can thus move away from the expressive theory underpinning Stevens' affirmation that "the imagination is the power that enables us to perceive the normal in the abnormal, the opposite of chaos in chaos" (NA 153), and see the "normal"—the "opposite of chaos"—that inheres in language. From this standpoint, the difference between poetry and the world is not so much that poetry conveys the imagination's perception of the world or the emotions those perceptions produce in us, but that the material substance of our language makes the original perception "disappear," as implied in my epigraph from Stevens' Adagia, which defines poetry as "a pheasant disappearing in the brush" (OP 198). Here we find a linguistic word-world that is distinct from the ontological world of being and that contains its own contingencies.

Being and To Be in Language

"To be" a thing—a pheasant, an eye, an objective—or "to be like" a thing are absolutely distinguishable in the discourse of philosophy, a discipline in which the to be of equivalence and definition and the to be like of resemblance or analogy must be prevented from overlapping. In traditional rhetoric, the former can construct statements of metaphorical equivalence, whereas the latter is a verbal incarnation of the simile. But according to one conventional conception of metaphor, the resemblance expressed in like is still implied even when it is elided in metaphorical statements[7] in which ontological resemblance can be said to be couched in the grammar of equivalence. In Stevens' writing, to be is most often materialized as copulae of the "X is Y" type, a form of equivalence that

Stevens systematically exploited in his *Adagia* for metaphorically "defin-ing" poetry itself: "Poetry is a pheasant" (*OP* 194); "Poetry is a pheasant disappearing in the brush" (*OP* 198); or the related "The tongue is an eye" (*OP* 193). The copula type is predominant in *Harmonium* too, al-though there, copular expressions sport with a full range of other usages of the verb *to be*. By using or overusing the verb *to be* as a means of over-lapping the signs of equivalence with the logic of resemblance, Stevens demonstrates yet another operation of language, the speculative play of artifice that will be the subject of this chapter and the next.

Although inquiry into the functions of the verb *to be* is at least as old as Aristotle,[8] the past few generations of linguists, philosophers, and literary critics have pursued it with particular diligence. It is convenient to begin with a widely accepted premise that we should discriminate be-tween two broad senses of *to be* that we find in various Indo-European languages, including English, French, and German. In one usage, *to be* means "to exist," "to be present." In English we can say, "A pheasant is in the field" (properly a locative) or "There is a pheasant outside" and give to *is* a semantic value of designating existence, whatever "existence" may mean and however existence may relate to language. The "meaning" of *to be* in an ontological statement is not commonly seen as problematic, although its function in metaphysics, since Kant at least, is debated. The second usage of *to be*—that of the copula—is particularly interesting for us, given Stevens' frequent use of it. The syntactic copula in such sen-tences as "A poem is a pheasant" or, let us say, "A poem is pheasanty," seems to have only a tenuous relationship with the verb *to be* used in statements of existence, especially in absolute ones like "Therefore I am." Although the nature and history of this relationship have not been conclusively elucidated, despite the efforts of linguists over the last hun-dred years, it is at least safe to say that the role of the copula is to link, and the linkage either states the equivalence of two terms (noun + noun) or defines a quality of one of two terms (noun + adjective); the formula it produces turns around on its own self.

The status of the copular syntagm "X is Y" should not be taken for granted. At the beginning of the twentieth century, linguists of "Indo-European," looking at languages not so very alien to English, French, or German, drew attention to the fact that even in Greek and Latin two forms for stating equivalence could exist: one using *to be* in the role of the copula—*omnia praeclara sunt rara;* and one juxtaposing nouns and/or ad-jectives in a "nominal sentence"—*omnia praeclara rara.* Emile Benveniste defined the nominal sentence as a sentence that has a nominal predicate containing no copular verb, in a situation in which one might normally assume the implied third person, present tense indicative of the verb *to be*.[9] Benveniste's extensive documentation of Greek and Latin texts allowed him to compare the usage of these two forms—which he called verbal and nominal, as I will also do[10]—and to conclude that the nominal sentence (i.e., noun + noun or noun + adjective, with no intervening verb) was usually used to state general truths, whereas the verbal copula was used when it was important to indicate a temporal or other particular relationship between an event and its enunciation.[11] Study of languages outside the Indo-European family provided a broader base for truly comparative studies of a cluster of linguistic phenomena that included the semantics and syntax of the verbs *to be* and *to have*, as well as various ways of expressing equivalence by joining an attribute to a subject. And it appeared that so many language groups from Sumerian to Amerindian have used various forms of nominal sentences rather than verbal statements to express equivalence or identity that, as Benveniste wrote, the list of inflected languages that lack nominal predication, such as present-day Western European languages, is shorter than the list of those that have it.[12] Thus, by the middle of the twentieth century, it was possible to put our modern European languages in perspective and see how peculiar they are in using the verb *to be* as a copula to predicate equivalence.

Examples provided by Ernst Locker are also instructive in relativizing modern European languages' use of the "verbal" copula.[13] They confirm, as Benveniste had said, that the verbal copula is a rather unusual form if we compare its use in English, French, or German with the nonverbal statements of equivalence (what Locker calls the nonverbal copula) that are the rule in non-Indo-European languages.[14] Within Locker's project of defining a universal grammar, the verbal copula exemplifies the general principle that Indo-European languages, in contrast to many other languages, privilege the verb as the key element in the sentence. What we need to realize is that using the verb to predicate equivalence—as in "A poem is a pheasant" in English—is in no way "natural." Rather, it is totally remarkable.

Benveniste and Locker draw rather different historical and philosophical conclusions from similar data. To Benveniste, the copula *to be* in our languages is something that was added on after the establishment of an existential sense. Its usage was extended from the existential to the copular function, and this constitutes a lexical "fall." In Benveniste's words, it "must have had a definite lexical meaning before falling—at the end of a long historical development—to the rank of 'copula.' "[15] Others have correlated this lapse with a modern perception that the full sense of "existence" is unavailable through language, and that we delude ourselves when we think we can state metaphysical truth. To Locker, on the other hand, the use of the verbal copula in European languages (Derrida's "*supplément de copule*") probably derives from the verbalization of a demonstrative particle and precedes the use of *to be* as a verb to state existence.[16] For him the copula is a trace of the human mind acting, not of a "fall."

Locker goes beyond linguistic description and claims to measure the degree to which various languages remain close to objective "reality" or, on the other hand, implicitly attribute a preponderant role to "human ideas."[17] The dominant role played by verbs in modern European languages is a sign for him of the activity of ideas transforming things. And the copula is one instance in which modern Indo-European languages deform "reality" by replacing it with a strong intellectualized view of it. In Locker's conception, while the copula produces a fallacious view of reality, its use nonetheless correlates with a power that he understands to have an enormous impact on practical and political "action," including the colonial expansion of powers using these languages.[18] Locker's view is an extreme case of considering that these languages encourage the speaker to think he or she is representing "reality." The copula in such a view is an exemplar of the kind of language that gives at least an illusion of mastery to its user, especially in that users commonly consider it as a means of asserting the "truth" (such as the "truth" Locker himself seems to claim when he writes of a fallacious view of reality).

A highly sophisticated medieval version of this belief in the truth of *to be* can be found in Saint Anselm's *Proslogion*, in what Immanuel Kant would later call the ontological argument for the existence of God. In Kant's view of Anselm's scheme, the postulation of qualities (God is omnipotent, good, etc.) forms the basis for the proof of God's existence. But Kant argues that this examination already *presupposes* God's existence and therefore cannot prove it. Moreover, the grammatical formulation with *to be* cannot tell us anything new about the subject or its attributes. This is because

> Being [in the copular form] is obviously not a real predicate;
> that is, it is not a concept of something which could be added to the

concept of a thing. It is merely the positing of a thing, or of certain of its determinations, as existing in themselves. Logically, it is merely the copula of a judgment. The proposition "God is omnipotent" contains two concepts, each of which has its object—God and omnipotence. The small word "is" adds no new predicate, but only serves to posit the predicate *in its relation* to the subject. If, now, we take the subject (God) with all its predicates (among which is omnipotence) and say "God is" or "There is God," we attach no new predicate to the concept of God, but only posit the subject itself with all its predicates, and indeed posit it as being an *object* that stands in relation to my *concept*. The content of both must be one and the same; nothing can have been added to the concept, which expresses merely what is possible by my thinking its object (through the expression "it is") as given absolutely.[19]

Thus, for Kant, the verb *to be*—used either as a copula or as a verb of existence—can play no role in rational theology, because the positing of "being" cannot be the object of a logical demonstration. This means that the copula can have no metaphysical truth function. Rather, Kant implies, when we use the verb *to be* to join a subject to an adjective or another noun, we are primarily establishing relationships between one concept and another. Kant's perception means that we are mistaken in thinking that when we use the verb *to be* we are actually reaching the "being" of the grammatical subject and its attributes.

Jacques Derrida has tried to put linguistic analysis into perspective by placing philosophy in the forefront, arguing that philosophy always precedes linguistics, not only historically (the founding text, Aristotle's *Categories*, was a work of philosophy) but also conceptually.[20] For Derrida, there can be no linguistics without a philosophy to provide it with concepts. Philosophy is not, he implies, determined by linguistic or grammatical structure. Derrida sees Benveniste's linguistics as wrong on both historical and conceptual counts when it attributes to Aristotle an "unconscious" linguistic priority.[21] He warns us that it is specious to argue that our belief systems (systems that rely on "classical ontology") have failed as a result of some "accidental" inability of the copula to express being. The conclusions arrived at by linguistics point to a malaise that is actually much deeper. Looking back to Nietzsche, Derrida also expresses dis-ease with philosophy's harping on the loss of the metaphysical ground that has disappeared with the collapse of assumptions of semantic plenitude, assumptions that have as a symptom the "fusion of the grammatical and the lexical functions of 'to be,' " in Derrida's terms. Toward the end of "The Supplement of Copula" he puts it this way:

> It is a great temptation, in fact hardly repressible, to consider the growing predominance of the formal copula function as a process of falling, abstraction, degradation, as evacuation of the semantic pleni-tude of the lexeme "to be" and of all the other lexemes which, like "to be," have been allowed to wane or be replaced. When we investigate this "history" (but the word "history" belongs to this process of mean-ing) as the history of meaning, when we ask the "question of being" as a question of the "meaning of being" (Heidegger), are we not limiting the destruction of classical ontology to a sphere constituted by the reappropriation of the semantic plenitude of "to be," by the reactiva-tion of lost origins, etc.? Are we not making the supplement of copula into an historical accident, even if it is considered structurally neces-sary? Are we not expecting to find a kind of original fall, and every-thing that such a perspective would imply?
>
> Why does the horizon of meaning dominate the questioning of both the linguist and the philosophical thinker?[22]

Derrida thus pinpoints a philosophical nexus that has influenced criticism in recent decades. Some linguists, philosophers, and literary critics bewail the denial of a referential base for language, as though tak-ing *to be* as something other than ontologically representational meant that language would become mere babble or mere convention. The rup-ture between an empirical reality principle and language is feared as hav-ing the power to destroy not only the descriptive ability of language but also its ability to express metaphysical meaning, with the concurrent dis-appearance of center, safety and Law. Mallarmé, Joyce, and Beckett might seem to demonstrate this. Yet, as we shall see in the next chapter, the untranslatability of Kant's refutation of the ontological proof of the existence of God into Chinese means that the predication of ontological reality is by no means a "natural" function of language.[23] It also means that the attribution of this function to English, for example, whatever its history, is a culturally and linguistically constructed phenomenon and one worth examining using other assumptions than the query about the "meaning" of *to be*.

English speakers, much more than French speakers, to stay within the Indo-European world, are suckled on the conviction that, as in Stevens' practice of insurance law, nuances of language are justified only insofar as they translate nuances of "reality."[24] If we look inward rather than outward from Locker's idea that Indo-European users' transposal of the idea of being onto the dominant idea of acting or doing is related to the status of the verb in their languages, we cannot avoid being struck by the fact that the inflections that characterize English indeed privilege the verb disproportionately. English invests the verb with the ability to express mood, aspect, tense, and sometimes number, often with excruciating precision. It is only by convention that we restrict the sense of "A poem is a pheasant" to the general truth value Benveniste says was expressed by the verbless nominal sentence in Homer's Greek and in classical Latin. Tense and mood are defined in relation to the speaker in his or her situation of enunciation. Strictly speaking, if I say a poem *is/has been/was/must be/ought to be/shall be* a pheasant, I am affirming it in relation to me as speaker or enunciator. I am relating historical time to my time of utterance (*is/has been/was*) or may be revealing a deduction (*must be*), a moral preference (*ought to be*) or my will (*shall be*). I can evoke nuances ad infinitum merely by modifying the various auxiliaries and grammatical forms of *to be*. It might give me a sense of mastering knowledge about the world and mastering the world *tout court*.

One commonly invoked alternative for a writer or reader is to treat language as a game in which orders of coherence are no longer representational. In their different ways, Mallarmé and Beckett, for instance, offer examples of disrupted games in which the rules seem to have been blurred or forgotten. Indeed, in Wittgenstein's chess-game image, the presence of chessmen does not suffice to make a "game." Players also need to know the rules that will guide their moves. Language, like chess, needs both the pieces and the rules—as well as players—in order to be played.[25] What I would like to emphasize is that the strategies of games are always played out by making and changing relationships. The game need not be trivial but may work through dangerous imbalances and require life-enhancing or life-threatening engagements. The players of the game need not think they are affirming statable "truth," as someone like Locker says users of Indo-European languages have traditionally been convinced they are doing; they may not claim as the primary interest of language its ability to represent ontological truths such as Shelley's external or internal "impressions"[26] or Stevens' heightened sense of "reality" or "imagination"; but players can be aware of producing other kinds of complex patterns that demonstrate their very relationship with language and the finely tuned delicacy of the power they wield within writing.

"Being" and Language in Poems

Derrida has seen that the academic disciplines of philosophy and linguistics have boxed themselves into a restrictive view in which the expression of semantic "being" and the establishment of ontological meaning are interdependent. His essay on the copula avoids proposing a way out of the quandary symptomatized by the way *to be* has been encrusted with ontology. In refusing closure he seems to suggest cutting through disciplines. Our groping for a third way can hardly avoid encounters with philosophy and linguistics, but it must independently derive tools from the material form of the word. This is where semantic "being" exists in the sign without the putative reference behind it forming any necessary relation. For this is where the writing and reading subjects can ask themselves about language as a vector of other possibility.

Stevens' work with "being" was not limited to problematizing the expression of transcendence, or weighing the transformations of the object world that gives us pleasure, or transmuting that perceptual pleasure itself. Among Stevens' responses to a general quizzicalness about "being" in language and its expression, we find Stevens, beginning with his early work in *Harmonium*, playing with a demiurgical power of language before existence, before being. One crucial work in his exploration of this possibility is "The Apostrophe to Vincentine" (CP 52–53). On the surface, Stevens is playing here with the traditional device of apostrophizing one of his many muse figures, while inserting her in a lapidary narrative about the writing process in the guise of a metaphor of painting. The problem of her "being" before the poet-painter's work on her is posed in the first of the four sections. In stanza I he tries to represent Vincentine without referring to any precompositional characteristics.

I

I figured you as nude between
Monotonous earth and dark blue sky.
It made you seem so small and lean

And nameless,
Heavenly Vincentine.

Readers of the poem have seen the poet-painter as initially disrobing Vincentine,[27] thus leaving her "nude" in the first line, and depriving her of some presupposed identity. This initial deprivation could then be what makes her appear to be symbolically "nameless." The stakes for the rest of the poem would lie in repairing the effect of the initial manipulation by reconstituting a more faithful image of her "Heavenly" form. But the very word "figured" hedges the question of whether this is a figure, metaphor, trope, or transfer made by the speaker as a substitute for something else (and thus a changed or even distorted representation of reality) or whether it is the sign for a new invention. This ambiguity is reinforced in the second section, which begins, "I saw you then, as warm as flesh, / Brunette," where "saw" also has two areas of semantic connotation, one implying "considered" and one implying "drew in my eye."

Indeed, the actual creation of the fictive situation might be seen as the very subject of stanza I. The poem starts off with the metrical regularity of the iambic tetrameter (with an ironic hint of relief only in the doubling of the unstressed syllable in "Mono*tonous* earth"), building up momentum. But by the fourth line a hesitation arises, the final four feet of the section are divided into two lines, "And nameless, / Heavenly Vincentine," and the reader has to take an extra breath before taking the title's cue to apostrophize "Heavenly Vincentine." The delayed emphasis on the direct address brings out the paradox of addressing her by name on the one hand and saying that she seemed "nameless" on the other. For it is only on completing the fictive act described in the poem that the speaker should be able to speak his creature's name post facto in the past tense. This is made explicit by the closing lines of the final section.

IV

And what I knew you felt
Came then.
Monotonous earth I saw become
Illimitable spheres of you,
And that white animal, so lean,
Turned Vincentine,
Turned heavenly Vincentine,

And that white animal, so lean,
Turned heavenly, heavenly Vincentine.

It is only here, at the end of the poem, that the artist's creature becomes something that can be addressed in the fictive present of the poem's writing. Thus there is a suspicion that what is being narrated is a creative act that ends in inventing a name for what had been formed and come alive, and that the poem is a palimpsest or rewriting of a hypothetical poem-painting in which Vincentine's name could not logically have preexisted.

This is not just logical nonsense. This partially self-referential poem narrates a poem-painting coming into being in a reordered and compressed Creation, in a world that is already no longer "without form and void" (Gen. 1:2). It enacts the coming into a name and the sense of a previously nonexistent Vincentine and/or a void Vincentine (the shell out of which this predecessor to the "Paltry Nude" will issue). There are already some givens: earth, sky, pigment. Vincentine is made not out of clay but of pigment. The "whited green" that makes the new creature a "Green Vincentine" in II seems to be created by the artist out of the mere daubs of color he has on his palette ("monotonous" and "dark blue" to set off "nude" in section I; "warm" and "brunette," and "whited green" to make a "Green Vincentine" in II). They establish the tactile and visual qualities of something "small and lean," but they only hint at any potential for life, as when she is seen as being "as warm as flesh." For in this poem it is not the creator who breathes life into this insubstantial collection of qualities. It is the creature herself who initiates the "walking" and "talking" among "human others" (III) and constitutes the "what I knew you felt" of the poet-painter's awareness (IV). The creature herself even transforms the creator's original view of the earth into "Illimitable spheres" of herself. In the first stage of the process, then, the poet posits a "you" and clothes it with attributes, as it were, allowing the creature herself in a second stage to realize a potential for animation, to progress from the animate to the human to the communicative and finally to transform or metaphorize herself into an ideal form (perhaps akin to a Platonic form) both "heavenly" and victorious. The pictorial "being" that is built up in the poem is an allegorical "figure" for the work of a painter that transcends his original conception and even his original materials.

Now in one sense, the new knowledge the creator has of Vincentine is already implicit in the first quality he gives her: "nude," therefore uncovered and potentially discovered. But what is notable is that it is section IV's turning of "Turned Vincentine, / Turned heavenly Vincentine" that gives Vincentine a second metaphorical life, a life that is no longer merely physical (referentially: painted, animal, human, visionary). Vincentine is said to become what was only a name before. Schematically, this is what happens:

(I)   Heavenly Vincentine →
(IV)   Turned Vincentine,
        Turned heavenly, heavenly Vincentine.

"Heavenly" as an adjectival epithet (in I, "Heavenly Vincentine") moves to the middle of the line and loses the capital "H" of idealization but expands grammatically into a predicate adjective (in "Turned heavenly") before returning—ambiguously—to its role as an adjectival epithet. This fact is hammered home by the final juxtaposition in "Turned heavenly, heavenly Vincentine." Contrary to what happens in Zulu, a language in which "The man is big" and "a big man" have the same word order[28] the repositioning of the adjective is grammatically significant in English. And in Stevens' poem, joining "heavenly" to the copular verb "Turned" (a copula that means "became," "now was") gives this creature of the mind a semblance of existence. The creature earns both modifier and name herself—a small victory (Heavenly Vincentine *vincit* in the narrated past) for her.

Even such an allegorical reading may remain ontologically charged if we take "existence" as the hidden ground of the copula and the other language surrounding it. If we cut across the language-versus-world dualism, it may seem that the reader's only alternative is to be like Vincentine's sister, "the paltry nude," who is frustrated and "discontent" because the poetic activity of the poem remains "meagre play" (CP 5–6), a mere language game. As we have seen, at the climax of the poem, "heavenly" in "Turned heavenly" is no longer a nonassertive epithet (according to the conventions of English, though not of Zulu), but it joins the ranks of other attributes that are predicated (according to ordinary understanding, though not Kant's) of the creature. If we remember Kant's injunction that *sein*, "to be," can be considered as a bogus predication, then "Turned Vincentine" and "Turned heavenly, heavenly Vincentine" can be seen as only using the semantic surface of existence and asserting change within it; "That . . . animal . . . / Turned Vincentine" and "Turned heavenly" could be better understood as juxtaposing two already preconceived concepts. Nonetheless, though preconceived (as they may appear in section I), they have another—increased—sense in their new position. Section I's epithet and name turn out to be conventions whose efficacy we should question. When the poet literally turns given words around in a different order, it is with a thrill of discovery. He discovers the hidden potential within language.

There is a degree of exactness in the way Stevens fashions lexis and syntax. He builds on oppositions such as the initial semantic opposition in "The Apostrophe" between earth and sky and its overlapping with heavenly; the logical opposition between "nameless" and the name "Vincentine"; the philosophical and grammatical oppositions between qualifier/adjective and substance/noun (II, "Your dress was green," "Whited green," "Green Vincentine"); the grammatical opposition between the epithet and predicate uses of "heavenly."[29] The play of adjectives here does a great deal to reveal how things happen when a speaker-artist dares to expose the contrived nature of the rational structure that usage imposes on language—acting out the message of the much later "It is posed and it is posed. / But in nature it merely grows" of "Add This to Rhetoric." It shows us that the delineations of English lexis and syntax are both given and malleable—that is, that they are amenable to the recombining, reshaping, and transposing of artifice.

The permutations allowed by the rules of English are what allow interaction or dialogue between the fashioner and his own artefact. Thus, on the level of the allegory of "Vincentine," the speaker twice affirms, "Yes," to Vincentine's "walking" and "talking" (III). He is attuned to her being "Voluble" (III). During the course of the poet's work, Vincentine's existence, her being "warm as flesh" in the words of the poet and not in the flesh itself, contributes to the progressive transport generated by language and allows the original figure to become "Illimitable spheres of you"—you, Vincentine, my language who is more than my individual eye-I and more than my individual knowing. My language acquires a status of superior being when the unveiling of its particularities produces new discoveries. The text becomes a place that shows the ability of the speaker to play with the rules that accepted classifications of language seem to rest on, to enter into a dialectical relationship with his word-fiction, and to learn from the malleability of linguistic material.

The particularity of Stevens' linguistic play lies in the surface forms of grammar and more especially the various surface forms of the copula

and of prepositions. Differences in use of the copula are not so great be-
tween English and French, for instance, as to make Stevens "untranslat-
able" into French. Nor do differences in the usage of person, tense, and
mood pose insurmountable problems, though some nuances have to be
generalized or, on the contrary, narrowed down ("they were" becomes *ils
furent* or *ils étaient,* for instance). But between English and Chinese the
differences in the grammar of "being" are enormous, and Stevens' insis-
tent use of copulae (to say nothing of the definite article and preposi-
tions, which are also totally different or lacking in Chinese) would be a
major source of frustration for his Chinese translator. When Shelley
writes that the "grammatical forms which express the moods of time, and
the difference of persons and the distinction of place are convertible
with respect to the highest poetry without injuring it as poetry," he is re-
ferring to the great narrative poetry of the Mediterranean world.[30] But in
Stevens' work, the underlying existential drama can be caught only in
brief glimpses through the imagined dialectic between speaker and spo-
ken. Stevens' probing into the functional core of language is a world
away from either philosophy or linguistics. These disciplines have pro-
duced, or claimed to produce, an overlay of forms of the *logos* (word, idea,
concept, ground) on *physis* (the given world, nature) or deductions mod-
eled on this overlay. Stevens' poetry, on the contrary, produces not an
overlay but a script that tests the rules.

The word-worlds that Stevens explores in his poetry and that be-
come his poetry are not to be found in the strangling exactness of the on-
tological version of philosophy or the scientific version of linguistics. "As
the reason destroys, the poet must create" (*OP* 190). In his lifelong ad-
vance toward "the exact rock where his inexactnesses / Would discover,
at last, the view toward which they had edged" ("The Poem that Took
the Place of a Mountain," *CP* 512), Stevens often uses the bogus gram-
matical exactness of techniques that turn words in all directions in order
to release a third kind of creation from within their shackles. This re-
quires more than affirming Vincentine's small victory over stale word-
painting and stale apostrophe. Stevens goes about the task, in part, by
laying bare the pseudolimitations of lexis and syntax—as he does with
the attributes and epithets, aided by the copula "turned," in "The Apos-
trophe to Vincentine"—to write a new kind of exact but expanded Eng-
lish. Writers work with living languages, with their present forms,
current usages, and inarticulate history. It is when Stevens denudes,
loosens, and extends the rules that govern lexis and syntax that he breaks

away not only from past poetry but also from philosophy and science and deploys language's previously unsuspected "Illimitable spheres" of itself.

It may thus be possible to free interpretation of the dualisms that pervade Stevens' and most critics' concepts. Modernist experiments in the visual arts and literature are often understood as undermining previous conceptions of representation and mimesis. As Richard Rorty hypothesizes from a metaphysical and epistemological perspective:

> One could see Borges and Nabokov, Mallarmé and Valéry and Wallace Stevens, Derrida and Foucault, as guiding us out of the world of subject-and-object, word-and-meaning, language-and-world, and into a newer and better intellectual universe, undreamt of since the Greeks first made those fateful distinctions between *nomos* and *physis*, *episteme* and *poiesis* which have haunted the West.[31]

But Rorty argues against such a focus, saying that such writers only make sense when they can define themselves against a persistent and vigorous Parmenidean realism. The essential irony of their position would be lost could they not take as a dialectical foil a view in which truth is measured by reference to the "hard fact" of world or mind. In order to be interesting as a word-game, "modernist" writing needs to situate itself in opposition to the dominant understanding of language as a picture of mind-world.[32] If we consider Stevens from another angle, on the other hand, and look at the areas where irony is less dominant than construction and againstness is less active than affirmation, we are directed to his use of the English language, not his palette of concepts. And it is in the internal workings of language, rather than in its function as an ironic or "straight" picture of a mind-world, that we can find a new focus.

To explain it another way, we can take two examples from *Harmonium* that illustrate the lexical and syntactical role of *to be* in copular formulae: "The only emperor is the emperor of ice-cream" ("The Emperor of Ice-Cream") and "I was myself the compass of that sea" ("Tea at the Palaz of Hoon"). Taken literally, the first sentence seems to assert that the emperor of ice-cream can be identified as the only emperor worthy of the name; the second sentence seems to state that the "I" played the role of the compass and could thus be identified with it. In the broadest sense, the sentences assert that X is equivalent to Y and, inversely, that Y defines X in some way. Yet taken as metaphors in which both terms are given, it is obvious that these equivalences are not meant to delimit characteristics ("A rhinoceros is a large pachydermatous quadruped") but rather to enable an expansion of reference. The statement of equivalence serves to join facts that are different in nature or, as Stevens might have said, distinct in "reality." *Rapprochements* or connections are made verbally between magisterial commander, say, and ice-cream maker, or between a self-sufficient sun god and the surrounding aqueous sea. In Stevens' disjoined *Adagia* and in many disparate and experimental early poems, the primary function of "definitions" or statements of identity (using *to be*) is to affirm the appropriateness of linking together two names from different spheres and not, as realists have maintained, to assign the appropriate name to the thing. To go one step further, when such "definitions" appear in *Adagia* in terms like "A poem is a pheasant," they stress how crucial it is to find the predicate most appropriate to the subject—not necessarily within the reality of the empirical world, the world of desire, the "imagination," or the literary canon but within the confines of the linguistic formula itself. Relationships of linguistic proximity become the very stuff of poetry, and *to be* is a privileged space around which the poet can turn strange new relationships. The challenge is to avoid reducing language to a mere game and to entertain new relations for their exploratory potential as a poem moves beyond its initial statement.

4

&

"Being" and a Place for Speculation

As the reason destroys, the poet must create.

—*Adagia* (OP 190)

"Being" and Inertia

The English of Wallace Stevens' poems can be seen as a theater in which various manifestations of "being" in language contend. Whether or not we concur with Derrida's critique of Benveniste's view of Aristotle, it is futile, I think, to try to characterize Stevens as giving an "unconscious" priority to either linguistics or philosophy. Clearly, Stevens is the child of nineteenth-century epistemological concepts, traceable in the complex connections that lie just under the surface of his poetry but also visible in explicit references to "seeing and being" and "self" (the subject-object dichotomy), recurrent nineteenth-century philosophico-literary vocabulary like "reality," "imagination," and "the life that is lived," and thematic statements about theological constructs, including "Theology after breakfast sticks to the eye" ("Les Plus Belles Pages," CP 245). This being said, his interest in the philosophical mode, like that of most literary people, is subordinated to that other undefinable one of serving the advance of "poetry." His thought on epistemological and aesthetic subjects was unsystematic, his access to philosophical predecessors amateurish, even dilettantish. He quoted from the works of philosophers from Pascal to Bergson to Whitehead, but also culled considerable information secondhand from contemporary academic writers such as Dr. Joad and Rogers, whose *A Student's History of Philosophy* provided Stevens with summaries of philosophical writings.[1] At the same time, Stevens refrained from formulating any precise conception of language, unlike the French poets with whom he might have distant affinities: Mallarmé and Valéry are justly reputed for analyzing language, and Valéry is hailed for trying to develop a theory of poetic language. Instead, Stevens' own "conscious" categories are primarily philosophical rather than linguistic.

On the other hand, Stevens' poetry needs to be read as text that explores the very compositional possibilities of English grammar within a place of its own construction. As we have seen, the copular usage of *to be* has been viewed either as an ontologically empty or fallen sign, or as an empowering one. Stevens' insistent use of the copula of being as a linguistic sign for predication directs us, however, to consider instances of "being" as links in a poetic structure that partially detaches itself from the need to ground grammatical predication in an ontological assumption and thus shifts the value of composition away from external (whether "real" or imaginary) referentiality toward an internal speculation within and about the limits and possibilities of specific linguistic structures.

Thus, just as we found Stevens explicitly testing the limits of metaphor, we can see him experimenting with the basic building block of English, *to be*, and testing its limits. The pressures on this verb are particularly strong, as we have seen, because of the demands placed on it for embracing "truth" in Western metaphysical tradition. The failure of this verb, then, may accompany the flagging of poetic energy. This is shown in one of Stevens' early poems, "Gubbinal" (1921, CP 85), where the verb *to be* maps a *via negationis* leading to a dead end. It is as dispirited a poem as Stevens ever wrote, the effect of its copula being diametrically opposed to the creative, life-giving "turn" that makes Vincentine "heavenly, heavenly Vincentine" (CP 53).

The complex play of references to being in "Gubbinal" alternates imaginative metaphorical language in the tercets with a description of contemporary society in the couplets. The tercets and couplets exploit two different grammatical uses of the copula.

> That strange flower, the sun,
> Is just what you say.
> Have it your way.

The world is ugly,
And the people are sad.

That tuft of jungle feathers,
That animal eye,
Is just what you say.

That savage of fire,
That seed,
Have it your way.

The world is ugly,
And the people are sad.

The tercets pair nouns (noun "is" noun / the sun "Is just what you say") in statements that seem to predicate acquiescence and confirm an implicitly negative judgment of a poet's sun metaphors. The speaker's flippant "Have it your way" belittles an implied commentator's pretextual comments, which, we assume, themselves belittled a metaphor-maker's protean names for the sun; the speaker's acquiescence in "Is just what you say" is ironical. But the work of predicating the sun metaphors breaks down in the third tercet where "That savage of fire, / That seed" are left grammatically suspended, deprived of any copular complement. These metaphors for a creator-destroyer sun are revealed to be "just"—merely—barren names once they are bereft of the "is" predicate. Retrospectively, what is confirmed is the nominalizing copula's inability to invest the "strange flower," "animal eye," and "savage of fire" metaphors for the sun with vestiges of "being."

The couplets complement a noun with a modifier in attribute position (noun "is" adjective) to form a counterstatement to the tercets, seemingly without irony. The simple aesthetic and affective qualifiers, "ugly" and "sad," are attributed to the sociopolitical "world" and "people," excluding any natural, mythical, or poetic connotations. Such down-to-earth descriptions of the social world seem utterly transparent compared to the somewhat rococo metaphors of the tercets. But does either form of copular predication have any validity or "truth" value in itself? An impoverished "truth" it would have to be. It is as though two impoverished usages of to be are strategically opposed to each other, sharpened by the poem's referential contrasts between flowery metaphors and realistic predicate adjectives, metaphysical ground and social world, the metaphorical and the "literal," the potentially poetic and the mundane.

If the speaker's ironic abandonment of the metaphor-maker's figures for renewal is devastating, his own *tristitia post bellum* is no more fruitful. His own laconic couplets can only describe his lassitude and malaise. Whereas motifs of tropical luxuriance engender a creative process in several other early poems such as "Hymn from a Watermelon Pavilion" (CP 88–89) or "Nomad Exquisite" (CP 95), in "Gubbinal" they fail to develop. The momentum of the "Forms, flames and the flakes of flames" of the slightly earlier "Nomad Exquisite" is repressed in the tercets of "Gubbinal" and even chastised by the couplets. The speaker's common sense acceptance that *to be* represents some sort of ontological reality as it is given proves to be totally unproductive. It produces inertia and not "a pheasant disappearing in the brush."

The black sun of melancholy seems to shine on this poem, and the very inertia of the use of the copula seems to me a sign, then, of the human poet (the real writer) behind the speaker examining two facets of how to express—or rather how not to express—being in poetry. The fallacy of straining for ontological reality is revealed in both moves, without the poem reaching toward any further, new purpose. The poem's logical outcome would be aphasia, in which the speaker's ability to speak—and thus his ability to be in his speech—would atrophy. The biographical Stevens' poetic voice did temporarily become almost silent after the 1923 publication of *Harmonium*, two years after he wrote this poem. But with the exception of this hiatus between 1927 and 1932, Stevens would continue to pursue the fullness of poetry, even 35 years later as age dimmed his former sense of freshness, joy, and meaningfulness, even when he would write to one of his longtime correspondents that "[n]othing seems particularly to matter nowadays."[2] Along with "The Sun This March" (CP 133–134), "Gubbinal" is one of the few poems Stevens ever wrote in a voice suffocating with helplessness. Is it any wonder that he placed the earlier "Nomad Exquisite" considerably *after* "Gubbinal" in *Harmonium?*[3]

"Gubbinal" merits attention because it suggests something about commonly accepted but unstated expectations for language. The poem's forms of predication glaringly expose the assumptions made by Western metaphysics and common sense that predication can "live" only when it is ontologically valid, whereas in this poem copular predication reveals only the speaker's inability to say more. The metaphorical names are not in themselves worn-out or "wormy," but they are placed in a debilitating context. The linguistic context is limited to repetitive copulae; the narrative context is limited to the ironic suppression of poetry. Together they illustrate the first half of the sentence from *Adagia* that I have placed at the head of this chapter: "As the reason destroys." But it does not satisfy the adage's main clause: "The poet must create."

Language as Place

It is, in sum, what Cook has called "Stevens' desire for a place that is a poetic home"[4] that dominates his work up to "Notes toward a Supreme Fiction" (1942). His places of and for poetry are often rendered as specific geographic or social scenes named Connecticut, Tennessee, North Carolina, Florida, Hartford, and Yucatan, to cite only a few examples from Stevens' rich store of place names, but they are also generically a "Gallant Château," "The Public Square," "the shadow of a pine tree" ("Six Significant Landscapes"), or "the sun" in which tails "glitter" and "the wind" in which feathers "bluster" ("Ploughing on Sunday," CP 20). Such places are also artistic and mental scenes within which to develop an impression or a thought metaphorically.

The practicalities of building both referentially and linguistically within places or contexts are indicated in "Theory" (CP 86–87), a poem that first states and then illustrates how dependent our identities are on what Henry James called the "accoutrements" of our daily lives. Stevens' imagery specifically singles out the enclosing spaces within which definitions can be made into "portraits."

I am what is around me.

Women understand this.
One is not duchess
A hundred yards from a carriage.

These, then are portraits:
A black vestibule;
A high bed sheltered by curtains.

These are merely instances.

The synecdoches for environment seem both to limit ("not a duchess") and enable the construction of a socially recognized identity. But in any case, "instances"—the times and places we stand in—are only part of a vast repertory of many possible environments in which we can portray ourselves. A great Stevens byword, "merely," in the last line, describes the incompletion of the preceding images, while it also demonstrates the inadequacy of developing any "theory": any thought-out theory would also be "merely" a synecdoche.

As synecdoches, the "carriage," "black vestibule," and curtained bed occlude as much as they denote. Other signifiers for rich, mysterious objects and shadowy places of secret comings and goings could replace them. English words fashion our social identity, but there exists a large range of choices available to us outside the poem, in the resources of English that are not exploited here. Stevens' playful use of *to be* in this portrayal of portraits also orients us toward confronting suave choices that write of our own relation to language. In addition to the accoutrements referred to, language also differentiates one subject from another. Or more accurately, we use it to build a homeplace for constructing or crafting our identity. Stevens' doubling of "These are" in "These, then are portraits,"[5] and "These are merely instances" designates *to be* as being neither a "fallen" copula stripped of ontological sense, nor an imperial copula that asserts its control over reality. Here it indexes or points deictically to the self-referentiality of the poem, in contrast to "I am what is . . ." with its reference to a world external to language. *To be* is a versatile verb that can be an emblem for what happens when we make language itself our defining home.

"Theory" theoretically indicates the range of possibilities within which language constructs a fiction made to be read. By signaling the constructedness of language, it overcomes the parodistic irony of its contemporary "Gubbinal" and accepts a synecdochal approach not only to the word-world relation but to the linguistic place, the range of lexis and syntax actually exploited within a text. It proposes, then, some emblems (both referential and linguistic) for the construction of a fictive theoretical space or place as it also constructs a fictive relation to the world, not just making itself a metaphor for artistic or mental activity, but differentiating itself from the external world.

The difference between the object-world and the word-world remains skeletal in "Theory," but numerous other poems from *Harmonium* develop a surface complexity to foreground the deployment of poetic/

linguistic space in such a way as to show that language itself is a place for a speculation within its own terms, on the basis of its own relations. A poem that does this with particular intensity is "The Snow Man" (1921, *CP* 9), which has been seen as revealing what Vendler calls "a terrifying blank."[6] Certainly this is the nexus of the poem, that without which it could not exist. Yet, the poem's own "presence" has a seductiveness that is attested to by both the quality and the quantity of critical attention it has received.[7] Its "bare rigor" was appreciated by a reviewer of the first edition of *Harmonium*[8] and it has since attracted critics concerned with issues of consciousness and the traces of romantic problematics in Stevens' poetry. Its cognitive implications have been inferred from its grammar and lexis and the poetic form they are cast in. Fundamentally, readers see it as a meditative poem, and many would agree with some variant of Bloom's estimate that the poem both states and enacts a rejection of the pathetic fallacy.[9]

The Snow Man

One must have a mind of winter
To regard the frost and the boughs
Of the pine-trees crusted with snow;

And have been cold a long time
To behold the junipers shagged with ice,
The spruces rough in the distant glitter

Of the January sun; and not to think
Of any misery in the sound of the wind,
In the sound of a few leaves,

Which is the sound of the land
Full of the same wind
That is blowing in the same bare place

For the listener, who listens in the snow,
And nothing himself, beholds
Nothing that is not there and the nothing that is.

The poem is logically structured along two grammatically dependent hypotheses. The first hypothetical act (ll. 1–7) involves the specular, as if one's "mind of winter" were going to be mirrored in the glittering visual and tactile fullness of the natural scene. The second hypothetical act (l. 7–15) withdraws thinking from the first mode of visual clutter by enacting a complicated *praeteritio* ("One must have" x "*not* to think") that introduces the auditory aspects of the scene. Timothy Bahti has written that when we consider the poem as it moves across its formal space from beginning to end/ending, the effect of the "logic of this turn in the middle . . . is to call the scene *to* the mind and, in the immediate negation, to call the mind *away* from it. It is an abstraction that renders concrete."[10] Human consciousness in such a reading is drawn away from the sound of the wind and the concatenation that ensues. The imagined subject's reaction is defined only in terms of its negation: not thinking of a human emotion, "misery." This would be what it is to have a mind of winter or, as Macksey suggests in one of the earlier phenomenological interpretations, to practice the "chastity of the intellect" that is the kernel of Santayana's definition of skepticism.[11] It keeps the hypothetical subject of consciousness—a snow man like the title's—safe from projecting himself onto the scene or confusing his own emotions (if he has any) with the nature of his surroundings.

From the points of view of the imagined speaker and the potential reader, on the other hand, refuge is not possible. The poem's imagery progresses from a place that is overfull to a place that is bare lexically but full in another way. The turn following the "January sun" (l. 7) leaves the first of Janus' faces in our minds while displaying the second face that is less suggestive semantically but more intricate syntactically. The "thinginess" of the beginning of the poem is underscored by the presence of a rich repertory of Germanic words, set off by the French-like "regard." The two French senses of "considering" and "looking" imbue the first tercet with the temptation of detachment, but paradoxically, despite the negation of the "turn in the middle," this possibility is counteracted by the willfulness of "behold" in the second and final tercets. There is no slackening of attention. Even the principle underlying the choice of vocabulary mimes this meaning. The referential movement goes from species to genus, from narrowly synecdochal "instances" (see "Theory") to more inclusive ones: from "pine-trees crusted," "junipers shagged," and "spruces rough" to "the sound of the wind," "the sound of the land," "the same wind" and "the same bare place," and finally to the triple "nothing." The words for texture and light are seemingly drawn from a huge repertory of terms that differentiate among particular things and visions, whereas the words evoking the sounds heard are reduced to plain words that do not differentiate. But these words—"wind" and "land," and "sound," "same," and "nothing"—are differentiated by being repeated in similar but not identical syntactic contexts. The circling repetitions of nouns and prepositions, as well as alliteration, consonance, and assonance, of this second half may be said to produce phonetically the monotonous opaqueness of the wind's speechless voice.

In the final embedded clause the "listener" is "nothing himself" and "beholds / Nothing that is not there and the nothing that is." Most readers have argued that "nothing" is either an index of absence or a sign of "no thing," that is, something other than a reified "thing," and therefore a noumenal and unutterable beyond. Pushed to their breaking points, such arguments read the poem as merely punning or, more threateningly, as nihilistic, especially since the listener is the ultimate object "For" whom the wind is blowing. It is true that even on the most literal level of the sentence's grammar, the final two lines of the poem are open to numerous readings, the most contradictory constructions involving the poem's strong closing use of *to be* in "the nothing that is." This form can either represent the absolute use of "is" to mean "does exist," or it can be an elliptical form for the locative: "the nothing that is there." Thus we have an ontological statement and a self-reflexive statement at the same time. What is more, their further interpretations seem to be mutually exclusive: on the one hand we have the nothing that exists rather than the nothing that does not exist, and on the other we have the nothing that is not there or the nothing that is elsewhere. Yet, as I shall show, one of the acutest senses created by the poem is that the final "is" is the positive final point in the excursion established by the language of the poem.

What is the effect of this balancing act? Although "The Snow Man" indeed referentially presents the temptation of accepting the void of or beyond thought, the poem has the power to eliminate a restrictive view of "nothing." Placing it in a locus of "there" also creates a sonorous context of fricatives, heard in "No*th*ing *th*at is not *th*ere and *th*e no*th*ing *th*at is."[12] Its broader context is a murmuring repetition of sibilants (/s/), perhaps a miming of a windlike, leaflike, landlike sound. The local, provincial character of "the nothing" is also something. "[T]he nothing that is" marks the only "being" in the poem, the end of the excursion, but not a dead end. It introduces in extremis an artificial differentiation between "nothing" and "the nothing." The definite article makes "the nothing" the user's own, familiar "nothing," a word artificially marked as willingly used and willingly predicated by that absolute "is." *Is* is among our most familiar language objects or sites yet it becomes slightly exotic here and suggestive not only of worlds that are concealed or revealed by language, but also of the place *not* outside of language but made by it. In this sense, "nothing" or *no thing* is metonymic for "no place," and "the nothing" is the place where the "nothing" that has replaced the self (l. 14) is—that is, the place where the sound of the language is structured by the poem's grammar and syntax.

It is in part because of the fullness of the first half that we notice the spareness of the second half and shift our attention from the luxuriance of lexis in the first to the intricacy of syntactic repetitions and relations in the second. If we can have a mind of winter, not seeing this as "misery" is one of the non-ontological activities the poem invites us to participate in. Like the jar represented in "Anecdote of the Jar" (CP 76), the poem can be understood as not "giv[ing] of bird or bush" while yet having "dominion" over all: its representational authority over nature is ambivalent, while its patterned word-world is clearly the sign of the power of artifice and of the artificer to create this syntactical thing.

In the second part of the poem the artifice of linguistic construction is signaled by the density of prepositional constructions, particularly the insistent repetition of *in* and *of* as a tactic for creating relationships of proximity. The denied misery is thus situated (ll. 8–13):

> . . . *in* the sound *of* the wind,
> *In* the sound *of* a few leaves,
>
> Which is the sound *of* the land
> Full *of* the same wind
> That is blowing *in* the same bare place
>
> For the listener, who listens *in* the snow (emphasis added)

Rather than having full semantic meaning, prepositions are function words that establish relations between other words. Here *in* is an obvious place marker. The relation established by an even less precise *of* in "the sound of" "the wind," "a few leaves," and "the land," although it indexes authorship or origin, is particularly ambiguous and seems rather to point to substance, on the model of "Full of." The connections worked among these phrases recall the process of "Domination of Black" (which precedes "The Snow Man" in *Harmonium*), in which the "leaves themselves /

Turning in the wind" set off a seemingly self-perpetuating sequence of im-
ages that become involuted and blur the source of the threatening sound
of the peacocks. So in "The Snow Man," the turning participial phrases
confuse our notion of any primary or originating authority in nature. The
repetition and rhythmic variation worked with the function words *of* and
in foreground instead the English language as the place or locus within
which the predicated lines of inclusion are blurred.

That by now familiar marker, the verb *to be*, also plays a role in this
move toward a pattern of nondistinction that, against all of our ingrained
trust in the ability of language to bring forth the reality principle, height-
ens the extra-ontological and intralinguistic materiality of the poem's
speculative activity. Many critics have considered that the principal
metaphysical allusion in "The Snow Man" is Emerson's "Nature," in par-
ticular the famous passage in which Emerson describes himself crossing
"a bare Common," and finding himself on "bare ground" where he be-
comes one with nature, through the vehicle of his "transparent eyeball."
"I am nothing," he says; "I see all."[13] But as Cook remarks, "The Snow
Man" is less an allusive poem than a riddle poem,[14] and it plays not only
with the content of paradox but with paradox itself.[15] Linguistically, it is
a tautology that is at the crux of the poem's linguistic extra-ontological
speculation. A tautology is usually in the form of a verbal copula. A tau-
tological proposition is a definition in which the definer adds nothing to
the defined, thereby allowing the proposition to be automatically
"true."[16] This is what we find in the bridge between the third and fourth
tercets of "The Snow Man" in a formula that brings close to each other
the sounds represented in the landscape (ll. 8–10):

> . . . in the sound of the wind,
> In the sound of a few leaves,
>
> Which is the sound of the land

"Which is" refers back either to "the sound of a few leaves" or to each of
"the sound of the wind" and "the sound of a few leaves." The relation be-
tween the second "sound" and the preceding "sound of the wind" is un-
easy. If the land may temporarily seem to be the supreme figure in the
groping movement toward definition, its originary power is overturned
by "the sound of the land / Full of the same wind / That is blowing in the
same bare place" (ll. 10–12). This makes the wind the supreme figure,

the dominant force in the scene and the moving principle of the syntax. We should note in passing that the "is" of "is blowing" fleetingly suggests a spurious moment of existence before becoming a mere auxiliary. But what is interesting about the longer structure around "which is" is that it makes the wind both container and contained. Although being full of something and being something are not quite the same thing, we cannot help noticing that Stevens has his copula "is" create a tautological definition that turns back on itself and conflates land and wind and, metaphorically, earth and air, body and breath, graphic signs and sound waves.

The pattern created in the quasi tautology here illustrates one of Ludwig Wittgenstein's statements about tautology generally, that "the conditions of agreement with the world—the representational relations—cancel one another, so that it does not stand in any representational relation to reality."[17] Stevens' copular "which is" sets up a formula that is somehow "true" by its formal structure but may not represent "reality" as a proposition; the "presenting relations" "cancel one another." But the formula is not empty, just as the zero of arithmetic is not empty but is part of the "symbolism" of arithmetic.[18] Rather, it brings into its scope new terms ("wind" → "leaves" → "land" → "place," and finally → "nothing") even as it repeats the old ones ("in the sound," "of the same," "in the same," and various combinations of these words). The concatenation adds new "worded" spaces to what has come before without reaching back to erase.

It seems to me that the reader's eye and ear are made to look at and listen to English as the very specific, even provincial locus of meditation—indeed, as the meditation itself. The poem creates an environment in which we may meet light, texture and form, and in which we can establish relations. There is a quasi-iconic effect of first depositing "The Snow Man" as title and as potential observer/experiencer on the beginning edge of the poem (the text that describes the scene). We perceive that our "behold[ing]" is parallel to the snow man's, a beholding that moves from without to within the word-world. The locus of meditative activity is the very words of the poem, which are emitted by an anonymous, hidden speaker.[19]

Let us come back again to "the nothing that is." Bloom is not the only critic to have lingered over the sense of this last phrase. Whereas Miller sees the "nothing that is" as "being," showing that being is not like other things, Bloom sees it rather as "a trope-undoing trope." His interpretation, although it has a totally different orientation than mine here, points to an identical necessity of considering the poem as a continuum in which the first half is not erased by the turn in the middle. On the level of the poem's fiction, the beholder or the beholder's surrogate remains implied with some form of human intervention through language. The resulting artefact is the work of a highly disciplined artificer. The challenge this poem presents should not be reduced to ontological decrypting of a referent alone. The intimate exploration into language is facilitated by the concealment of any personal voice. But the obvious aesthetic pleasure readers have procured from both the "glitter" and the "misery" parts attests to an intense engagement with the voicing of the vast yet regulated possibilities of the English language.

Beyond the Province of English

Stevens' speculative stance seems "foreign" to the tradition of philosophical and poetic writing in the English language and, as far as I know, in Germanic and Latinate languages generally. His poetry is even the polar opposite of that of as radical a French poet as Mallarmé, who disarticulates grammatical functions rather than making them more dense, and who gradually eliminates the signifiers of being rather than foregrounding them.[20] Specific philosophical and poetic influences that have had an impact on Stevens' writing have been identified, including such well documented sources as Vico, Coleridge, William James, Santayana, I. A. Richards, Charles Mauron, Henri Focillon. But of course the originality of Stevens' work cannot be accounted for by historical or positivist reference to the presence of these or other sources.

To feel more at ease about taking non-ontological speculation seriously in a culture that does not do so, let us step once more beyond the province of Indo-European languages and consider a contrasting philosophical tradition that has had no significant debate about "being"—the Chinese tradition. To my mind, it is helpful to nuance the Sapir-Whorf hypothesis that language "determines" a culture's concepts and entertain the notion that, as A. C. Graham, a scholar of Chinese philosophy, has put it, "the thought of a culture is guided and constrained by the structure of its language."[21] To nonspecialists it is the intersection of philosophy and language, and not the plausibility of influence in one direction or the other, that is illuminating. As we have seen, Western philosophy has made metaphysical questions about "being," the ground or truth of existence, a central issue, and it has argued those questions with help from the verb *to be*. Chinese philosophy, on the contrary, has channeled most of its energies into debating social and ethical questions and codifying rites for maintaining harmony between earth and heaven. It has broached metaphysical questions, even such ones as the "existence" of the spirits honored in prescribed rites, only peripherally. As for the language that vehicles this tradition, it is indisputably the case that there is no verb in Chinese that denotes both existence identified by ontological being and what Western philosophy has called quiddity ("thinginess," substance) the way *to be* in its existential usages does in English. In addition, the copular relationship, which, as we have seen, is indicated in English with *to be* in such sentences as "A poem is a pheasant" and "A poem is pheasanty," is expressed in classical Chinese by mere juxtaposition of a noun or adjective with the initial noun: "Poem pheasant" and "Poem pheasanty." This means that, as Graham points out, in order to translate Kant's refutation of Saint Anselm's ontological proof of the existence of God into Chinese, three different Chinese words are needed to transpose Kant's different usages of *to be* (Kant's *sein*). In addition, it would be necessary to coin a modern neologism to translate existence (in pinyin transcription: *cunzai*), which would also have to be extended to cover the copular use of *to be*. This coined term would have no function in Chinese, as Graham says, "except in the translation of Western philosophical arguments."[22]

In Indo-European languages, on the contrary, there is a linguistic potential for arguing "being" that is bodied forth in philosophy, and conversely there is an implicit assumption about being that has been subsumed latently in much of our linguistic experience. Broadly speaking, descriptions of the world written in English are usually regarded as assuming the existence of something, the thing or object of the description, in order to be valid, and the reality principle is "naturally" shown forth in copular predication or in a "there is" type of statement. Poetry is no exception to this tendency. Thus Shakespeare can say, "Thou art more lovely and more temperate," as Emily Dickinson can write, "The Brain—is wider than the Sky—." In classical Chinese, on the other hand—in this case precisely because it has no copula—when the ninth-century poet Du Fu writes that the country lies in ruins but that nature's mountains and rivers remain, his five-character regulated verse literally says, "Country ruined, mountain river [landscape] there." It should be noted that (1) what I have translated as an adverbial-sounding "there" is also a preposition meaning more or less "at," or, more idiomatically, "is at"; that (2) the Chinese makes no distinction between the singular and plural nouns I give in my transposition; and that (3) "ruined" is indistinguishable from other forms of the Chinese word *po,* which elsewhere might translate as any person or any tense and thus mean "he ruins," "I have ruined," "they will ruin," etc. Chinese structures do the work of painting a picture without recourse either to any word for "being" or "idea" of it. In traditional lyric poetry, whether regulated verse (*shi*) or verse imitating a song pattern (*ci*), we find writing that is highly descriptive, yet the question of whether it corresponds to an existential situation, either in the empirical world or in the world of the poet's imagination, would not come to mind.

As should already be apparent, a Westerner reading classical Chinese poetry is struck by the "absence" of the verbal copula but also, in correlation with this, the "absence" of any marks of tense, only rare marks of aspect and mode, and lack of distinction between singular and plural. Indeed, the Chinese language is fundamentally different from Indo-European languages in having neither inflections, such as declension and conjugation, nor tense, such as past versus present. Classical Chinese is an almost purely analytic, as opposed to synthetic, language, and depends as such on word order rather than inflection or morphology to produce grammatical sense. Modern Chinese, while adding suffixes to mark number for nouns and pronouns and suffixed particles to indicate verbal aspect such as types of the perfective, departs little from this principle. English, on the other hand, nuances through inflection: we have only to think of the multiple forms of *to be:* not only the simple forms *am, is, are, was, were, being, been,* and *be,* but all the nuances produced by the adjunction of modals and other auxiliaries, *will/shall, can/could, has to/have to, ought to, must,* to say nothing of the subtleties of the subjunctive as opposed to indicative mood (*if I were*). I would suggest that such detailed distinctions—and even their understood presence in the repertory a writer chooses from—heighten the sense not only that, as Ernst Locker would have it, the mind is actively seizing the world, but also that the kind of accuracy we aim for is an accuracy in relation to a world that preexists language. The forms for these distinctions harden or fix the reality principle in Indo-European languages in ways that Chinese cannot or at least does not. Thus even with a very simple and ordinary shift in tense Shakespeare can modulate from "Thou art more lovely" to

"But thy eternal beauty will not fade" and refer to two seeming ontological realities, beauty in the present and beauty in the future, both attached to the speaker's time of utterance. More strikingly, and more subtly, the poet can also then conflate these two ontological times into a projective present, stated by wagering that his own verse will live into the future, but using the present tense, first joined with the modal *can*, then alone: "So long as men can breathe and eyes can see, / So long lives this and this gives life to thee." The sense of projection beyond the allotted time of the loved one's life becomes significant in the context of what has preceded, in the previously articulated shift from present to future tenses, both assumed to represent ontological times in our tradition.

A. C. Graham, who is one of the rare scholars to bring to the surface the underlying assumptions of classical Chinese philosophy, describes the difference between Western and Chinese discussions of "being" as follows:

> Thinking in terms of Being [in Western languages], we start from an object which on the one hand is, exists, on the other hand has properties. Thinking in terms of [the Chinese] yu [to have; or the locative function], we start from an environment which we may or may not determine as "the world", which has, within which there is, the object; arriving at the object we find that it has, that within it there are, form and colour.[23]

Instead of *to be*, then, Chinese, like many other languages, has recourse to *to have*, a synecdoche, as it were, positing an imagined place that is a field or a space for something to be named and accrete attributes. His description is also a good fit for the process by which Stevens' "The Snow Man" is built from hypothesizing "hav[ing] a mind of winter." Language is the "real" place. Graham's insistence on language as a place within which properties can arise and relations take place shows us a language that is above all a creative, productive, experimental environment. The hard "reality" of phenomena or of their supposed noumenal ground is not denied, but it does not come under consideration in classical Chinese, whereas Stevens in the "The Snow Man" in effect orients readers not only toward the linguistic environment but in a second, metaphysical direction.

The "being" aimed at by the Chinese language is not literal reference but a web of enabling relationships that create a dynamic description. Thus, classical Chinese will play with the contrast *shi-fei*, "this is it-that's not," as a dynamic field for balancing and rebalancing hypotheses. Or as Jacques Gernet writes, describing the divergence between Western metaphysical philosophy and Chinese philosophy:

> Our own philosophical traditions, which owe so much to 'the sugges-tions stemming from certain grammatical functions', are founded upon categories considered to be universal and are concerned with ab-stractions and ideas that are stable. Chinese thought, in contrast, rec-ognizes only functional classifications and oppositions. It is concerned not with 'yes' or 'no,' with being or non-being, but with contraries which succeed, combine with and complement one other; not with eternal realities but with potentialities and tendencies, phases of flow-ering or decline. In the place of the idea of law as an immutable rule, it favors that of a model or schema for development.[24]

Whatever the relation between the cultural expressions of a lan-guage and the structures of the language itself, Graham's and Gernet's broader perspective can help us see that on the one hand, cultures borne by Sinitic languages do not rely on nuances of a universal reality princi-ple affirmed in relation to a speaker but focus on the developmental processes allowed by linguistic classifications. Yet they may also create sophisticated bodies of philosophy and poetry as well as powerful politi-cal empires (*pace* Locker). And on the other hand, a comparative view allows us to see that the supposed Western "fall" of *to be* and metaphysics need not be considered a disaster if we may heal our "loss" by exploiting underestimated elements of our own languages. Stevens, it seems to me, points us precisely in this direction in much of his experimentation with the vocabulary of *to be* and function words of place, as in "The Snow Man."

Looking at Blackbirds

There is one early Stevens poem that strikingly musters the ambivalence of *to be* and combines it with signs of place like prepositions to create a movement with a double effect: it both unmakes the logical expression of ontological being, and creates a new linguistic field for speculative explo-ration. "Thirteen Ways of Looking at a Blackbird" (1917, CP 92–95) is, from my way of looking here, one of Stevens' primary testing grounds for combining older uses of metaphorical and symbolic meaning with new nonrealist and nonidealist—non-ontological—uses of *to be*. Although widely applauded, it has received surprisingly little close attention.[25]

Sections I and XIII embrace a sequence of great diversity and even dispersal, unified, it might seem, only by the presence of a referential blackbird (or blackbirds) in each section. Each of the thirteen sections demonstrates a fragmentary instantaneousness that relates it to Imagist poetry of the period[26] and may distract us from the fact that the framework itself creates a very strong sense of location or setting; that is, it posits a spatial context and indicates the extent of this context for the sequence it embraces.

I

Among twenty snowy mountains,
The only moving thing
Was the eye of the blackbird.

XII

It was evening all afternoon.
It was snowing
And it was going to snow.
The blackbird sat
In the cedar-limbs.

The closing section XIII reiterates the sense created in section I of a solid geographical or "natural" landscape. Through the Stevensian technique of prepositional foregrounding, Stevens attaches the very grammatical subjects of his sentences to the material stuff of signifiers like "Among . . . snowy mountains" and "In the cedar-limbs." The referentiality of the setting might be thought of as preexisting since there is a pretense of artlessness coupled with inertness, as though nature's handy perches were simply ordinary givens. They offer themselves as the place for "the only moving thing" to begin a series of movements that finally still themselves in XIII. But of course, this assertion relies on a premise of ontological fullness—somewhere—in nature, in the speaker's choice from among external givens, or in the human imagination's constructs from nature. The past tense of the frame may contribute to this sense.

In section I, the given, "Among twenty snowy mountains," is both enticing and imprisoning. The tight chiasmic embrace of "A-*mong . . . moun*-tains" encloses the playful euphony of the adjectives "*tw*-en-*ty*" and "sno-*wy*." Movement intervenes through semantic reference, but it is enacted through the play of signifiers when the spell of the phrase is loosened in the second line by the advance of regular iambs and the "rhyme"[27] -*ing*, unstressed in "moving" and stressed in "thing." The final "moving" of the sentence's subject, the "eye of the blackbird," moves us from a natural given to an imaginative or imaginary one, still ontological, in the movement that is necessary for the flight of the poem. The paradox of predicating this imaginative and emotional reality—a bird's eye is anatomically incapable of movement—stresses its metaphorical value.

Indeed, as a synecdoche for the activity of the viewer and a metaphor for the work of a poet, that roving, moving "eye" signifies the initial impulse for the movement needed to find "thirteen ways of looking." The blackbird's eye represents the shifting, animated, spirited world of creatures in the midst of the frozen world of geology. It also forms part of a delicately traced visual image that we might imagine as contrasting the dark glint of the blackbird's eye with the supposed whiteness of the mountains, a tiny eye point with a vast expanse, and lively and attentive movement (fictive and anatomically impossible though it is) with frigid immobility. Considering the blackbird's potential symbolic import as a bird of ill omen, this function of glinting, shifting, living, moving must relativize any simple contrast between its blackness and the white background. The eye of the blackbird must embrace a range of symbolic meanings across a spectrum from the benign to the malign, like Melville's whale. Although ominous in its blackness,[28] it is also promising for its ability to escape all but the determinism of movement itself. We have seen in "The Motive for Metaphor" how a demiurgical chain of unexpected transformations can be set off by "Desiring the exhilarations of changes" (CP 288). For besides leading back to the quasi-ontological eye of the blackbird, the "moving thing" also implicates the emotions of the looker who is moved. The eye of the "I" implicitly scans the frozen landscape to pick out the one object that moves or that moves him—that is, the only object that signifies: blackbirds. The "I"'s desire determines the terms in which the fiction of the poem can be constituted.[29]

The verb form "was" in this case predicates the first step toward fulfillment of the speaker's purpose, which is to examine one object from different perspectives; it exemplifies his method, which is to create a kind of necessity that will engender the rest of the disparate poem. The verb *to be* functions in its semantically "fallen" form of copular equivalence. In addition, the prepositional-geographical setting of "Among twenty snowy mountains" makes the locative function predominate over that of any supposed existence. The bird's reality even as a fantastical or imagined object is, in this perspective, not essential for the poem to be "significant." The poem might be compared to "Six Significant Landscapes," where the poem's "scape"—its status as a made artwork—is projected into the foreground as the poem is built up. As in those "Landscapes," the settings here form a verbal context of both location and equivalence.

The use of the vocabulary of empirical reality and reason helps to underscore the ways in which "Thirteen Ways of Looking at a Blackbird" deploys Stevens' exploration, outside empirical reality and beyond reason but within English syntax as the place of speculation beyond ontology. Within the frame of the poems section XIII boasts glaringly of the strangeness that projects the poem beyond ontological illusion through the triple repetition of *to be*. "It was evening all afternoon," describing afternoon as "evening," is strange in itself, but of the strangeness of relatively simple paradox that we find here and there throughout Stevens' work. The snow falling casts an unnatural or supernatural pall over the referential "afternoon" of the poem's end, hinting at impending death through predication of the blackbird's immobility and reference to cedarlimbs. More interesting here is what happens in a sequential reading that makes "It was evening" (noun as time adverb) into "It was evening all afternoon," changing "evening" into an adjectival attribute. The grammatical role of the impersonal "It was" also changes as we read. It takes a further grammatical "fall" as an auxiliary in "It was snowing," and a deeper plunge as the auxiliary of an auxiliary in "And it was going to snow."

Without going into even more technical detail, it seems obvious that the incremental construction of the lines not only builds up the potential semantic polysemy, but that it also plays with the grammatical functions of impersonal *it*, the shifting suffix *-ing*, and non-ontological *was*, making us aware that such signs as these cannot be identified semantically. Section XIII exposes the central requirements of the English language's grammatical logic and grammatical constraints: the use of subject and verb in predication, even when subject and verb are merely functional (for example, *it was*), and the use of inflections, especially those protean ones like *-ing* that can be moved to different parts of speech such as verbs, adverbs, nouns, adjectives. Thus, by keeping Stevens' lines in their linear context—and we will see in the next chapter how important linear construction is in Stevens—we perceive that the strangeness extracted from language by Stevens extends far beyond the semantic, into the functional core of grammar, that place where the rationality of statements of being in our tradition is constructed.

This functional core is strikingly represented in "Thirteen Ways" in a repertory of several functions of that most common of linguistic resources, the verb *to be*. The first four sections contain six examples of *to be* in twelve lines, using two of its eight simple forms (not to mention its numerous combinatory forms), *was* and *are*. Several functions are represented by these forms, however, from the copula of equivalence of noun plus noun (I, "thing / Was the eye" and III, "It was a small part") or noun plus adjectival attribute (II, "I was of three minds"), to atemporal existence (II, "there are"), to a generalizing eternal or logical copula (IV, man and woman "Are one" and man and woman and blackbird "Are one"), in which the predicate hesitates between adjective and noun. This repertory is complemented later with a passive function (VIII, "the blackbird is involved") and extended to auxiliary and modal functions (XII, "is moving" and "must be flying;" XIII, "was snowing" and "was going to snow").

The verb *to be* contributes to making strange while respecting English grammar even in sections that seem to disorient the least. In section XII we seem to find a mere symbolic code: "The river is moving. / The blackbird must be flying." The parallel syntax and verb forms do the job of establishing iconic and syntactical resemblance. The metaphorical sense broadens from a deduction ("must be") that the two movements illustrate the same flow of the universe and that the two images are emblems of the ongoingness of the poem. However, the *-ing* form of "moving" and that of "flying" are not necessarily the same, for whereas "moving" can mean that the river is in the process of flowing or that it is a "moving thing" or moves the viewer as in section I, "flying" cannot function implicitly as an adjective without breaking the rules governing English grammar. Thus, along with showing the non-ontological functions of *to be*, this small couplet is a prism revealing the arbitrariness of

English grammar, and it makes us hesitate not only about the rules of metaphorical resemblance, or its supposed basis in described empirical reality, but also about deduction and its basis in linguistic logic.

The first four sections, however, constituting our way into the poem, play a predeterminant role in foregrounding *to be*. They encourage us as readers to problematize the question of "being" we will encounter in later sections in other developmental schemes. The speaker in the opening sections I to IV reaches into language and removes it from its common sense and ontological ground. For instance, the speaker predicates himself saying that he "was of three minds" (II), not two. He then proceeds not by exegesis but by a simile in which he trickily deploys the tactic of reshuffling mere letters: He strips "three" of its *h* to make "tree," pseudo-ontologically puts it back in "there are," and leaves the "tree" again, through the copular bond of "are," to produce "three blackbirds." This is the new definition of "I" as sleight-of-hand man. Switching tactics, the speaker's trinity of minds and trinity of blackbirds give way in section IV to another trinity consummated by a simpler copular use of the verb *to be:* "A man and a woman and a blackbird / Are one." The paradox begotten of this copula may be an even more convincing play against ontology. "Are one" suggests the common-sense possibility of the union of flesh, love, knowledge, social life, and being within the semantic paradox of "one" being two. Including the blackbird in the "one" of man and woman in the second statement introduces the difference of an alien species, making the union a perhaps unholy one. In this vein, the resolution of the two statements into a hypothetical third statement of the implied syllogism would produce nonsense: A man and a woman *are* a man and a woman and a blackbird.[30] The minor point is that syllogism is in any case for Stevens an example of philosophical or rational language that has no validity as poetic statement. What Wordsworth in his *Prelude* called the "syllogistic words" of a wizard are an apt simile for the logic chopping of rationalism, in that both wizards and rationalists "unsoul" the mysteries that bind humankind together into "one brotherhood."[31] The major point lies elsewhere: equivalence in poetic language is shown to result from the accretive movement from "man" to "wo-" + "man," to a second movement that adds "blackbird;" poetic unity is created by the syntactic parallel of "Are one." That is, it is the copula that is the unifying force of the speaker's world. Semantically or lexically weak, it obtains its strength from establishing pivotal relations and balancing forces. It is a point around which degrees of distinction and equivalence, and diversity and unity, can be deployed experimentally.

Such moves take place within very small poems whose referential boundaries are established by visual-spatial images. In sections I to III these images are expressed with the verb *to be* combined with prepositions which incorporate it into the locative function. In addition, the "tree / In which" we meet the "three blackbirds" in II signals a unified grammatical and graphic space created by language for the poet's creative free play. This is given phonetic expression in section III, where the blackbird thing and "blackbird" word "whirled *in* the autumn winds." Who knows what the antecedent of "It" is in "It was a small part of the pantomime"? (Is it "The blackbird," the whole preceding sentence, or the phonetic play?) "It was," however, is what holds the speculative balancing act together among the vast possibilities of which the poem illustrates just a few. The "pantomime" is not just a "natural" mimicry but also a linguistic one, the great space of English.

Although it is difficult to extend such readings beyond the merely self-reflexive or metaphorical, we notice that the semantically weak locative is foregrounded as one of the main structuring principles for the extra-ontological cognitive work of the poem. Once the principle of location has been firmly established through the verb *to be*, it is constantly reiterated in other verbal contexts. The prepositional phrases have extremely diverse syntactic functions, as in:

"The mood / Traced *in* the shadow / An indecipherable cause" (VI)
"the black bird / Walks *around* the feet" / "Of the women *about* you"
        (VII)
"the blackbird is involved / *In* what I know" (VIII)
"the edge / *Of* one *of* many circles" (IX)
"the blackbird flew *out of* sight" (X)
"*At* the sight of blackbirds / Flying *in* a green light" (X)
"He rode *over* Connecticut / *In* a glass coach" (XI)
"The blackbird sat / *In* the cedar-limbs" (XIII) (emphasis added)

The referential looking denoted in the poem is focused on delimited spaces or even on the very elements that delimit them. Language is an analogous space whose limitations or boundaries are thus also inherently defined through a process of foregrounding and reiterating linguistic functions rather than affirming semantic meaning.

This is one of the senses of sections VI-VII and IX-XI, in which the locative is joined with verbs of filling, crossing, tracing, walking, flying, marking, riding. Inscribed within the space under a Roman numeral, they suggest the various motions of drawing, barring, scratching, dotting, jotting, coloring, and running off the page effected by the writing. The location is the necessary precondition, whether the frame be a "long window" or "shadow" (VI), the positioning of women "about" the men (VII), "the edge / Of one of many circles" (IX), "in a green light" (X), or the "glass coach" in which a man goes riding "over Connecticut" (XI). Both "looking at" a natural blackbird in a natural world and attempting resolution by logic are displaced by speculation (also looking, even spying) of another sort. On the one hand, this new speculation should avoid the fantastical deformations imagined of the "thin men of Haddam"- Adam (VII) or mistakes made despite seeming transparency (XI). On the other hand, it should deal with the material given by the "shadow" inscribed within the writer's frame rather than pursue an irretrievable and "indecipherable cause" (VI). Crossing and walking around within the poetic context and testing it metaphorically by flying "out of sight" (X) graft small-scale but bold experimentation onto an acute awareness of grammatical artifice and convention.

Symbolic conventions are also subordinated to the foregrounding of grammatical ones. Among the archetypal spatial symbols Stevens evokes in "Thirteen Ways" is the circle, dear to Saint Augustine and Emerson.

IX

When the blackbird flew out of sight,
It marked the edge
Of one of many circles.

Stevens' image disperses the unifying mystical force of Saint Augustine's God whose center was everywhere and circumference nowhere. Stevens' circles are akin to the material illustrations with which Emerson opens his essay, "Circles": "The eye is the first circle; the horizon which it forms is the second."[32] The circle is indeed that through which we see and the limit of what we see. But whereas Emerson goes on to say that "throughout nature this primary figure is repeated without end," Stevens, rather than looking for a First Idea here, affirms an undifferentiated plurality that strips his circles of the Ideal that Emerson calls in this essay "the highest emblem in the cipher of the world." The linguistic circles Stevens inscribes in this poem are not all variants of the same but all differently shaped spaces of looking as well as of speculating. The role of locative constructions, of which the word *circle* is a semantically full sign, is to establish the linguistic architecture of "Thirteen Ways"—a confined space of verbal looking or speculation. What is beyond the circle is not seen; its edge erects a boundary for the thought of the poet.

The liminal situation of the poet's vision in section IX is paralleled by the situation of his language in it: it signifies, on the one hand, the constraints given by language, materialized in an "edge" at the end of a line, a graphic shape that borders on the void but is saved from conclusion by the following line, "Of one of many circles." If there are other circles, with other edges then, the "edge" mentioned here is the only one that is related to this blackbird. The section also affirms a movement that surpasses or passes over the edge of any single circle—the section's metaphorical unity—into a plurality of other circles or the space containing those circles. Each section in "Thirteen Ways" inscribes its own distinctive logico-grammatical movement within a specific syntactic space that has only tangential rational or ontological relevance.

As poets have always known, the acceptance of certain material limits allows creativity to concentrate itself. Stevens' limits are less the traditional ones of versification than the ambiguous boundaries of the grammatical functions of some of the most common words in English, most strikingly *to be* and prepositions. The reference to the *panto-* = "all" and *mime* = "imitation" (III) affirms an ambition to point beyond the minutiae that are denoted. It would be wrongheaded to deny the idealist aspirations of Stevens' project, or to overlook his search for a concrete poetic utterance that would be adequate to some metaphysical or noumenal form like "The thing I hum" that "Appears to be the rhythm of this celestial pantomime" in "Landscape with Boat" (1940, CP 241–243). But his chosen medium, language—not clay, paint, dance movements, or musical sequence—must find "all" it can do in its own terms. And in "Thirteen Ways" we discover that language inevitably narrows itself in order to expand and circumscribes in order to "whirl" (related to Old Norse *hvirfill* = "circle, ring, summit") as "in the autumn winds" (III). Stevens' English shows that its power comes from revolving within a space it is familiar with in order to make strange new relationships within it.

As a last movement in this chapter, then, I would like to look at sections V and VIII, which signify the difficulty of the poet's balancing act. They illustrate in particular the impossibility of choosing between external and internal speculation. In imagistic terms, sections V and VIII suggest alternatives: the pleasure felt during the blackbird's whistling, as compared to that felt after it in V; a rhythmic or sound-oriented model for poetic knowing, as compared to the primarily cognitive and/or symbolic model of the blackbird in VIII.

V

I do not know which to prefer,
The beauty of inflections
Or the beauty of innuendoes,
The blackbird whistling
Or just after.

On the level of the signified, but on this level only, section V seems to propose an ontologically "full" choice between "The beauty of inflections / Or the beauty of innuendoes," that is, for example between the modulations of voice (parallel to the "whistling" of the blackbird) and the meaningful suggestions that come to the mind with a slight delay (parallel to "just after"). On the level of the metaphors, there is an impossible choice between poetry itself and its resonance in the mind. This relatively simple metaphor becomes a complex place of poetic rather than ontological speculation when we consider the playful use of etymology in "inflections" and "innuendoes." We recognize that the word "inflections" illustrates the principles of English word building, like the use of different prefixes already present in Latin (*inflect, deflect, reflect*) and the Anglicization of the marks of different parts of speech, such as the common substantive suffix *-tion* here, or such forms as *inflected, inflectional, inflexibility*. It thus belongs to a large family of regularized and domesticated English words derived from the Latin root, *flectere*, now considerably impoverished in terms of its morphology—that is, its inflections. The hidden genealogy of the word "innuendoes" is quite different. Despite sharing with "inflections" the *in-* prefix meaning "in or toward," "innuendo" derives from the ablative case of the Latin gerund and is thus less a fixed thing and more a function or means. Appropriated as an English noun, its unusual *-endo* form nonetheless separates it from the static abstractness of -*tion* and relates it to musical terminology like "crescendo" and "diminuendo." It suggests not only by its etymology (*nuere* = "to nod") but also by its form a process or unfurling. It brings with it the functional or relational aspect of *innuere* = "to nod, to signify." Contrasted with the unbending bendingness of the word "inflections," the word "innuendoes" moves toward another gerund, another holder for that moving suffix -*ing* but a Germanic one this time: "whistling." The blackbird's inflections increase in sensuousness through this encounter between Latin and Old English. Interaction between the Latin and Anglo-Saxon roots of modern English can also be found in the spurious parallel between "prefer" and "after," words that dimly mime each other in look and sound but are in fact constructed along entirely different principles.[33] "Prefer" and "after," verb and adverb, delimit a temporal location within which the section unfurls and moves forward. What should come first is undecidable, as is what can happen in the "after" after the section's end. Such play with root meanings, real and spurious kinship, and metaphor suggests both nonreferential speculation within the poem and semantic inference beyond the limited sphere of the poem.

The necessity of this doubleness is stated allegorically in section VIII.

VIII

I know noble accents
And lucid, inescapable rhythms,
But I know, too,
That the blackbird is involved
In what I know.

The triple "I know" counters the "I do not know" of section V, but it articulates a disturbing discrepancy ("But") between light ("lucid" ← *lucidus* = "light, brilliant, pure") versus dark ("blackbird"), and linear movement ("accents" and "rhythms") versus circular containment ("involved" ← *volvere* = "to roll, turn"). The speaker must submit himself to the requirements of aesthetic forms implied by the "noble accents" and "lucid, inescapable rhythms," just as he must accept the quotidian materiality of "the blackbird" and the necessary symbolic grounding implied by the circle of being "involved." Sound and bird are locations into which the speaker is inevitably taken by the prefix *in-*. Yet the "I" is greater than the "blackbird," which is only a part of what he knows. The two halves of the section do not balance evenly. In the speculative process, which is linked to vocal utterance and music here, the movement inward is only part of the larger movement forward, enough to stop the progress of this particular section but not enough to dry up the poet's utterance. The sound of the word "no" is repeated three times in the form of its homonym ("know") and once in "noble." "I know" forms a three-step staircase in the spatial layout of the poem, a descent from "noble accents" (chiming with "noble ascents"?). Yet it is a "yes" to knowing "in" the parts of language that can be loosened from purely referential and semantic bonds, in parts where the poet's inner ear listens to the sound patterns of the poem. This is also where Stevens' possibility lies.

The material signs that allow for such linguistic cross-fertilization, alternation, and overlapping as we find in section V are especially visible in Stevens' early poetry, though present throughout his whole poetic oeuvre. Such etymological and morphological play suggests a *jouissance* in the doubleness of Stevens' relationship in and to language, a pleasure to be found in the doubleness of constraint and possibility in language. The poet works from within it to reach his "objective," "the truth not only of the poem but of poetry" (*Adagia, OP* 190). The blackbird's constantly shifting "meaning" does indeed give it a Moby-Dick-like ambiguity of good-evil, loving-fearsome, vital-deathbound traits, while the web of morphological resemblances and syntactic modulations through which it moves confer on it that rational "decreation" that is so typical of Stevens' poetry up to "Notes toward a Supreme Fiction" in the early forties.

The blackbird thus becomes a figure of the very language that effects a realignment of cognitive activity within language. Language means both the denotative, symbolic, and metaphorical space of its signifieds and the textual space of the signifiers, such as the word "blackbird." Hence the insistence on grammatically marked location throughout the poem. If Stevens' poem speaks of its own condition of being determined by its linguistic history, it also allows the poet to "create" beyond the provincial boundaries his own linguistic culture has erected. If the language deceives, then the shock may represent a danger for knowledge, as when the passenger in the coach "mistook / The shadow of his equipage / For blackbirds" and was pierced by fear (XI). Or if its activity surprises the observer and transforms the objects, as in "blackbirds / Flying in a green light," our values may be shaken like the "bawds of euphony." We are warned too that something false can be taken for that play of possibility and constraint represented by the blackbird in its varying linguistic contexts. If the blackbird seems to have an effect on every section's context and changes the reader's sense of what Stevens called "reality" in it, it is also the case that each local verbal or linguistic context changes the blackbird and changes the effect of the whole on us as we become aware of how our linguistic culture works cognitively.

The various contexts created throughout the "Thirteen Ways of Looking at a Blackbird" might be considered from the romantic point of view as haphazard attempts at defining or identifying the writing subject's relation to an object that is already ambiguous in itself and is a symbol rich in potential for producing hopes and fears. But here the emphasis would be on subject and object. If we place an emphasis instead on the "writing," the sections individually create an expectancy. The various dubitative stances of such sections as II, V, VI, VII, and VIII reveal an unavowed search for perfection. But a poem like "A man and a woman / Are one. / A man and a woman and a blackbird / Are one" (IV) stands only on the decidedness, not the ontological or logical value, of the copular "Are one." The destabilization brought about by extra-ontological strategies forces meaning out of the visible world of natural looking and its invisible counterpart, into the world of language and *its* place in the poet's and reader's world.

In this sense, the ill omen of the blackbird's color and the number thirteen are counterbalanced—though not entirely counteracted—by a counterethos of what I called before the "optimism" of section V. Poe's raven can only reiterate "Nevermore," but Stevens' blackbird becomes a signifier that enables the proliferation of ever new contexts. The speculative activity of "Thirteen Ways" consists less in creating cognitive knowledge about some hypothetical truth than in creating a poetic being, both as the text is being listened to and looked at and in the post-poem silence, beyond the bird's whistling and the hearer's listening, and beyond the confines of the page.

Part III

5

❧

"Contemporaneous" Language in "The Man with the Blue Guitar"

> The only possible order of life is one in which all order is constantly changing.
>
> —*Letters* #328

Beginning with "things as they are"

The 33 stanzas of "The Man with the Blue Guitar" (*CP* 165–183) are bound together by a more or less iambic tetrameter couplet form, a core of minimal vocabulary, the recurrence of certain "talismanic phrases,"[1] "rhetorical disjunctiveness,"[2] and a tension between solid affirmation and loose, accretive syntax. Both because of and in spite of the poem's particularities, critics have almost unanimously seen it as a testing ground for procedures that would be used in Stevens' later work and thus as a watershed or "centerpiece"[3] in Stevens' poetic development. Its language, or more precisely the way its own language constructs a word-world through relationships along the chain it creates, is one of the poem's obsessive subjects. To my mind, "The Blue Guitar" is the poet's most radical realization of the non-ontological possibilities of the chain of language, an experiment taken to its furthest reaches. Its context is also, as we shall see, particularly significant in that the turbulent mid-thirties gave Stevens a heightened sense of rupture with the historical past. In this sense it is a poem with a message about the precarity of language generally and poetry in particular.

Questions of ontology and representation occupy the poem's opening scene, which sketches the confrontation between a putative audience and a guitarist. It is the audience's catch phrase, "things as they are," in section I that is in a sense the germ of the poem. This audience is reacting against a type of art that is like Stevens' own early work. The accusation is that he deforms the "green of day" on his "blue guitar" and thus does "not play things as they are." In this world of realists, "things as they are" signifies that there is an empirical reality that language can and should mimetically represent. But in section I, the guitarist recognizes this demand only to exclude it from the range of his blue guitar, on which "Things as they are / Are changed." Furthermore, the speaker that subsumes the entire poem paints this shade of difference into the opening scene by confronting the day's "green" with the guitar's "blue."

The audience also induces a tension in the man's performance by demanding that the "tune" be "beyond us," on the one hand but "yet ourselves," on the other. One facet of this dichotomy is identified by Harold Bloom, who sees the audience as asking for transcendence, "the Whitmanian impossible."[4] Indeed, this yearning, whether seen as a metaphysical aspiration or as a poetic project (as in section VI), shows us that the poem is haunted by the weight of assumptions that we have seen Stevens struggling to exorcise. It seems that here too Stevens "must," as the audience demands, contend with the romantic debate over reality and imagination that anchors Stevens' very words to the vocabulary of a former time. Wordsworth, using the vocabulary of sensationalist empiricism, wrote that poetry's business was "to treat of things not as they *are* . . . but as they *seem* to exist to the *senses,* and to the *passions*" and as worked upon "in the spirit of genuine imagination."[5] Without the work of the mind and the emotions, there is no human "life." In Wordsworth's scheme, the phrase "things as they are" refers to the order of objects as they exist independently of humankind. They become phenomena in the way they "seem" to exist and their potentially objective qualities are surpassed by the creative work of the imagining subject. For Wordsworth, then, "things as they are" do not figure in poetry. A few years after writing "The Blue Guitar," Stevens, by a sophistic play of definition around a copula, would turn this phrase around while agreeing in spirit with Wordsworth. In his lecture, "The Noble Rider and the Sound of Words" (1941), he would displace the boundaries of "things as they are." He would say that indeed the "subject-matter" of poetry should not consist of mere empirical objects but rather "the life that is lived in the scene";

however it is this "life," and not the "external scene," that constitutes "reality" and this newly defined "reality" "is things as they are" (*NA* 25). This temporary equivalence does not so much contradict Wordsworth's implication that "things as they *are*" are the opposite of "things as they *seem* to exist" to the senses and passions as it does enlarge the scope of what is relevant to human consciousness and feeling and include the change of "things as they are" within it.

There is another, polemical, side of "things as they are." Indeed when Stevens first published "The Man with the Blue Guitar" in October 1937, in *The Man with the Blue Guitar and Other Poems*, the statement of purpose drafted for the dust jacket promoted this new poem as "deal[ing] with the incessant conjunctions between things as they are and things imagined" (*OP* 233). This he contrasted with "Owl's Clover," published the year before, which had as its effect, the dust jacket reads, to "emphasize[] the opposition between things as they are and things imagined" and thus "isolate poetry." Although the reference remains hazy, "things as they are" may signal the audience's adoption of the catch phrase used by Marxist criticism to indict the rise of fascism abroad and labor conditions at home in America.[6] For, as Alan Filreis has abundantly shown, Stevens, like his fellow artists and poets of the midthirties, was necessarily drawn into the fray over the subject matter and purpose of art in chaotic times. One of the four poems of "Owl's Clover," "Mr. Burnshaw and the Statue," was written in response to the lambasting that Stevens' *Ideas of Order* (1935) had suffered in the review written by Stanley Burnshaw for the October 1, 1935 issue of the radical Marxist journal, *New Masses*. Among the class defects Burnshaw found in Stevens' writing, he criticized Stevens for failing to "sweep his contradictory notions into a valid Idea of Order."[7] Although Stevens makes numerous, traceable, and developed references to current events in "Owl's Clover," as Robert Emmett Monroe has claimed,[8] he still refuses to systematize or resolve "contradictory notions." Thus he obviously ‗ rings together the registers of high culture and the facts of colonial war when he parodies the holy and aestheticized "Seraphim of Europe" as angels "sighting machine-guns" or "Combatting bushmen for a patch of gourds" (*OP* 87), while the poem as a whole stresses the cleavage between a language reserved for art and the languages of everyday life. "The Man with the Blue Guitar," written over a year later, abandons such direct reference and leaves the audience's "things as they are" tantalizingly open.

Whatever the phrase may echo or connote, however, the performer's first move puts the problematic in place in terms of representation, as we have seen: "Things as they are / Are changed upon the blue guitar," he says. He thus implies that the audience's desire for relevance represented in the mimetic "green" of the day is misplaced. But he also inverts the order of the audience's "guitar"/"are" rhyme, initiated in "blue guitar"/"things as they are." (This fertile rhyme will be reiterated, with variations in placement, in I, II, IV, VI, VII, XIV, XVII, XXVIII, XXXI, and XXXII.) In inventing the quasi chiasmus "they are / Are changed," he also emphasizes the agency of the guitar behind the new mode of "being." This mode is not one of existence but of the pseudocopular "Are changed." At the outset, the reader can infer that whatever "things as they are" may include, the tune-song-poem cannot fail to establish a difference, a turning from "are" to "Are changed," a transfer from existence to rupture of identity. This reminds us of the narrative and rhetorical movements of the early "Apostrophe to Vincentine."

This "Are changed" presages the ambiguous shifting the guitarist will practice within his own discourse once the audience's voice disappears as an independent instance (or in echo) after section VI. The sequence revitalizes the audience's "things as they are" nine times in ways that show it cannot be a fixed, polar concept but only a metaphor with shifting emphases. Although the narrating persona, the guitarist, and the audience all speak in consonance with the possibility of fully representing "being," the guitarist's statements acknowledge a certain complexity, a delay in the possibility of resolution. The guitarist's assertion of change takes into account the newness the thing acquires with each succeeding moment but especially the newness of the form that language brings to the thing by placing "old" words in varying contexts. When the guitarist first brings the human and "things as they are" into the same sphere, they are diluted ontologically. A spurious hypothesis—"If to serenade almost to man / Is to miss, by that, things as they are" (II)—seems to be reduced to moving the words of the "serenade" in "Say that it is the serenade." Stevens' play with two copulas and the contrast of "almost to man" with "Of a man" also bring this stanza into the mode of speculation of "Thirteen Ways," but replacing looking with "saying" or playing a serenade. Later, in section VII, "things as they are" can be more symbolically conflated with the forces of life and a creative "us," as opposed to the moon, which is "Detached from" both "us" and "things as they are" (VII). And later still, the phrase returns to an artificial resolution of the romantic dilemma, touching on Goethe's "Dichtung und Wahrheit" and echoing an even more distant Lucretian *De Rerum Natura* (XXIII). But here the full, fixed, existential sense of "to be" is confounded as the reader becomes aware that in any modern poet's *De Rerum Natura*, "things as they are" cannot neatly distinguish the spheres of "Dichtung" and "Wahrheit" (XXIII). If we reach either distinction or, on the contrary, resolution of the two in "Confusion solved," it is, by the spurious etymological force of these words (*fundere* and *solvere*), an implosion, the opposite of ontological definition.

The poem's final experiment with "things as they are" is the result of a long sequence of janglings, chatterings, serenades, rhapsodies, ai-yi-yi's, chords, discord, drifting, shifting, substitutions, and all kinds of "playing," which are methods not of representation but of surprise. In XXXII the performer finally posits destroying "the crust of shape," meaning the borders within which qualities can collect. Casting away the "rotted names" himself, the performer no longer heeds "things as they are" but asks, "You as you are?" The answer is the new tautological copula, "You are yourself." As the Franciscan don in section XXIX will show us later, neither "you" nor "yourself" is a stable entity. In the movement of the song, the statement of their equivalence is only one verbal conjunction in a constantly moving economy of shifting pairs. Of "you as you are," so with "things as they are," the originating phrase. Throughout his meandering song, the guitarist questions the fixity and "thinginess" of "things as they are," and at the same time plays with antilogical and nonontological extensions of "being," as he did with the copula and other functions of *to be* in "Thirteen Ways of Looking at a Blackbird." The present shift recommends a change in emphasis, from the seeming ontological mode to a mode in which the guitar's poetry engenders extraontological speculation and composition.

The Audience's Opening Demands

In the audience's hostile position the performer seems to infer a program that he will unwork. This ethos characterizes V, where the audience expands its initial demand for fusion, in what, to my mind, is the only section besides the first one in which the voice is unambiguously that of a represented "us" speaking to the performer as "you."[9] Like the younger Stevens' pensive woman in "Sunday Morning," the audience is dissatisfied and needs compensation. Unlike the woman, it is impatient and imperious in articulating its own desire. It orders the guitarist with "Do not speak to us of the greatness of poetry" (V), and tells him what his poetry "must" (deontic obligation in I and V) and must not do. It seems almost surprisingly to crave yet reject the kind of philosophical and epistemological satisfactions Stevens played with in the poetry of *Harmonium*. As Harold Bloom writes, the audience "makes the wrong demands upon a poet, yet centers always upon Stevens' earlier self."[10] Ontologically, the audience desires the implicit fullness of "Ourselves in poetry" and "Ourselves in the tune" as a compensation for the disappearance of God in "empty heaven and its hymns" and the disappearance of meaning in the object world of the "bare" earth (V). It rejects the prescriptions of traditional poetry implicit in the "vaults," which in this context recall Vergil's and Dante's transcendent orders most obviously, as well as Orpheus' search for his Eurydice.[11] However, it also rejects this guitarist's shape-shifting and artificial "serenade" (II). It is clear about abolishing the old myths while requiring the satisfactions of fullness.

Within section V the audience's sense of a loss to be filled is most patent in the harping use of *to be* in "There are no shadows" at the start of the section. Combined first with the locative complements, "in our sun" and "anywhere," it crescendos to an absolute statement, abstracting itself even from spatial inscription. Contrary to what we have seen in the example of writing in Chinese, the verbal construction of section V cannot be read as pointing to a place that allows us to approach further description, nuance, discovery. When the audience uses "There are no shadows in our sun" as the context for defining "Day is desire and night is sleep," it limits "in our sun" to a place of unnuanced polar opposites. It is the intensest place where "desire" and "sleep" are absolute and complete in themselves during their assigned times. The "anywhere" in "There are no shadows anywhere" then eliminates all interest, all desire, all significance of place itself. It creates an empty place, "flat and bare." In the final stage, the disappearance of any locative to complement "There are no shadows" empties the place where being can be recognized. Retrospectively the word "shadows" becomes the sign for referential existence, "no shadows" for nonexistence.

This being has its metaphysical component in the image of "empty heaven and its hymns," expressing the loss of the ground of being and its measure. We sense here an acute form of the nostalgia that Stevens spurns in poems written just before "The Blue Guitar" (like "Farewell to Florida" or "How to Live. What to Do" [*Ideas of Order*]) or just after it

("Of Modern Poetry," "Arrival at the Waldorf," and "Landscape with Boat" [*Parts of a World*]). The sense of loss is only rarely hinted at by the performer himself, as in XV (which I will discuss in chapter 6) and in XXXI where loss is referred to existentially in a locative: "There is no place, // Here, for the lark fixed in the mind, / In the museum of the sky" (XXXI). The "shriek" that replaces the lark-haunted Shelleyan tune is a reminder of Stevens' earlier "againstness" in regard to quaint metaphors like the one here of the "bubbling sun." In recalling an earlier mode that would be "fixed," the performer shows how embroiled the audience's initial discomfort seems to be, not only in the old metaphors themselves, not just in "empty heaven," but also in its "hymns"—that is, in its need to find ontological fullness represented in language.

The performance shows that one of the things that is "wrong" with the audience's demands in V is that despite discontent, it can only imagine changing terms within the old mode of sheer existence, the "things as they are" and the existential statements ("There are") that inscribe them in space. Its effort to change registers works no better. When it substitutes new signs for old ones, when "Poetry // exceeding music" displaces the architectural or geometric images of "torches wisping in the underground" and "the structure of vaults upon a point of light," it becomes almost solipsistic and tautological. It boxes "Ourselves in poetry" into a tightly constrained poetry/guitar metaphor chained to layers of the prepositions *in* and *of* in the final two couplets. Its made-to-order forms implode, like "Confusion solved" (XXIII).

The performance of section VI brings out what was only implicit in the previous section—the audience's latent desire to stabilize "things as they are" but also themselves in it. Although the section contains the "us" of the audience and the "you" of the performer, it can be conceived of as either the direct discourse of the audience or the performer's echo of his detractors' style. The first part of the section is unpredicated, a static picture assumed by a mask. It ironically transforms the audience's protest against "change" into the debilitating "nothing changed":

Yet nothing changed, except the place

Of things as they are and only the place
As you play them, on the blue guitar,

Placed, so, beyond the compass of change,
Perceived in a final atmosphere; (VI, 4–8)

Exclusion and restriction mark this image. It is paradoxical because one circle is transcended (that of "the compass of change") only to reach another—a "-sphere" that is final or fixed. The audience is merely taking given spaces and making a few minor adjustments of "place." Indeed, change in the sense of transformation is unbearable for the audience, whereas it is the guitarist's basic working assumption. With heaven abolished, "us as we are" and "things as they are" are metonymized by the ruling metaphor of "place" denoted by terms of local topography—earth, ourselves, vaults, sun, heaven, atmosphere, guitar. Whatever the audience's unstated political and social agenda might be locally, its telos prescribes hard and fast ontological definition.

It is instructive to see how the performer at the end of the poem recalls the audience's ambiguous desire to impose a restrictive finality onto language. In XXXII, for instance, he challenges both the ontological and poetic potentials of the audience's particular rhetorical strategy when he again addresses his antagonists directly:

> How should you walk in that space and know
> Nothing of the madness of space,
>
> Nothing of its jocular procreations? (XXXII, 5–7)

The guitarist's distinction between "that space" and "space" implies that a closed system ("that space") will never allow the joy of expansion of "Nomad Exquisite" or the free speculation of "Thirteen Ways of Looking at a Blackbird," and that it may prevent the "procreations" of passing life on to future generations. On another level, this retrospectively associates the audience's desire as it is expressed in section VI with the stillness of death; for ironically, the furthest reach of its inferable ontological/spatial system is an eschatological "final atmosphere" (*atmos* = "vapor"). Unlike the defunct "smoky dew," it promises no redispersal.

Section XXIX is the most interesting debunking of the audience's demands. The performer at first seems to satisfy the audience's nostalgia by endorsing "degustations in the vaults" as a sacred space, balanced by the secular one "beyond the cathedral, outside." But although achieving polarized stability might answer the audience's demands, it would be a fatal reduction, the falsity of which is reinforced by the speaker's oblique allusion to T. S. Eliot's "still point,"[12] when he evokes balancing things "To and to and to the point of still." The performer demonstrates the moving transformation of "to and to and to" by leaping beyond "the point of still," in a series of infinitives that only increases the swaying movement while indeed saying that " 'the balance does not quite rest' " and that somehow " '[t]he mask is strange, however like.' "

It is false to consider that "being" can be transposed by art into another medium, for the speaker debunks his balancing act with: "The shapes are wrong and the sounds are false. / The bells are the bellowing of bulls." Indeed, the phonetic shift of signifier from "bells" to "bellowing" to "bulls" illustrates that the linguistic material itself changes and does not merely represent. Thus it seems both a surprise and an outgrowth of such an evolution when the persona picks up the idea of strangeness and likeness again in closing the section by saying disjunctively of the priest: "Yet Franciscan don was never more / Himself than in this fertile glass."

As we saw in chapter 2, Stevens' metaphors can be "fertile" by being allowed to follow changes in the very material form of words; here the strangeness brought about by these changes is what finally allows the speaker to use the copula and equate the don with "Himself." We might be tempted to see an allusion to harmony and total realization within a transcendent order here (especially since "Himself" requires a capital "H" at the beginning of a line). However, the guitarist's limiting locative, "in this fertile glass," unlike the audience's system of spatial expressions, makes no claim at being complete and true, or at covering the whole space. Rather, it shows itself to be relative to something like the "jocular procreations" (XXXII) of the word-sounds that procure it. The "glass" reflects a perception of his self produced by a series of refractions of sound, the audible analogy of the Other as in the "mirror stage" described by Lacan.[13] Being "Himself" is an incomplete state mediated by reflection. Just as "one mask" and then its parallel "another" can be said only to be "like" in this section but never balance beyond perpetual strangeness, the image of self will reveal its own incompletion in the "fertile glass." It will produce a series of ricochets between self seeing another as other sees oneself, ad infinitum. It escapes the strictures of truth versus falsity by claiming the necessary incompletion and nonfiniteness of any representation and the need to step outside an ontological scheme.

In sum, then, one of the functions of the audience in the opening sections of "The Man with the Blue Guitar" is to provide a foil for later developments. The first six sections of the poem contain a zigzagging sampling of what the poetry may contain or reject. The performer seems to understand that the audience wants the poem to "sing" about "a man," and not the idealized form (though parodied) of "a hero's head, large eye / And bearded bronze" (II). The unidentifiable voice of section III, with its ritual dissection of "man number one," extends the scope of such ideal forms of man (the modern replacement of "empty heaven") to include the contemporary political dictator who is part of "things as they are." The historical evolution of hero worship is concisely encapsulated in sections II and III. Yet the performer must resist reducing the (representation of the) guitar to a "place" for a "composing of senses," as is shown at the end of the ambiguously voiced section VI when it encloses the guitar's potential in a suffocating embrace:

> The tune is space. The blue guitar
>
> Becomes the place of things as they are,
> A composing of senses of the guitar. (VI, 12–14)

If we look at the historical evolution of the Latin word *spatium* we can see what will happen in the guitarist's tune: the acceptation of this word grew from a restricted one of "race course" or "arena," and hence an enclosed space, to that of "open area," "expanse," "distance," without any connotation of enclosure, and finally to the sense of "lapse of time," "duration," which shifted the emphasis from space to time. The performer too will need a length of time to respond to the audience in his own poetic manner, for his experiments in making and unmaking semantic and syntactic closure will be unfurled during the human time of language's syntagmatic development. By keeping his speculation always moving, the performer will not only resist the conservative ontology of verbal fixity and stability, he will also keep any art fashioned to fulfill the audience's needs in a state of becoming, what the performer will later call "a thing yet to be made" (IX).

The "pressure of the contemporaneous"

As Joseph Carroll has succinctly noted, much of Stevens' poetic career "occurs in an extended period of public crisis. In every volume, from *Ideas of Order* to *Transport to Summer*, the 'pressure of reality' leaves its impress in poems of public concern."[14] At this point we need to consider the substantial gestures made in "The Man with the Blue Guitar" to engage art with contemporary social and political problems. The audience does not say what kind of content would fit the historical occasion of a poem written in the first half of 1937, but the performer's song is rife with unspecified yet unmistakable allusions to the "news." We will see that Stevens uses such allusions rather differently in "The Blue Guitar" than he did in *Ideas of Order*, first published in 1936, before "Owl's Clover." In *Ideas of Order*, Stevens' images of ideological clashes and threats to the political order function primarily to sever Stevens' ties with the poetry of his *Harmonium* years. Thus, in "Sad Strains of a Gay Waltz," written in 1935 (CP 121–122), the waltz is used as an outdated emblem of self-confident elegance and social aloofness. It is "no longer a mode of desire." Hoon also returns here to be criticized for not recognizing "the figures of man." These emblems are displaced in the middle of "Sad Strains" by newsreel-type images of social unrest, images depicting

> . . . these sudden mobs of men,

> These sudden clouds of faces and arms,
> An immense suppression, freed,
> These voices crying without knowing for what

The poem stages the persona's failure to "know" what in poetry might satisfy the crowd's ineffable desire, a need sublimated in the unnamed demonstration or strike. He can only hope against hope that "some harmonious skeptic" will find a "music" capable of taking this new social reality of raging men into account. Thus while "Sad Strains," along with "Mozart, 1935" (CP 131–132), explicitly disavows *Harmonium*'s occasional poses of désabusé or melancholy aesthete, it also raises newly actualized questions for Stevens about how or whether poetry can be a haven from or antidote to social dissolution.

　　With the publication of "The Blue Guitar," critics generally recognized the broadening of Stevens' subject, his new "vaguely political contexts" and "ideological subject-matter,"[15] whether for good or ill. As we have seen, the contemporary literary world was highly polarized ideologically, and art movements and literary journals (like *New Masses*, or *Partisan Review*, which solicited poems from Stevens) were pressuring Stevens to take a stand. Now leftist readers saw Stevens not only as including images of the modern world of social and political violence but as leaning toward their own ideological position in denouncing fascism, for example. Filreis summarizes the situation by saying that "reviewers of *The Man with the Blue Guitar and Other Poems* tended to reiterate the guitarist's argument by ascribing to it a new and satisfying ideological harmony between themselves and the modernist moving from right to left."[16] But to us two thirds of a century later, the critical discourse seems "vaguely," bewilderingly, general because it hides the particular behind the veil of unsaid assumptions.

It nonetheless seems obvious today that Stevens' language, especially after *Harmonium*, is borrowed not only from the language of poets, philosophers, and the Bible but also from the speech, texts, and images available to the wider American public. Its concerns bear some relation, albeit sometimes oblique, to the common collective and national anxieties of the moment. Standing before an audience at his alma mater, Harvard, in December 1936, Stevens spoke for the generally shared perception of all when he said that the "pressure of the contemporaneous" had become "constant and extreme" since the previous World War ("The Irrational Element in Poetry" [*OP* 229]). During the late thirties and into the early forties Stevens acknowledged the pervasive influence of the media, as in "The Noble Rider" where he evoked the "extraordinary pressure of news" with a series of sinister puns on the common conflation of "news" as events and "news" as discourse or "description" of it (*NA* 20).[17] The particular acuity with which cataclysmic events were felt far beyond the regions where they were occurring was due to the growing impact of the press and the radio. Stevens' poetry of the thirties feeds partially on the givens behind the "news," as much as that of such generational contemporaries as William Carlos Williams, T. S. Eliot, and Robert Frost does, as different as the result may be. Stevens' verbal images too can even be seen as overlapping with the expressions of more politically engaged poets.[18] Thus the "mobs" of Stevens' "Sad Strains," for instance, are related to the "mass" in "America rises in a wave a mass / pushing away the rot" in Muriel Rukeyser's "Movie," also written in 1935. And in "The Man with the Blue Guitar," we may therefore read the guitarist's final offering, "Here is the bread of time to come" (XXXIII), not only as a solemn ritual substitute for the Eucharist but as a poetic performative of the "bread lines" that formed in American cities.[19] The "bread" in Stevens' poem, however, also exceeds the social and religious spheres to span innumerable spheres of the fictive "we," including not only the "scholar" (XXIV), "Franciscan don" (XXIX), "Geographers and philosophers" (XXVII), Picasso (XV) and Goethe (XXIII) but also actor (IX) and acrobat (XXV), as well as political opponent or "adversary" (X), and "employer" and "employee" (XXXI), whose common names are given in the poem.

Stevens' strategy in "The Blue Guitar" differs from both the "againstness" of "Sad Strains of a Gay Waltz" and the social criticism of the poetry of political protest. It includes appropriating the vocabulary of current discourse but blurring the borders of the discursive categories of the moment, be they those of capital versus labor,[20] communism versus fascism, or the aesthetic versus the political. Thus Filreis shows, for instance, that one of Stevens' images of demagoguery ("The Blue Guitar" X) is just as applicable to Stalin, Hitler, or Mussolini and that it could also apply to Roosevelt, although contemporaries took it for the Nazi or Fascist dictator.[21] In addition, the dialogical texture of the poem allows Stevens' performer to have it many ways. The very openness of the audience's initial terms leaves the performer free to juggle with object and subject, outer and inner, natural world and human kind, time now and all time, local sociopolitical context and individual desire—the audience's inferable expectations and his own play with words. This makes it particularly difficult to decode any fundamental "occasion" or reference among the poem's dizzying, polymorphous possibilities.

It is striking that both then and now criticism has focused on Stevens' imbrication in the local—that is, the American—perspective on these troubled times, and in particular the right-left debate as it was linked to American social unrest and given form by American political parties. On the other hand, Stevens at this time had not only already started his imaginative and artistic association with Europe without ever visiting it,[22] but he had also extended both his anxieties and sometimes his discourse beyond ordinary provincial boundaries. A clue to his scope can be found in "The Irrational Element in Poetry," Stevens' Harvard address:

> We no sooner say that it never can happen here than we recognize that we say it without any illusions. We are preoccupied with events, even when we do not observe them closely. We have a sense of upheaval. We feel threatened. We look from an uncertain present toward a more uncertain future. (*OP* 229)

Stevens' reiterated and anaphoric "we" drones on to embrace the American nation as a people that can no longer live "apart in a happy oblivion," while it also creates a rapport with Stevens' present audience, putting his local self in harmony with it before shifting to the impersonal but singular "One" of the poet. These two affective modes, however, are preceded by a direct appeal when Stevens says that "the end of civilization" is not merely possible but now "measurably probable" and asks his audience rhetorically, "If you are not a communist, has not civilization ended in Russia? If you are not a Nazi, has it not ended in Germany?" (*OP* 229). The "upheaval" that "we" fear is what has already occurred elsewhere. And he asks his audience to take an empathetic leap and think of the "end of civilization" as having already taken place, not within the local theater but for others, across the Atlantic.

This speech was given not only before the United States' entry into the war in December 1941, or before England and France's declaration of war on Germany in September 1939, but even before the start of the German Anschluss in March 1938. Stevens' anxiety about the immanence of mass chaos was increasingly articulated as of 1935 and 1936. 1936, it may be recalled, was not only the year of labor disputes in the U.S. leading to the expulsion of the CIO from the AFL, but also of the outbreak of the Spanish Civil War and the remilitarization of the Rhineland by Hitler in defiance of the Treaty of Versailles.

It has been noticed that the 1936 poem, "The Men That Are Falling" (CP 187–188), can be read as elusively referring to the ravages of the Spanish Civil War.[23] Indeed its title (taken up later in the poem) may remind us of press photographs that were to play an innovative role in exposing the human horror and pathos of this particular war and wars since. *Life* magazine, which started appearing in November 1936, began with its very first issue to display large-sized photographs of the human suffering endured by the victims of the Spanish war. It may even be possible that Stevens saw or heard of Robert Capa's famous photograph of the Republican soldier falling, arms spread, rifle in hand. Although it was not reprinted by *Life* until July 12, 1937, after Stevens had written "The Men That Are Falling," it had already appeared in the French magazine *Vu* in September 1936 with a large caption, "Comment ils sont tombés" ("How They Fell").[24] Even if Stevens may not have gone out of his way to see such images, he could not avoid being exposed to some of them at the office or probably on his own living-room coffee table, and echoes filter subliminally or consciously into his poetic vocabulary.

"The Men That Are Falling" is a poem that cushions part of its song and part of a soldier's delirium in a holy hush but works up to a brutal exhortation that condemns the waste of war. The reference works both as a cry of horror and as a meta-image of register and style that typify modern, ideologized war: "Taste of the blood upon his martyred lips, / O pensioners, O demagogues and pay-men!" Here we are reminded both of the polarized positions of Franquist Fascists and their leftist opponents of several stripes and of the hyperbolic register of their discourse. At the same time, both referent and sign highlight a generalizable truth about the manner in which murderous wars in modern times are fomented by demagogues and their "pay-men" cliques. If we ignore the Spanish Civil War, this level of meaning will still remain. The linguistic forms of the poem reveal the powerlessness of those who fight and those who look on aghast, and the modern manipulation of passions and interests through ideological rhetoric. This is how Stevens can maneuver between a putative news reference—and even news discourse—and the general phenomenon while he plays with the singular and the polysemous, the encrypted and the readable. In 1937 "The Man with the Blue Guitar" would take this procedure one step further by dispersing flitting references across its long trajectory. It would encrypt news items and news discourse within it in ways that are both more specific yet placed in more polysemous contexts, and thus more hidden than in "The Men That Are Falling." Thus section XVI of "The Blue Guitar" picks up the allusion again as "men as they fell," but it inserts it into an elemental, archaic image:

> The earth is not earth but a stone,
> Not the mother that held men as they fell
>
> But stone, but like a stone, no: not
> The mother, but an oppressor . . . (XVI, 1–4)

The oppressor figure has the effect of a tyrannical god or plague before becoming the "oppressor that grudges" the men their death, which extends the metaphor into a metonymy for the political tyrant. Thus a phrase similar to one that relates to the Spanish Civil War in another poem is cut off here from any continuous description of a known situation and disperses a communally shared image or phrase in a defamiliarizing context.

With hindsight such an image is an indication that Stevens' work from 1935 to 1936 contains encodings of a somewhat premonitory dread, a dread in which the specter of war looms large. Indeed, it seems to me that references to international events and "facts" perceived as harbingers of worldwide destruction of human institutions and the human spirit are more present in "The Man with the Blue Guitar" than has been generally acknowledged. The "end of civilization," which Stevens said had already occurred in parts of Europe by the end of 1936, is a significant context of the overlapping and polymorphous allusions in this poem.

We should remember, moreover, what serious scrutiny the many manifestations of this threat were receiving in the mid-thirties. On the one hand, scholars became interested in both the manipulative uses propaganda was put to in totalitarian regimes and the psychological mechanisms it depended on generally. The media were understood to play a fundamental role in the way parties and pressure groups seized control over the minds of the public. The manipulative uses of the media were considered to be of danger not only to the totalitarian systems implanted in Europe but to the rest of the world as well. For instance, O. W. Riegel, in *Mobilizing for Chaos* (1934), cited radio broadcasting as "the most single factor in domestic political and social control in communication in modern times." His analysis of the mind-warping psychological effects of the media, propaganda, and the "corruption of the news" covers primarily Germany and the Soviet Union but also contains a warning for the United States. He concludes with the chilling title, "Toward a New Dark Ages?"[25] As for the coverage of other aspects of totalitarian regimes, besides the hardening of the Soviet regime, the several stages of the rise of National Socialism during the mid-thirties figured in frequent news items. During the winter and spring of 1937, while Stevens was composing "The Man with the Blue Guitar," the *New York Times* provided extensive and varied coverage of Nazi events, from Hitler's New Year's proclamation to the National Socialist party, to a series on the Berlin Auto Show and promotion of the "small cheap car" that would become the Volkswagen, to boycotts and protests in America over the supposed Nazi activities of German groups in the United States, among other Nazi-related events. Comprehensive book-length studies also appeared. By the middle of the decade, Hitler's procedures, including the founding of secret societies, visual and verbal symbol-making, and mass spectacle and "exaltation," had been detailed. Readers were warned that the Nazi "hero-cult" and "Messiah mythology" were potentially explosive and they were informed that Hitler's *Mein Kampf* expressed no scruples over the "rightness or wrongness of [the] undertaking" it advocated.[26]

In conformity with Stevens' experimental and innovative precedents, readers can expect "The Man with the Blue Guitar" to make strange the ever present "nominal subject" of the threat of war and the means of control used by demagogic regimes. We have seen that one such reference to "him who none believes, / Whom all believe that all believe," that is, "the pagan in a varnished car" (X), is so general that it could apply to Hitler, Mussolini, Stalin, or even Roosevelt (the latter is Filreis' primary reference, because of the open car Roosevelt rode in for his January 1937 inauguration).[27] In addition, of course, the juxtaposition of registers and references prevents it from being just a contemporary scene. Elsewhere too the specificity of allusions to news coverage of impending horror in Europe is almost masked by polymorphous juxtapositions, but there are patterns of reference that nonetheless fit together. In two instances (V and XVI), references to Nazism are masked by metaphors of light. Thus, the classical sounding "structure of vaults upon a point of light" is also an apt description of the decor Hitler had constructed for himself by Albert Speer: Speer used powerful projectors to create vaults of light over the tribune from which Hitler would whip up the fanaticism of the crowd.[28] What seems to be a highly literary metaphor may simultaneously be a proper denotation, resonating to deflate the relevance of poetic myth. It could be a topical example not only of the audience's rejection of outdated poetry, but also of its psychic repression of the visible chaos of its own world, a world it calls "flat and bare" (V). The danger of Nazi extravaganza is also present in the light image in XIV, in beams, first one then a thousand, "radiant in the sky," which are succeeded by "One says a German chandelier— / A candle is enough to light the world." This may suggest Emerson's modest but self-reliant single candle in opposition to the refinement and pomp of the multicandled German "chandelier."[29] But it is also any individual's single, well-informed judgment in opposition to the authority of the German *chancellor* (Hitler had been named chancellor in January 1933) and the recent acceleration he had given to German rearmament. The formal, impersonal turn of "One says" chillingly intimates that what might seem a mere phonetic slip may accuse demagoguery of planned deceptions. Thus the occult reference to contemporary politics—one among other simultaneous associations—slips itself into the phonetic scheme of the section while allowing the word-world paradigm to be dominant.

In contrast to these ironic encodings, the "Mechanical beetles" of VII is a clear warning about what people may become when they call the sun "good" even when it has lost involvement with human beings. The earth "alive with creeping men, // Mechanical beetles never quite warm" is a dangerous example of what happens when the loss of empathy or the ability to feel deadens the sense of moral and political judgment and abolishes the distinction between "good" and not "good." Spiraling in to the narrowest range of contemporary reference, or the "occasion" for the specific image, however, the beetle metaphor may also be read as an allusion to the Volkswagen car that was being promised in Germany as the answer to the average man's dreams—a car promised for production in 1937 that would allow him and his family to get about on the new Autobahn network begun in 1933.[30]

Perhaps if such encryptings have not been detailed in readings of "The Man with the Blue Guitar," it is because they are only small parts of more inclusive waves of heterogeneous reference, and the references of modernist againstness and the American political scene have fit more smoothly into the urgent concerns of two or three generations of critics, as I have contended. On the other hand, the very heterogeneity is part of the disorienting texture of the poem. Section XXXI brings heterogeneous references into a provocative proximity that states how difficult it is to keep the poem open to them all:

How long and late the pheasant sleeps . . .
The employer and employee contend,

. Combat, compose their droll affair. (XXXI, 1–3) (Ellipsis in original.)

This section's bird image prepares us for the Shelleyan reference to the lark later in the section and more generally suggests the sounds of birds that have been such important metaphors for English poetry and that, as such, nourished Stevens' creation.[31] It is also a private allusion to two sentences we have met in our examination of the copula, extracted from the *Adagia* Stevens was collecting in a notebook at this time: "A poem is a pheasant," and "Poetry is a pheasant disappearing in the brush" (*OP* 194, 198). The reference to labor disputes is not covert at all, but it jars; labor disputes cannot be influenced by poetry but are examples of what happens in nonpoetic discourse. With the play on latinate *cum* words ("contend, / Combat, compose") the reference extends the patently political " 'Here am I, my adversary, that / *Confront* you' " (X) (emphasis added) to a related sociopolitical sphere, while it also implicates the metaphorical artifice of all discourse that must "compose" and not simply represent.[32] This self-referential move taxes the discourse of labor disputes as well as that of poetry as self-forming and self-perpetuating. Furthermore, the two discourses never meet referentially in the section because employer and employee do not heed the presence of the "cockbird" (dawn's rooster, the new poetry's pheasant, or the old poetry's lark). "The Man with the Blue Guitar" reserves part of its pleasure for habitual readers of poetry, those who read etymologies and recognize subtexts from Stevens' own work and romantic poetry, for instance. Thus Stevens' material signs move to include the daily life of broader society in its reference while at the same time they expose how this society has excluded poetry from its daily life and exemplify why it indeed will not, or cannot, read Stevens except within the ongoing ideological debate.

The Appeal to a Community

The point is that writing an anonymous audience into "The Blue Guitar" is a way for Stevens to integrate a fictive community, a "we," into his poem. This "we" shares references of average citizens, people with jobs and families. It includes the "we" that Stevens evoked in his Harvard address in "We no sooner say that [the end of civilization] can never happen here than we say it without any illusions" (OP 229), where "we" includes both speaker/writer and listener/reader, and "it can never happen here" is a bit of journalistic propaganda Stevens has tucked into his speech. The "we" of the audience in "The Blue Guitar" has as its correspondents the actual "we" "here" in America who, like Stevens himself, read newspapers and magazines, listened to the radio, and discussed the current events of Europe and the Americas.

"The Man with the Blue Guitar" thus cannot be reduced to a finite set of hermeneutic possibilities as the audience might like it to be. It can hardly be said to be accessible to the audience represented in it but can be read only by the most literate of real-life audiences, perhaps only a modernist-trained audience attuned to the twentieth-century crisis of poetry's "wormy metaphors." The situation of the poem is akin to that of "Anecdote of the Jar" as read by Frank Lentricchia. In his provocative meditation on the function of anecdotes, Lentricchia describes an "anecdote" as a story that can be deciphered only by a group of insiders (although he does not call them by that simple name). The effect of the anecdote (and perhaps its purpose) is to cultivate social bonds created by shared references. As he puts it, an anecdote is "a social form which instigates cultural memory: the act of narrative renewal, the reinstatement of social cohesion."[33] Stevens' "Anecdote," however, resists any simple decoding by any one social group. It seems to quarrel with the community raised on the old poetry and, by its "plain-speaking syntax,"[34] to bring the poem into contact with a social class that is excluded from and exploited by the privileged class. Yet the poem cannot reach other than the privileged, who, although they may strive to work against the system of privilege, also necessarily work within it.

The "serenade" or "chattering" of "The Blue Guitar" also ambiguously extends itself toward these two different audiences, and even toward multiple ones. The fictive audience that is actually represented by "they" is familiar with the old poetry but scornful of it. It therefore seeks out a player not of pipes or lute but of the guitar, a musician who has both romantic and more "popular" associations. Shelley's "With a Guitar, To Jane" and "To Jane (The Keen Stars Were Twinkling)"[35] might exemplify the guitar's romantic connotations; the jazz guitar or American folk music and its outgrowth in protest songs of the 1930s, such as Woody Guthrie's, its popular ones. The new poetry, by acknowledging the place of the old and using its categories becomes recognizable as "poetry" to traditional readers. New readers, on the other hand, who do not read through the grid of the old norms, or who may have the folk or jazz guitar as their reference, may be excluded by the metaphorical play of Stevens' poem although they may understand the denotation and even some of the contemporary allusions we have looked at. Both groups will find it difficult to "read" the poem's strangeness.

The representation of the "fictive" audience shows the guitarist to be dependent on a community as an impetus for speculation.[36] The poem's performer will integrate some of the audience's terms into his discourse even as he makes its images and references polyvalent. He will imitate some of the audience's tricks of word placement (loose juxtaposition, the transposition of words relative to the line length, copular structures) even as he introduces numerous tricks of his own that will be the subject of my next chapter. Solicited to revitalize the old symbol system, he will, contrary to what he does in "Owl's Clover," juggle with the system. In all these activities the performer will perform suggestively rather than argue his poetic statements. He will use his authority in nonauthoritarian ways. This is all the more difficult since the audience seems to need conclusion, cogency and consensus. Stevens' performer declines the role of lawgiver (suggested by section V) or explicator and remains responsive to the public's sense of loss. He enters the relationship with a willingness to engage in a discursive activity that seeks not to refute but to modulate his audience's own terms experimentally and thus respect the fictive encounter that provides the impetus for the whole poem. The audience's terms keep recurring as the guitarist improvises, rehearsing rather than explicating previous statements as he goes along, acknowledging the audience's presence in XV and XXII, and even making its presence the *sine qua non* of significance as the guitarist comes to a close in XXXII and XXXIII.

The performer's willingness to include the other in conversation can be seen as contributing to the shifts in voice, tone, attitude, and language level that we encounter throughout the poem sequence. This is not Whitman's imaginative appropriation of all subject positions, "Absorbing all to myself and for this song," as he writes in section 13 of *Song of Myself*. Rather than "absorbing" and speaking in the place of the other, Stevens' "I" (which is expressed only in about half the sections) declaims, whimsically corrects and expands, or meditates as an actor would. Thus it rallies others to taunt demagogues with " 'Here am I, my adversary, that / Confront you, hoo-ing the slick trombones' " (X) or plays with the limits of individual personality in "Tom-tom, c'est moi" and "Where / Do I begin and end?" (XII). It entertains experimental, unpredicated positions, like that ambiguous one in VI that begins, "A tune beyond us as we are" (VI), but also one that would constitute a less grandiose model for the human self in XXI:

> A substitute for all the gods:
> This self, not that gold self aloft,
>
> Alone, one's shadow magnified (XXI, 1–3)

The persona takes advantage of what guitarist and actor have in common, the ability to express others' positions imaginatively without appropriating them, but with the speaker often remaining anonymous, as undefinable as the imagined "voice" in a piece of purely instrumental music.

The "works" "share[d]" by the sun (X) embrace the works we create with language. This is patent in the self-reflexive effect in VII, where the poet hypothesizes a change from a previous statement by asking, "When shall I come to say of the sun / . . . It is a sea." Language consists of "given," public signs that the audience and guitarist have in common. Instead of taking refuge in the hermetic environment of the anecdote, the language in "The Blue Guitar" elucidates the process by which we exploit the language that belongs to many environments. One of the functions of the audience's presence, then, is to initiate an oblique speculation on the social construction of discourse in relation to an undefined, heterogeneous community.

A number of distant repercussions of the opening shearsman metaphor can be read in this way. According to the *OED*, the second meaning of "shearman" ("shearsman" does not figure in the *OED*) refers to a metal cutter and can be related to the dissection in canto III and its final "Jangling the metal of the strings." The primary meaning is "one who cuts wool," a sense expanded by the guitar into metaphors of clothing. Thus, in section IX, the guitarist transforms the instrument's shapeless blue into

> The color like a thought that grows
> Out of a mood, the tragic robe
>
> Of the actor, half his gesture, half
> His speech, the dress of his meaning, silk
>
> Sodden with his melancholy words,
> The weather of his stage, himself. (IX, 7–12)

The clothing of the actor's speech defines his human condition. The guitarist's "fantoche" (XXX) is also an avatar of this clothed theatrical figure, and described as "Hanging his shawl upon the wind," he exits from the theater in which the "words" we use are shown to construct our ideas and ourselves. These fleeting figures strutting on the stage, it seems to me, implicate the audience not only as members of the same community, but as their *semblables*, their alter egos, their mirror images. As the Franciscan don in his glass (XXIX) I discussed earlier shows, the other cannot escape being the other in language, both "like" and "strange." The "glass" reveals a fluctuating experience conditioned by the fluctuations of the signifier; the actor or fantoche, clothed by the guitarist-shearsman, holds a glass up to us so that we can see what we are and what we are not as well as the surface we share with him. Thus in XXII, when returning explicitly to the relation between poetry and "things as they are," the poet will insist on the fact that our definitions are tributary to the apportioning that takes place within our shared language, relativized by the cognizance of "Or so we say."

Although the poet's task is primarily a solitary one, his language is not only the poet's material garb but his emblematic "other." The signs for shared references are drawn playfully—although the play is sometimes sinister—from a vast paradigmatic pool. Exact consensual reference for each case is not required, for situations are temporary and follow each other with a vital fluidity in the poem; more crucially, as with all Stevens' poetry, the fields of metaphorical "meaning" are far from stable or univocal. Such heterogeneous invention seems particularly crucial to poetry when we consider that references to the "contemporaneous" are bound to become irrelevant to future generations except as accompanied by explanatory paraphernalia. And then, because they have become ghosts of the past, their meaning and impact will have changed. Perhaps one of the effects of Stevens' oblique encrypting of current events and media discourse in "The Man with the Blue Guitar" is precisely to reveal the destiny of these references: their repercussions on readers will be ephemeral.

The kind of encoding practiced by Stevens is different from that practiced by writers who depend for their effects on other kinds of sources. Writers of "anecdotes," hermetic writers in the religious tradition, or poets like Pound address a small group of initiates and set up obstacles to the comprehension of outsiders. Pound's Greek quotations and Chinese characters may be decipherable by a select few who will have earned access to their hidden core, as are allusions to the classics and works of national literary and historical heritages. Besides reinforcing the bonds already existing among the community of educated readers, traditional literary and cultural references point to a faith in the perpetuation of a common heritage. Their history has demonstrated their perennial quality, users of such allusions seem to say; it is assumed that they will be perpetuated in the future and contribute to cultural continuity. The traces of this heritage—richly commented on by critics—may make the poetry "readable" by connecting it to its past, which is also our past.

Stevens, of course, exploited both obliquely and plainly our Western literary heritage, especially its Anglo-American branch, but by contrast, his allusions to the "contemporaneous" have no shared past. They have only a local present. They are signs of a rupture with the past that

Stevens saw as the main "fact" of the post–World War I era. The past was known, but as we have seen, Stevens said about the present and the future: "We look from an uncertain present toward a more uncertain future" (OP 229). Much of the past has been destroyed by the present: "Things as they are have been destroyed" ("The Man with the Blue Guitar" XV). The "uncertain future" that will be generated by the present time is almost blank. All that is known is that it will be different. "Contemporaneous" links that resonate today—links among "chandelier," "chancellor," "the structure of vaults upon a point of light," and the earth as an "oppressor" of "the men as they fall"—may fall on deaf ears tomorrow. Hence the need for a polysemy that reaches into many registers at once, encoding multiple layers of past as well as present signs. The multiplicity of parallel codes only serves to heighten the tension between the conflicting temporal scopes on which the poem's life depends. Read this way, "The Man with the Blue Guitar" becomes Stevens' most stunning accomplishment in relativizing his own "occasion" for writing: using puns and other word play to conceal the signs that derive from his society's news discourse signifies the precariousness of the poem's sense.

After paying only passing attention to the audience and its demands (XV and XXII), the performer of "The Man with the Blue Guitar" refocuses on the contemporary scene at the end of the poem. Here, "employee and employer contend" and the morning sun is "this posture of the nerves" (XXXI). He addresses the audience (XXXII) and then communes with them in "our bread" (XXXIII). He makes a neat division between the time of the workaday world and the time of performing poetry. The performer's temporal logic reserves a special time for the performance of poetry: "The moments when we choose to play / The imagined pine, the imagined jay" (XXXIII). This perfunctory division is induced by a self-reflexive partitioning of spheres and the practical need to end the performance. "Time in its final block," as the performer says, would be the time outside or beyond poetic performance. It is opposed to the time of poetic performance where the audience can experience another awareness of overlapping times. The "pressure of the contemporaneous" is put into the double perspective of an undefined past, which is the past of the English language, and the future's claim on the mortality of performer and audience.

Building the poem's own perishability into its metaphorical references, Stevens' guitarist also finds a way of countering the audience's insistence on spatial circumscription as a founding metaphor and as a compositional strategy. The hermeneutic relationship between contemporary audience and performer is overlaid with disruptions. For he does not fill the old spaces with new signs but finds ways of slipping among registers and making metaphors overlap only partially here, partially there, creating only fugitive patterns or designs. The "spaces" (metaphorical and literal) into which such fragmentary allusions are fitted differ each time and thus defer the reading of each metaphor to other succeeding parts of the poem. As I suggested earlier, this strategy exploits *spatium* in the sense of a "lapse of time" rather than a closed space. And it contributes to what makes "The Man with the Blue Guitar" an unrehearsed extra-ontological speculation rather than a work of elucidation, persuasion, or lawgiving.

The covert allusions to contemporary chaos that I have noted demonstrate a breach in language use. On the one hand, the audience desires "fitting" language with the world by the assemblage of authoritative and unitary symbol systems. They include those constituted by the literary heritage which the audience rejects, and those constituted by workaday discourse or the press, which the performer infers from the audience's demand for fixed mimetism. On the other hand, the performer insists on the inventive disruption of systems by layering multireferential fragments of language. The time of the performance presents itself as the only time during which the audience can experience a release from the defenses it has built up against unpredictable change. The language of "The Man with the Blue Guitar" may be seen as an experiment in giving language survival value in the face of the way dead language and propaganda serve the harbingers of totalitaranism and mass destruction. Its purpose is like that of the work of the imagination which, as Stevens would say in 1941, is that of "pressing back against the pressure of reality." It has to do with "self-preservation" (*NA* 36).

6

&

EXPERIMENTS WITH MOMENTUM ON THE BLUE GUITAR

> Poetry must resist the intelligence almost successfully.
> —*Adagia* (OP 197)

Tuning Up

Reading "The Man with the Blue Guitar" is like discovering a maze of constant difference among a limited number of reiterated leitmotifs. Stevens' other long poems do not strip themselves down to essentials the way "The Blue Guitar" does: "The Comedian as the Letter C" (1922, CP 27–46) creates movement by a comic-serious narrative of initiation, domestication, and engenderment of "Daughters with Curls" (CP 443); "Notes toward a Supreme Fiction" (1942, CP 380–408) peoples itself with a whole cast of "allegorical personae," as Vendler calls them, which, if they allow a play of their attendant "lyric genres and discourse that gives [the poem] variability and volatility,"[1] also give readers' imaginations and memories some concrete markers amidst the abstract issues the poem deals with; after the celebrated "Notes," poems like "Description without Place" (1945, CP 339–346) and "An Ordinary Evening in New Haven" (1949, CP 465–489) develop discursively, incorporating heterogeneous images into their ruminations. "The Man with the Blue Guitar" ostentatiously thwarts narrative or logical development, both across the whole and within many of its parts. As Robert Rehder has noted, the poem is "a unique order composed of unique elements, unalterable and, like history, irreversible. Stevens' order is an anti-plot, a system that connects without allowing any pattern to be formed."[2] Although Stevens' basic metaphors and copulas are made to fulfill the traditional referential and ontological functions of language, what these lexical and syntactic materials produce is what Rehder has called an "unpatterned" discourse. Thus the sheer sequential necessity of the verbal texture is given prominence, on a level furthest removed from reference.

The foregrounding of texture in Stevens' early poetry may at first remind us of Picasso's or Braque's cubist works, painted during the late teens when Stevens started writing the poems for *Harmonium*. In these paintings the guitar, fruit, and chessboard are necessary references, but what is new is that the new relations of reference and the new relations of shape and line also become objects of contemplation and speculation. "Blue Guitar" privileges traditional left-right, up-down reading, but the disruption of reference thrusts the sequential order of reading into our attention as an object of speculative activity itself. Signs and sounds establish patterns along not a narrative but a spatial line, a line of reading reinforced by the numbering of the 33 sections and the uneven procession of the 200 tetrameter couplets. As we shall see later, the linear form of signs and sounds also dictates our perception of linear time, which is, of course, particularly crucial in the reading and performing of long poems.

"The Man with the Blue Guitar" is unique in Stevens' oeuvre in the way it beckons readers, both through the very metaphor of the song the performer "sings" and "plays" and in terms of its abstract shape, to think of its linear form in terms of a succession of musical fragments. We might expect to find general patterns constituting full periods, rounded completions, the "espousal to the sound // Of right joining, a music of ideas" ("Study of Images II," [CP 464]), as in poems like "God is Good. It Is a Beautiful Night" (CP 285) or "The Planet on the Table" (CP 532). Or we might, as with avant-garde painting and music of the early twentieth century, hear it privileging rupture. This is the case of "The Man with the Blue Guitar" and many early Stevens poems.

The poem is duplicated metaphorically as a tune played by the guitar player, which the audience-antagonist defines as "The tune is space" (VI). Yet, to follow this metaphor, the audience's own restricted view of circumscribed space is transformed into a space that changes contours as the poem surges forward, languishes in self-complacency, contests, assents, meets a challenge, makes compromises, cuts its own momentum off. Stevens' persona takes full advantage of his extended scope to vary his procedures with a freedom that is characteristic of this poem yet unusual in Stevens' work. If we are willing to enter into the poem's movement, we find that the incessant shifts produced by these procedures create a momentum that engages our constant interest. I would like to explore this process as it contends with the making of broadly symbolic or narrowly metaphorical definition, in this, Stevens' most radical experiment in temporal effect linked with surface movement.

Before reading the poem's linear unfolding in space-time, however, we should consider three sections that threaten to pervert or prematurely abort the guitarist's exploration. The most violent of these is section III, which temporarily sweeps into oblivion the ideal of section II's "serenade" (L. *serenus, -a, -um* means "calm, clear"). The murderous conceit of section III represents tune-playing as the ritualized dissection of a living man. Its narrative logic and verbal aggression are a danger to both singer-player and poem.

III

Ah, but to play man number one,
To drive the dagger in his heart,

To lay his brain upon the board
And pick the acrid colors out,

To nail his thought across the door,
Its wings spread wide to rain and snow,

To strike his living hi and ho,
To tick it, tock it, turn it true,

To bang it from a savage blue,
Jangling the metal of the strings . . . (Ellipsis in original.)

It is relevant that this is the only section of "The Blue Guitar" in which the verb *to be* does not occur in one form or another: it thus neither approaches nor describes being, nor does it even set up relations through the copula. Having no attendant subject or conjugated verb, the act seems depersonalized. The heterogeneous voice of the poem becomes so undefinable here that it has even been read—mistakenly, I think—as being the work of the audience. The verbalization of desire seems to be self-authorized and thus defy all controls. The optative mood of the verbs allows the surge of violence to transform an unclaimed murderous wish into effective, aggressive action.

In terms of representation, the opening "Ah" is a stressed foot of desire as yet unsymbolized; it culminates in another trochee, in a "Jangling" that somewhat arbitrarily suspends the flow of energy. Within the connecting arc, an investment in destructive drives is doubled by the Stevensian tactic of expanding and controlling the semantic or symbolic development of a metaphor. The curious "metal" of the strings (last line), for instance, derives symbolically from the denotations of "dagger" and "nail." The section's fury, however, results primarily from the (guitar's) insistent play of sound. In contrast to the initial "Ah" of desire, violent infinitives ensure a regularity of beat that is a rarity for Stevens. The iambic insistence on the monosyllable infinitives, from "To drive" to "To bang," provides the poem with a basic impulse that inhabits the very language until it destroys itself. This becomes inevitable in the sequence that follows from extirpating the "living hi and ho" from the guitar's "savage blue," which leads to the poem's destructive "Jangling." Alliterations, assonances, and consonances (/d/ in 2, /b/ in 3, and so forth, to the /t/, /k/ and /i/ in "To tick it, tock it, turn it true") also underscore the unflagging beat of the iambic tetrameter and the final trochaic and self-thwarting "Jangling the metal of the strings . . ." The drives thus concentrate in rhythmic and phonetic repetitions that Julia Kristeva associates with the "semiotic," as opposed to the "symbolic" contribution to the construction of meaning.[3] Our attention is drawn toward the dynamic relationships among the signs over and above their referential function, especially as the lines of dependence and causality of this murder narrative are far from clear: Is the guitar's personifying "savage blue" the source of the torturer's energy or the place of the victim's torture? Kristeva, joining the purely linguistic with the psychoanalytic, would impute the drives to the unconscious of the speaking/writing subject (the real-life author), which is the pivotal object of her phenomenological and psychological quest. What may arrest readers of section III of "The Blue Guitar" is that its grammatical and phonetic strategies sidestep the usual ways of positing an organizing ego that would try to control the construction of coherent representational meaning. They thus foreground the ongoingness of the very linguistic process over motive or meaning, as the metaphoric transformations are nearly masked by the section's frenzy of sound and rhythm.

The "semiotic" fury of signifiers seems to compete with the attempt to nonetheless construct a symbol system through networks of metaphors for the "man number one" who is tortured and dissected in this section. This "man" is an extension of the "hero's head" (II). He is perhaps the poet-seer, the great man of history, but also a prefiguring of the thirties demagogue of section X and the single or solitary thinker reduced to himself of XII. He is the one who feels and knows, figured in other poems as the "pensive man" ("Connoisseur of Chaos," *CP* 216), the "glass man" ("Asides on the Oboe," *CP* 251), or "Adam of beau regard" ("The Pure Good of Theory," *CP* 331). But doesn't he also implicate the poem's number-one man, "The man bent over his guitar" (I)? This simple player is in any case a putative knower who endangers himself by experimenting. The "thought" of the tortured man, the guitarist's double, is extended metaphorically beyond the nailed bird toward Christ on the cross in one direction, and toward a butterfly pinned on a board in the other (prefiguring "all the flies are caught" in XI).

The "living hi and ho" in this pattern exemplifies an utterance that does not function primarily as a conveyor of symbolic "meaning." It is then that the possibility of life appears, on a literal level, since the (player's) stated goal is to extract the pre- or non-symbolic order from human sound and "turn it true." But this is effected only through sounds or even noises: the "tick-tock" of clock or hammer and the jarring "Jangling" of the guitar's strings.[4] The concealed speaker's uninhibited desire deconstructs the possibility of defining anything "true." The question may be, then, to what extent it is possible to sing man when symbolic, metaphorical signs are shown to have another face, a generally ignored or repressed face of meaningless and potentially destructive sound.

Metaphorical language channeled into harassing noise and destructive impulse is, however, only the first and most extreme of many inconclusive experiments in combining the symbolic and the semiotic that will accumulate as the poem moves on. The "living hi and ho" here prepares us for the later "ay di mi" (XIII) and "ay-yi-yi" (XXV), which appear in sections that are "about," respectively, the grammatical function of words and their varying position within syntax. Section XIII raises the issue of the relation between things in the world, or referents (expressed by the substantive "blue"), and the word (*blue*) as noun or adjective:

XIII

The pale intrusions into blue
Are corrupting pallors . . . ay di mi,

Blue buds or pitchy blooms. Be content—
Expansions, diffusions—content to be

The unspotted imbecile revery,
The heraldic center of the world

Of blue, blue sleek with a hundred chins,
The amorist Adjective aflame . . . (Ellipsis in original.)

The sound of "ay di mi" hesitates between the Latin pronunciation of the musical note *mi* that would rhyme it with "be" and "revery," and the anglicized reading that would rhyme it with "ay-yi-yi" and thus include the homonym for "I die." It recalls William Carlos Williams' even more contradictory *"Ay de mi,"* which is also a signature within a list of qualities of color, such as "Blood-bright," "flame-rust," and "pink."[5] Both poems imply the inescapableness of words of quality, but whereas Williams' poem strips all these qualities down to "white," Stevens' guitarist reveals the simultaneous potential of seemingly "full" color words to create a centripetal movement but also to "corrupt" or to burn themselves out in a self-consuming passion (indicated by the disrupted syntactic structure of the stanza, among other things). Overall, it is the extreme versatility of the word "blue" itself (as noun, as adjective, and as itself beginning with the letter *b* [*be*]) that dominates our reading experience. This versatility is generalized in terms of syntax in the ludic section XXV much later in the poem, where the juggler is explicitly given "symbols" that are overwhelmed by the sheer movement and rhythmic flux of the section and the surreal transformations that take place:

He held the world upon his nose
And this-a-way he gave a fling.

His robes and symbols, ai-yi-yi—
And that-a-way he twirled the thing.

. . . . .

And the world had worlds, ai, this-a-way:
The grass turned green and the grass turned gray.

And the nose is eternal, that-a-way.
Things as they were, things as they are,

Things as they will be by and by. . .
A fat thumb beats out ai-yi-yi. (XXV, 1–4, 9–14) (Ellipsis in original.)

From the destructive to the ludic, these three sections body forth linguistic textures whose function is only minimally to state referential if catachrestic meaning and primordially to reveal language as a texture that creates an arc of movement from its signifiers. The tentativeness of each of these arcs is made visible in the ellipses at or near the end of the sections. The anonymous rage of section III, with the ambiguous responsibility of its guitar's "savage blue," is not repeated again. Rather, in retrospect, section III clears the way for reading the section, and each subsequent section, as one moment—but not "a moment final"—in a movement that goes from here to there, from "this-a-way" to "that-a-way" (XXV), from one "like" to another "like" (XXIX), or from "this" to "that" (XXXII).

First Movement

The need to move on in "The Man with the Blue Guitar" is ingrained in the poem's formal structure in constantly varying ways. Although the overall structure is "unpatterned," if we read the sequence of sections as the verbal form of spatial and temporal momentum, we can perceive possible stages in the experience of reading as it becomes an experience of ongoingness. In the four ensuing "movements" I will treat a number of sections in the order in which they occur, using metaphorical constructs from within the poem as a guide.

A good starting point is the spatial metaphor the performer uses as a paradigm for the construction of the song or poem. As I intimated in chapter 5, the performer rejects the static finality demanded by the audience's rigid notion of "place" and "space." On the simplest level, the performer modulates "place" much as Stevens did in his earlier poetry, as in the metaphorical modulations of "Place of the Solitaires" (CP 60). In this early poem, the opening command involves the creation of a space of constant movement, invoked by the couplet:

> Let the place of the solitaires
> Be a place of perpetual undulation.

The rest of the poem only partially fulfills the opening conditions. Repetitions and substitutions occur: *-ation*, for instance, is repeated in "undulation," "cessation," "continuation," "iteration," the preposition *of* is disseminated throughout the poem, and the sound /o/ is reiterated in "no," "motion" and "most." But to use a musical analogy, what the poem calls the "renewal of noise" is a miniature theme and variation in the classical mode, in which change always recalls the original theme or motif. That is, the development is based on repetition of resemblance, marching in orderly rank from line to line. It perpetuates the same with only minor differences, ending with a simple variation in the final quatrain:

> And, most, of the motion of thought
> And its restless iteration,
> In the place of the solitaires,
> Which is to be a place of perpetual undulation.

The poem cannot fulfill its stated objective of "manifold continuation," because the poem's "motion" undulates or folds back on itself but does not move beyond its initial impetus. It seems governed by redundancy and overfull of "semiotic" noise.

Dissatisfaction with such redundancy verging on noise is encountered in section IV of "The Blue Guitar," which comes as an experiment in "life" after the destruction desired in III. To "pick" is no longer a metaphor of dissection and extraction (as in "pick the acrid colors out" in III) but of movement along the space-time of the guitar's tune playing:

IV

> So that's life, then: things as they are?
> It picks its way on the blue guitar.
>
> A million people on one string?
> And all their manner in the thing,

And all their manner, right and wrong,
And all their manner, weak and strong?

The feelings crazily, craftily call,
Like a buzzing of flies in autumn air,

And that's life, then: things as they are,
This buzzing of the blue guitar.

The opening question about the equivalence between "life" and "things as they are" is tried out by representing the crowd referentially, and then debunked at the end in the "buzzing" sound of skepticism. The "buzzing" is the guitar's way of reversing Hoon's solipsistic "hymns that buzzed beside my ears" ("Tea at the Palaz of Hoon," CP 65) but also of differentiating itself from the million people. The internal couplets merely accumulate a large, heterogeneous audience that recurs as the biblical "multitude" in XII. Here, "A million people" connotes the masses, American laborers or farm workers before their union organizers, or, in the perspective of my reading of allusions to Nazi demagoguery in the poem, European crowds before their leaders. The triple anaphora of the "manner" of the masses also demonstrates habit and accumulation, both in its verse form and its lexis. It propagates social, moral, and discursive repetition. In a mere repetition of their very selves, the mass-produced *Männer* (the plural of *Mann* = "man" in German) are undifferentiated from their collective identity. This word-play compresses normally separate "people" into a mass and erases all critical thought, expansion, or development. At one extreme we encounter the bludgeoning result of the audience's ethos, its desire for satisfaction in a "final atmosphere," and perhaps a trace of Stevens' resistance to his own leftist detractors. On another level, the reduction impedes the variety of the musician's basic material, either the building of a chord that would have pleasurable variety within it or the development of a melody over time. The performer needs the rest of the poem sequence to try out other responses.

The guitarist's ethos of pleasurable variety occurs in an extended structure of shifting conceits, one each in VII to IX, once the audience has fallen silent. We should remember (see chapter 5) that in VII the shearsman-sharer as contemplator and guitarist postulates a situation in which "the sun no longer shares our works"—that is, a situation in which people have no sense of belonging to a vital scheme of things and risk becoming mere "creeping men, // Mechanical beetles never quite warm."

The word-act by which the performer detaches himself from a vivifying source or pathos gives way to a literal hypothesis in "I stand." But this form of inactivity cannot be represented formally because the poem moves—although "moves" is a metaphor—on. This can be seen by the way the predication breaks down as sentences are replaced by incomplete infinitive questions, and "I stand" becomes "To stand" at the close of the section:

> Not to be part of the sun? To stand
>
> Remote and call it merciful?
> The strings are cold on the blue guitar. (VII, 12–14)

"To stand" illustrates the primary sense of the English word as well as of its original Latin meaning "spatial separation or distance." Stevens' "Remote," with the moving back of *re-movere*, itself confirms the stillness of the "cold" strings in the last line.

Thus the poem itself must move not back but forward if it is to vivify and overcome the cold. Aesthetic pleasure on the fringes of symbol systems is built into the structure of the poem by its emphasis on succeeding moments. These are not "spots of time" like the static epiphanies Wordsworth stages in his *Prelude*, but musical "meanderings" like the main body of Wordsworth's narrative. Indeed, in VIII, the atmosphere or weather is itself depicted as "rolling by," moving on.

VIII

> The vivid, florid, turgid sky,
> The drenching thunder rolling by,
>
> The morning deluged still by night,
> The clouds tumultuously bright
>
> And the feeling heavy in cold chords
> Struggling toward impassioned choirs,
>
> Crying among the clouds, enraged
> By gold antagonists in air—
>
> I know my lazy, leaden twang
> Is like the reason in a storm;

And yet it brings the storm to bear.
I twang it out and leave it there.

The struggle in the weather is metamorphosed into a musical struggle. It temporarily takes up the "cold" motif of VII, firmly separating it from its previous context (though keeping the musical connotation) and forcing it into the emotional field of "cold chords" that attempt to join with "impassioned choirs." Not only does the phonetic structure of these few lines verge on noise through their accumulated alliteration (/k/); but the metrical pattern, which was an insistently regular iambic, becomes temporarily chaotic in ll. 4–6.

    The guitarist's final predication ("I know") reinstates order. The copula—his "lazy, leaden twang / Is like the reason in a storm"—does not so much define the guitar metaphorically as situate the guitar within the performer's emotional and verbal world of "The . . . sky," "the drenching thunder," "the morning," "the feeling," "the clouds." Although the guitar's means are the opposite of the tempest's tumult, the guitar is also similar to the storm ("like" it). "[T]he reason in a storm" that the guitar resembles may denote "understanding," but it is more strongly related to "motive, cause." The guitar bringing the storm "to bear" is thus introduced by the disjunctive "And yet," for the very motive or movement must also stop itself. This balancing is resolved not logically or discursively but with a "twang" that, like "bang" (III), is a noise devoid of symbolic meaning. In this paraphrase, the "cold chords" in VIII intervene against the moving tumult of natural phenomena to thwart them in a single inharmonious gesture: the "twang" stops struggle but does not transform it into new movement. It creates a pure noise that allows temporary rest. A rest here is a space created by or on the guitar, but it is also a rhythmic silence, a "rest" in the musical sense.

    Anticipating my argument below, I would say that the space is immediately succeeded by another one, and that the silence is full of the rhythm of waiting. The temporal dimension becomes salient here. Moreover, this is confirmed when VIII's final "I twang it out and leave it there" is immediately followed by "And the color" that begins IX, almost as though the guitar had not brought a stop to the passionate struggle in which it had been involved. This initiates the third conceit in the series from VII to IX.

IX

And the color, the overcast blue
Of the air, in which the blue guitar

Is a form, described but difficult,
And I am merely a shadow hunched

Above the arrowy, still strings,
The maker of a thing yet to be made;

The color like a thought that grows
Out of a mood, the tragic robe

Of the actor, half his gesture, half
His speech, the dress of his meaning, silk

Sodden with his melancholy words,
The weather of his stage, himself.

The section's "arrowy, still strings" combine in a single pair of epi-
thets the double potential of the guitar as the place for poetry. First, "ar-
rowy" selects an image of lightning from among the numerous
suggestions surrounding the thunderstorm and its "gold antagonists" in
VIII. It perpetuates the potential recurrence of the storm that rages in
that section's first four couplets, while "still" refers to the effect the guitar
has on the storm at the end of VIII. But secondly, the "arrow" denotes
what can move through the air in time. In this association, the word
"still" may remind us of Zeno's paradox, in which an arrow, which is usu-
ally said to "move" continuously, is defined not as moving but as occupy-
ing a succession of infinitely small spaces and thus as remaining still
during infinitely small moments. This could be an apt description of
what we call the "movement" of ordinary language.

Yet by calling what is described a "movement," I am made to real-
ize that this is a metaphorical move meant to serve a critical strategy: it
will aid me to describe "The Man with the Blue Guitar" in terms other
than substitution, displacement, or aporia, which emphasize space, and
turn to signs that take both space and time into account (and later, time
alone), terms such as movement, motion, or direction. It is the "arrowy"
nature of the strings that will be given free rein in the second half of IX
(ll. 7–10), finally creating something like a sense of an ongoing, moving
direction. Here we find both Zeno's succession of spaces in which small

synecdochal displacements are realized, and a line leading from guitar and maker to "himself," who is both guitarist and actor-other. The sense of moving forward, it seems to me, is reinforced by the way Stevens plays with word placement, such as shifting the place of "the" and "his" across the lines, or using different parts of speech to produce enjambment. The grammatical suspension of this six-line clause (parallel to that of ll. 1–5, moreover) contributes to the impression that the form is not being pictorially "described" (l. 3) but that indeed the color of the section "grows" (l. 7) as synecdoches replace each other.

Allusions to section IX abound in the ending of the late poem, "Angel Surrounded by Paysans" (1949, CP 496–497), which provides a striking contrast to the original. As in a number of other later poems that seem to allude to "The Man with the Blue Guitar," the allusions naturally include echoes of semantic fields, such as the spectral quality of the metaphorical "shadow" or "apparition," clothing or apparel, weight and color, bodily movement, the self, but also quasi quotations and inversions. A few examples:

"Blue Guitar"	"Angel"
"And I am merely" →	"Am I not"
"half his gesture, half / His speech" →	"half of a figure of a sort, // A figure half seen"
"himself " →	"Myself "
"sodden with his melancholy words" →	"such lightest look"

The later poem also uses the movement of the same words (or forms of them) across the lines in different positions and grammatically varies enjambment to effect the turning of the accumulated phrases. More significantly, however, "Angel Surrounded by Paysans" culminates with a series of disguises around which the angel-actor asks rhetorically, "Am I not"

> . . . an apparition apparelled in
>
> Apparels of such lightest look that a turn
> Of my shoulder and quickly, too quickly, I am gone?

As Marie Borroff says of this closing: "The reiterative phrasing of 'quickly, too quickly,' in the last line of all, performs a minor holding action—a pause on the threshold of disappearance."[6] It unambiguously affirms the transitoriness of any meaningful mediating figure, but it does so in the sense of a limited duration that is perhaps consonant with the "occasion" of the poem—that is, the contemplation of a still life painting Stevens had just acquired.[7]

In "The Man with the Blue Guitar" IX, on the other hand, it is as though the "maker of a thing yet to be made" were singing of his series of invented conceits and the ruptures between them. He loosens the bonds of metaphorical construction by showing that indeed he is constantly moving beyond a present definition of "yet to be made," and uttering this "to be" in a way that both speaks about and performs a sense of moving experimentally in a direction that must be forward but otherwise is constantly being redefined. Within the structure of the whole, section IX confirms the work's direction toward a hypothetical future begun in VII.

Second Movement

What I am calling "direction" here subsumes what critics have identified as the poem's improvisational character, its abrupt starts and stops, its enactment of the heterogeneous and fragmented nature of experience. In his early *Poets of Reality* (1965), J. Hillis Miller saw that "The Man with the Blue Guitar" demonstrated Stevens' turn to a new style in which the "finished unity of his earlier poems" is "gradually replaced by poems which are open-ended improvisations, created from moment to moment by the poet's breath. They begin in the middle of a thought, and their ending is arbitrary."[8] Miller stressed the poem's phenomenological repercussions: Life "as it is" in the guitarist's poem "is a sequence of states of consciousness with neither start nor finish."[9] I would like to take a cue from the poem's conceit instead and consider that the composing and playing represented in the poem privileges the musical metaphor and that this can most forcefully be read as enacting a direction forward and taking the reader-listener with it.

The unavoidable comparison with music has of course been made. As Barbara Holmes states, critics have noticed Stevens' preference for writing "variations" or "improvisations," but they have rarely defined these terms precisely or applied rigorous criteria to the poems.[10] Stevens himself uses the word "variation" five times and "improvisation" four times. It is easy to see that a vague analogy might be made between the principle of musical theme and variation and "Thirteen Ways of Looking at a Blackbird" (CP 92–95),[11] "Variations on a Summer's Day" (CP 232–236), or "Chocorua to its Neighbor" (CP 296–302), for example, and even more loosely "Notes toward a Supreme Fiction" (CP 380–408). The late poem, "Thinking of a Relation between the Images of Metaphors" (CP 356–357), illustrates the classic form of variation in which the "theme" remains recognizable throughout the series. The second couplet provides a statement: "In the ear of the fisherman, who is all / One ear, the wood-doves are singing a single song." The lexical elements of the statement, and even letter combinations like *oo*, then recur in new combinations and new places and produce new words ("bass") to add to the "fisherman" and "dove."

> . . . The fisherman is all
> One eye, in which the dove resembles the dove.
>
> There is one dove, one bass, one fisherman.
> Yet coo becomes rou-coo, rou-coo.

"How close / To the unstated theme each variation comes," the poem then says self-reflexively. "Improvisation," on the other hand, which principally applies to the situation of creating while performing, does not necessarily imply the underlying cohesion of "theme and variations" yet nearly always exploits it. When Bach "improvised" a prelude and fugue on the basis of a hymn tune,[12] he had to reiterate the tune as a theme in various forms (varying the degree or tempo, for instance) as required by the rules of counterpoint or other rules of construction. And as Holmes correctly notes, even the jazz jam session, with its seeming freedom to the layman's ear, relies on "an 'ostinato bass figure' or some other thematic element (a melody or motive)," which it retains throughout.[13] Yet to show, as Holmes does, that "The Man with the Blue Guitar" is "a hybrid form, a cross between theme and variations and the on-the-spot performed piece, the improvisation,"[14] does not help us to enter into the strangeness of the reading experience.

It is the reader's and listener's subjective reaction to the work that makes it seem "spontaneous" or "improvised" or not, and that reaction is partially formed by the expectations the performer develops in us during his speculative activity. Creating a thing of words, and not nonreferential music, his strategy plays in part with expectations of metaphorical development. But more crucially, when we read Stevens' "Blue Guitar" from section to section, we have the "impression" that although we recognize certain recurring words and phrases, we are constantly surprised by the new syntactical patterns and other linguistic and prosodic ruptures of symmetry that interrupt what seemed to constitute a line of development. Holmes says that sometimes between sections we have "little preparation" for "leaping from one version to the next."[15] This is the main aspect of the improvisational technique that is relevant to reading "The Blue Guitar," for I think that this "leaping" with "little preparation" describes what happens both between and within sections and that it is one of the characteristic principles of "order" of "The Man with the Blue Guitar."

Whereas the sequence from VII to IX exemplifies "leaping" from one conceit to another and one pose or style to another from section to section, XI contains leaps within the small space-time of a single section. The guitarist's beginning strategy in XI is the construction of copular equivalences, with *become* in the first two couplets (instead of his usual *be*) emphasizing change and process:

XI

Slowly the ivy on the stones
Becomes the stones. Women become

The cities, children become the fields
And men in waves become the sea.

It is the chord that falsifies.
The sea returns upon the men,

The fields entrap the children, brick
Is a weed and all the flies are caught,

Wingless and withered, but living alive.
The discord merely magnifies.

Deeper within the belly's dark
Of time, time grows upon the rock.

In the first two couplets the reiterated copulas ("become" for *to be*) effect the initial transformation of living plants and humans into inhuman substrata: stone, cities, fields, and sea. The men seem all the more dehumanized since they are displaced by waves (suggesting waves of soldiers and waves of the sea) before being annihilated by them. The copular relations here merely make transfers from one known entity to another as does the surrealist art Stevens criticized. The only variety is produced by enjambment around the copula, but the seemingly random nature of this rhythmic ploy serves to heighten the strangeness of the copular transformations and have us notice that the copulas themselves make "waves" that produce troughs and crests in the syntax. This momentum could continue, but it is cut short.

A second movement begins after the rupture effected by the "empty" *to be* of "It is the chord that falsifies." The new transformations of an even more grotesque and mutilating scene are vehicled by a greater variety of verbs. Arbitrary entrapment and fossilization vaguely echo the ivy becoming the stones in the first movement while perhaps suggesting a view of flies caught in amber (presaging the "amber-ember pod" in XXX). The redundancy of "living alive" is a doubly sinister and cruel lie. A third movement begins with "The discord merely magnifies." Rhyming with "the chord that falsifies," it also similarly breaks the syntactic patterns (S + V + complement) and rhythm of the four preceding lines. It introduces a further variation with the final couplet's "Deeper," which nonetheless recalls the adjectival line "Wingless and withered." Finally, the closing couplet recuperates the potential fecundity of the women in the first movement in the sinister "belly's dark" of a now impersonal, archaic "time."

Our discomfort derives from the series' abrupt representational and syntactic shifts. The four initial transformations effected with "become" are not systematically undone or redone in the second and third movements. Instead, once the men and children have been neatly dealt with, the poem proceeds through primarily haphazard changes. Among them we find a semantic cluster of "brick," the initial "stones," and "the cities," and another of "weed" and "ivy," but also a phonetic cluster extending from "women" to "*m*en in *w*aves," "*w*eed," and "*w*ingless and *w*ithered." Finally, in a graphic move, "flies" (which are metaphors for human victims) operate a distortion of "fields" and even "falsifies"—partially reiterating "the buzzing of flies" in IV. Paralleling the lack of thematic coherence, such prosodic asymmetry destabilizes these second metamorphoses, as in "brick / Is a weed."

The empirical-realist reality of this compressed narrative seems to depict the erasure of human individuality by "waves" of chaos. Civilization as we know it, as Stevens might say, is blotted out by the freezing of time in the "return" to both natural and fossilized states. Preservation is guaranteed but in a degraded and helpless form. Set within its historical context, the section appears as a grotesque image of the organized chaos perpetrated by such Nazi events as the opening of concentration camps for party opponents, book-burnings (both 1933), or subsequent German rearmament, rampage orchestrated in German cities, or mass spectacles complete with the "chords" of rousing music. However, a unitary decoding, or even plural and contradictory ones, cannot account for all the strangeness readers experience in reading this section, in context or alone. The variety of leitmotif and syntax overrides our impression of the kind of underlying thematic unity that Stevens himself, on the contrary, attributed to XI when he paraphrased it:

> The chord destroys its elements by uniting them in a chord. They then cease to exist separately. On the other hand, discord exaggerates the separation between its elements. These propositions are stated in a variety of terms: ivy on stone, people in cities, men in masses. (*Letters* #406)[16]

It is interesting that even Stevens' musical terms are loaded with spatial connotations, as if visualizable location signified by "in," "on," or "between" exerted mastery over the tension produced by a less patent motion or direction toward, and as if the musical metaphor were pertinent primarily to a spatial reference. But it is by considering not the spatial but the temporal dimension, I think, that we can account for the texture of "improvisation" that many readers attribute to the poem. Surprise interruptions in the ongoing development are most fruitfully considered as analogous to the production of musical time, as contrasted to interruptions in structure that we call "fragmentation," which emphasizes space.

Most professional writing on music is too arcane to be of use here. It is safe to say, however, that since Schoenberg and Stravinsky started considering music as a "form," most musicology has outwardly abandoned the traditional view of music as either "expressing" or "meaning" something, such as the celestial harmony, universal force or will, or human emotion. Contemporary approaches focus on the psychological effect of music (the listener-reader's response), the composer's intention, syntactic permutations (as seen in Valéry and Mallarmé), or the theory of signs, for instance, yet even such approaches are interlaced with a reading of "meaning," expressive or cognitive, though not necessarily referential. In this vein, Anca Rosu, in her interesting reading of sound patterns in Stevens' poetry, bears in mind Stevens' wariness of transparent referentiality while interpreting sound in terms of nonreferential meaning. What is relevant to us here is that in calling the "very symmetry of sound" a "foundation of the real," she also incidentally makes "time" antithetical to the "real" in music when she says of Stevens' visual poem, "The Poems of Our Climate" (CP 193–194): "As it becomes almost a song, the poem does to the temporal flow what usually music does: it patterns it, contains it, makes it tame and human."[17] However, it seems to me that falling back on the teleology of the creative act diverts attention from the very foundation of musical reading and playing, or "interpretation"—the deployment of a tempo of sound and silence across expository passages and transitions. Moreover, not only is discourse on temporal development central to music criticism, but experiments with tempo and rhythm have marked twentieth-century music just as much as more obvious experiments with new scales and new instrumental and noninstrumental sounds.[18]

I would argue that Stevens' experimental discontinuity and random change also have the effect of heightening our awareness of time— that is, of time as a distinguishable parameter of experience. It cannot be claimed that this was part of Stevens' conscious project for his poem. Nor can such a psychological effect be clearly demonstrated as being produced by any particular work. Yet if it is true, as Rudolf Arnheim has claimed, that neither space nor time is "usually a component of the perception of events,"[19] there do appear to be occasions when they indeed become a conscious "part" of experience. Arnheim says that the "Time experience" can happen in listening to music when "components of a piece are perceived as separate systems, for example, in the overlappings of a fugue." Although we do not ordinarily experience time consciously because the musical voices are usually "tightly integrated in their musical flow," Arnheim considers that in some modern music the melodic flow is fractured in such a way that when "even short intervals are strong enough to turn elements into self-contained point-sized systems, Time is called upon as the only substratum in which the fragments can organize. Accordingly the listener experiences 'waiting for the next tone.'" This can also be salient when the listener is waiting for the climax or finale. The melodic and harmonic structure may have been deployed so that a "goal is established in the awareness of the listener and acts as an independent system toward which the music is striving."[20] Fragmentariness, in his view, is not alone sufficient to produce that tension. Rather, the perceptual and psychological tensions that serve as its catalyst result from the structuring of "systems" and the shifts that lookers or listeners operate while moving from one to another.

This explanation of the experience of time passing in music provides us with an analogy for what happens in section XI of "The Blue Guitar" when the two "Point-sized systems" of metaphorical movements are cut off, the first with "the chord," the second with "The discord." The definite articles imply the known, yet the reader cannot know what chord or discord arises here. "The discord" is not the semantic negative of "the chord" as a group of simultaneous notes, although its polysemy may include an ear-grating vertical structure (as a slightly forced parallel to "the chord"); it also connotes the sound of quarreling people or a jarring sequence of words. In each of these readings "The discord" occurs to stop the description of a mutilating, dehumanized, Kafkaesque scene. Each of the two music-oriented sentence-lines—"It is the chord that falsifies" and "The discord merely magnifies"—unexpectedly arrests the miniature system of the preceding scene of transformation rather than permuting within it. We might expect the persona to launch into a Whitmanian catalogue or to make explicit the relationship between the women, men and children, for instance. Or we might expect him, in the second series, to develop the metaphoric areas of dehumanization or fossilization. The "waves" and the return of the "sea" denote a swell, a growing amplitude, a movement toward, but these are countered by the musical metaphors. The series of shifts leaves time as the basic "substratum" for organizing the fragments. "The Man with the Blue Guitar" taken as a whole seems to make time particularly salient because of the way the metaphorical rapprochements seem to change system irregularly, often within individual sections, as in XI, or from one section to the other.

It may be enlightening to consider a parallel—a fortuitous though suggestive one—between the texture of "The Blue Guitar" and certain musical compositions by Alexander von Zemlinsky, a Viennese composer and Schoenberg's teacher. Theodor Adorno has described the general strategy of Zemlinsky's Third String Quartet (1924) in terms that could apply to Stevens' poem when he writes of Zemlinsky's "readiness to interrupt the movement, never pursuing a rhythmic impulse beyond the point where it naturally comes to rest: the antithesis of anything mechanical. This waxing and waning of impulse is characteristic."[21] Note the vocabulary of this translation that carries the notion of horizontal development (as opposed to vertical chords) into the area of temporal change ("impulse," "movement," natural "rest," "waxing," and "waning"). Similarly, as we have seen, the metaphorical structure of section XI of "The Blue Guitar" is subjected to "waxing" and "waning," or, in a more exact translation of Adorno's "*Nachlassen und Wiederaufleben*," abating and reviving. The rebirth of the next system follows quickly upon the "chord"'s interruption of the previous movement. Each series of ongoing transformations is no more than a sketch of its own internal logic. Any potential amplification is merely potential, globally thematized in the metaphor become synecdoche of "time" that we have seen in the final couplet: "Deeper within the belly's dark / Of time, time grows upon the rock." The delaying of "Of time" to the beginning of the last line can be read as playing with our sense of a tension between anticipation and delay, between the spatial inscription of "within" and "upon" and the syntactic movement toward a climax that comes all too soon, and between putting off the inevitable and initiating a new problematic.

This juncture in Stevens' poem makes apparent the complex work of his performer's fictive improvisational art. It is the work of structuring the audience's patience through its perception of time. Thwarting the reader's desire to decode here a line, there a couplet, here a sentence, there an entire section, the performance leaps ahead in a direction punctuated with sudden stops. Against all expectation, in shorter and longer movements, what readers perceive is their own demand for unifying constructs on many levels—the modulation of image clusters of poetry, the narrative development of plot in fiction, the movement of harmonic and melodic line in music—and their own dependence on the unfolding of the artwork in time.

Third Movement

Arnheim's phenomenology of perception applied to music and the visual arts helps us to see that only certain kinds of composition heighten our awareness of time. The incompressible nature of time in performing a horizontal score is what characterizes music generally as compared to the visual arts or even literature. A reflection on the aesthetics of music provides the happiest critical metaphor for describing the way Stevens puts his metaphors into his syntax, the timeline of language in "The Man with the Blue Guitar." The fact that, with the exception of program music or "concrete" music, music is an art that is purely non- or self-referential means that representation is not an issue, either in realist-empiricist or idealist modes. On the other hand, discourse about music necessarily shares metaphors used to describe other arts or other experiences. Thus Victor Zuckerkandl would raise his discourse to a high degree of abstraction in writing about the temporality of music, yet use the "natural" linear metaphor of a stream to distinguish listening to "the stream of events in time" from listening to "the stream of time itself":

> Our foreknowledge is concerned with the stream of events; our hearing is concerned with the stream of time . . . The expectation that I feel upon hearing a tone in a melody is not directed toward any *event*, toward something that is to become present; it is directed toward futurity, toward what can never become present. It is not expectation *of something*, a feeling whose object is an event in time; it is pure expectation, which has time itself, the eventuation of time, as its object . . . Without leaving the present behind me, I experience futurity as that toward which the present is directed and always remains directed . . . Heard as a succession of acoustical events, music will soon become boring; heard as the manifestation of time eventuating, it can never bore.[22]

Foreknowledge of "events," then, explains only part of the aesthetic pleasure we take, for instance, in rehearing a piece of music—or rereading a novel or poem—when we know what "events" are coming. This is the pleasure of seeing or hearing something new that we had not noticed before. Different details, different patterns, different meanings become perceptible, and we enjoy the experience of discovery within repetition. The phenomenon is particularly obvious when we listen to or perform music and Zuckerkandl thought that music's particular nonreferentiality could point to the processes that are at work in the appreciation of all the arts. This allowed him to isolate more easily another level on which the exact content or "event" is only part of what we experience. That is, we may also experience the expectation itself and live the adventure of temporality through the temporality of the work.

Time, the vector of all experience, is the very "thing" in music. When in "The Blue Guitar" XI "time" itself is named, we learn the significance of metaphorically presenting this poem as a tune that is improvised on the spot. The series of transformations that began as "things as they are / Are changed upon the blue guitar" (I) is based not just on the transfer from one medium to another or from the empirical world to the world of words; the "transfer" involves what is not a transfer at all because it rests on a "thing"-less, empty thing—time. As I implied earlier, time's momentum, a continuity made perceptible by ruptures of rhythm and tempo, is the ground of musical production. It is "present," though not always consciously experienced, in the appreciation of all artistic works, as Zuckerkandl suggested, but also as the metaphorless and nameless "thing yet to be made" (IX) in poetic language.

The means by which the poem uses a speculative technique to keep moving forward in time only occasionally include named reference to time but disperse references to music across the whole poem. In a minimal selection, we find, for humanly produced music, sixteen sections containing references to the "guitar," seven that name "play(ing)," three that mention "strings," two each "chord(s)," "strum(ming)," "compos(ing)" or "song," and one each "serenade," "pick(s)," "twang," "trombones," "prelude," "discord," "orchestra," "Good-bye, harvest moon" (take-off on popular song), "psaltery," "lute(s)," "duet," "refrain," "bar," "beats out," "music," and "rhapsody." Six sections contain no explicit references to music (XIII, XXI-XXII, XXIV, XXVII, XXX), but including birds, wind, and sea would have produced a different count. Stevens' later and largest poem, "Notes toward a Supreme Fiction" (1942, CP 380–408), takes on a new sense if we take "notes" in the musical sense and see the titles of the poem's three parts as describing together, with an extreme exactitude, the nature of musical sequence: "It Must Be Abstract," "It Must Change," and "It Must Give Pleasure." Words, like sequences of notes, are also abstract forms that change and give pleasure in doing so. And the pleasure of temporal expectation is one of the pleasures most intensely produced by "The Man with the Blue Guitar." In particular, the musico-temporal adventure is an implicit measure of the poem's self-reflexive speculation.

Section XII embodies just such a speculation about the production of the guitarist's own poem, while making part of its self-reflexiveness semiotically rather than symbolically perceptible.

XII

Tom-tom, c'est moi. The blue guitar
And I are one. The orchestra

Fills the high hall with shuffling men
High as the hall. The whirling noise

Of a multitude dwindles, all said,
To his breath that lies awake at night.

I know that timid breathing. Where
Do I begin and end? And where,

As I strum the thing do I pick up
That which momentously declares

Itself not to be I and yet
Must be. It could be nothing else.

This section seems to begin arbitrarily with a new thematic or metaphoric inspiration that cuts off the growth announced at the end of XI in "time grows upon the rock." At the same time, it exteriorizes or makes sensible the image of section XI's "time, time" growing hidden within a place of generation by chiming the sound form of tapping on drum or guitar in "Tom-tom, c'est moi." More than developing a metaphor for musical time, this transition serves as an attention-getter that makes musical time audible. And we experience "waiting for the next tone," as Arnheim said about the special experience we have when the composition shifts from one "system" to another without warning. The "tom-tom" becomes phonetically associated with the player's own breath only at a pause mid-section, in "*tim*id breathing," which may be the section's way of criticizing the narrowness of the definitions the player will attempt to construct in the second half of the stanza. The word "strum" (/tm/ → /strm/) adds to this. Thus the sound technique enacts both "temporal" and thematic dimensions.

In reading this section, the reader may experience a process of constant destabilization and expectancy itself. The grammatically irregular enjambments, the suspension of "where" at line end (ll. 7 and 8), the thematics of filling and dwindling, expansion and reduction (a common denominator throughout much of "The Blue Guitar")—all play with "c'est moi" as it is led through various equivalences (I = guitar; men = hall; noise = breath; that which is not I = that which is I), to the triple play of the copula at the end of the section. But the temporal experience is more dependent on a thread of syllable-signs that runs through the section producing seemingly fortuitous transformations, from a fullness that risks being overfull to a reduction that risks becoming empty: "shuffl*ing*" and "whirl*ing*" are bred with *"breath"* to produce the player's *"breathing,"* which is replaced by the guitar *"thing,"* which becomes the background of "no*thing* else" than the 'I' the player plays (note the ambiguity of that which "I pick up," which could be "picked" on the guitar as an echo of IV, or merely incidental to it). Once again, what Kristeva has identified as the "semiotic" failure to produce meaning lurks here behind the strict grammatical control the player exercises (see section III). The player's playing with the verb *to be* also presents surprising quirks of form, in which the relation between the form of the word and the sense of the poem's shifts seems underdetermined: we move from the performer exhorting others to cry out, "'Here am I, my adversary'" in X, to the several new forms of *to be* in XII: "c'est moi," "The blue guitar / And I are one," and the paradoxically alogical last couplet:

> That which momentously declares
>
> Itself not to be I and yet
> Must be. It could be nothing else. (XII, 10–12)

Something—perhaps the section-song, what it represents, or what it bodies forth in sound-words—declares itself not to be me, but as player I say that it nevertheless "Must be." The strange detachment of this verb ("Must be") from its subject ("Itself") and "Itself" from its antecedent ("That which") helps confuse the identity of the final subject of "It could be nothing else."

These indeterminacies and negations at the section's end answer the spuriously apocalyptic question, "Where / Do I begin and end?" The Latin *momentum* (← *movere*) which serves as the root of "momentously" means "moment of time, particle" and "movement, moving power." The evasive subject is thus situated in a complex of pronouns that punctuate a single moment of time. It may have pretensions of expanding the previously reduced "timid breathing" into realms of the spirit, of carrying us from the orchestra's ordinary time of repetition, through apocalyptic revelation, and finally into a time that is the pure temporal dimension of the "thing"'s poetic space. But these peter out. *Momentum* also means "the space within which a movement is produced" and, in Quintilian, "moments or points" in an exposition, thus emphasizing the internal, finite borders of linguistic activity, both spatially and temporally. "It could be nothing else" indeed puts an end to any expectancy of future development. In an allegorical reading, since the poem is self-derisively caught "on" the guitar, metaphors of finite spatial relation may indicate "where" sense resides without ever naming what that sense is; at the same time, the guitar produces a series of synecdochal moments that tend to evade the audience's "moment final" (VI) and, in the context of the whole poem, stave off or defer the final reduction into poetic versus unpoetic "moments" that will mark the poem's end in XXXIII.

The temporal dimension may also become perceptible when a self-reflexive section seems to privilege the static. This is what happens in section XV. The internal development of the section precludes any narrative development. It refers to a "picture," a drawing, etching or painting, an ekphrastic representative of the spatial arts. As in Keats' "Ode on a Grecian Urn," the poet formulates questions about the "now" of contemplation, but whereas Keats focuses on the scene of sacrifice represented on the art object, Stevens' persona immediately extrapolates from the object's perplexing qualities the better to focus on his own society and himself as possibly "deformed," "dead," "cold." The unintelligibility of the art image becomes a trope for the persona's disorientation in modern times.

XV

Is this picture of Picasso's, this "hoard
Of destructions," a picture of ourselves,

· Now, an image of our society?
Do I sit, deformed, a naked egg,

Catching at Good-bye, harvest moon,
Without seeing the harvest or the moon?

Things as they are have been destroyed.
Have I? Am I a man that is dead

At a table on which the food is cold?
Is my thought a memory, not alive?

Is the spot on the floor, there, wine or blood
And whichever it may be, is it mine?

As the section moves on, the "hoard of destructions,"[23] being a *fait accompli*, "Now," is shown to result from changes in the course of society's and the individual's life. The isolation of "Have I?" hints at both a finished process of change and a present state of dispossession. Thus the ekphrastic moment is a sign no longer of cultural continuity but rather of individual death and cultural forgetfulness. A popular song ("Shine on, shine on, harvest moon," misremembered here) is meaningless because two signs of nature's (cyclical) time—the harvest and the moon—have become empty. Similarly, the "wine or blood" of sacrament or brawl cannot be identified. Mere signifiers remain. Cultural forgetfulness is the equivalent of a "memory" that is "not alive" because the momentum of culture has been broken. This is enacted by the repetition of unanswered questions and the insistence on copular equivalences and locatives in the second half of the poem. Temporal immobilization is figured as disparate objects without momentum among them.

The destabilized equivalences we find so often in "The Man with the Blue Guitar" are particularly anguishing in XV because they shrink the discrete moments of the section's progress into a succession of static images subsumed by a picture metaphor. Among the heterogeneous images only the "table" with food on it seems to link up with a still-life "picture" of the eucharistic "wine or blood." But it is primarily the sentence structure that creates a broken rhythm by varying the length of the sentences that complement the copulas ("Is this picture," "Am I a man," "Is my thought," "Is the spot") and auxiliaries ("Do I sit," but "Have I?" alone). As the eye roves across this series of pictures, and the ear listens from pause to pause, and the duration of each varies, the sense of direction is intensified and we may, according to Zuckerkandl's description, live in "pure expectation," not of something but of continuation or arrest in "futurity" itself. The temporality of the text itself becomes salient, then, as part of our reading experience.

Fourth Movement

Between sections III and XXIX of the poem, the performer displays his virtuosity as player-singer in ways so varied that not even the most flexible conceptual scheme can both give an overview and reach into the lived experience of reading the poem word-by-word, couplet by couplet, section by section. Four sections chosen from the second half of the poem (with the exception of the last four sections) will have to suffice to illustrate the diversity of Stevens' styles, which, borrowing again from music, are as various as the movements of a suite or partita's sarabande, bourrée, gigue, allemande, courante, minuet. They explore rhythmic and motivic possibilities while respecting the specific instrument's tonal range and possibilities for fingering.

Sections XVIII and XIX both use the music metaphor to point to the unfurling patterns of signifiers that override semantic content. Though having certain spatial affinities and exploring locative situations, they reduce and expand the "I"'s desires by always looking forward.

XVIII

A dream (to call it a dream) in which
I can believe, in face of the object,

A dream no longer a dream, a thing
Of things as they are, as the blue guitar

After long strumming on certain nights
Gives the touch of the senses, not of the hand,

But of the very senses as they touch
The wind-gloss. Or as daylight comes,

Like light in a mirroring of cliffs,
Rising upward from a sea of ex.

The ostensible theme of this section is that of trying to give form ("dream," "thing") to sheer sense perception in a world of mere objects. Although Stevens had been working on the question since the early poems of *Harmonium*, this is the first use of the word "object" in his poetry. The spatial fixity of "I," "object," "dream," "thing," "hand," and "wind-gloss" drifts into vaporous diffusion until crystallizing in the final vision of cliffs and sea. In a free speculative movement within language, words like "dream," "thing," "senses," and "touch" are displaced into new syntactic positions. Exploration couples affirmation with negation, as in "A dream no longer a dream" and "the touch of the senses, not of the hand."

The music metaphor referentially detaches the "dream" from the referential content of language. Stevens' persona is broaching the highly charged issue of the Paterian ideal (one Stevens had no sympathy for) of an art that "is always striving to be independent of the mere intelligence, to become a matter of pure perception, to get rid of its responsibilities to its subject or material."[24] The only art in which perception is present in unmixed form is music, for as Pater says elsewhere, "in music it is impossible to distinguish the form from the substance or matter."[25] His oft quoted "all art constantly aspires to the condition of music" (pronounced at a time when abstract painting and sculpture had not yet been born) implies, in the terms of Stevens' poem, that the "thing" and the "senses" (sensation) are one in music. Music allows the world's "object[s]"—which can be a distraction from aesthetic concentration in figurative arts like literature or (nonabstract) painting—to be forgotten, left behind in the "sea of ex."[26] The "touch" of "strumming" approaches what in Pater's view it is music's privilege to be able to effect without appealing to thought[27] or codes of ontological reference. The "senses," we should notice, are reiterated as "the very senses as they touch," with "The wind-gloss" delayed to the next line. The "senses" seem to first touch each other or move themselves: they also are the very subject that strums. Agent, means, and effect are fused.

The delusion of achieving pure sensation in language without statable meaning is indicated by the "wind-gloss." Stevens' version of the romantic Eolian wind harp links the nonreferential medium (music and sheen, then light) to verbal interpretation through glossing. The same tension is figured in the preceding section, XVII, in which the blue guitar, whose "animal" (anima) parts "propound" and "articulate," is compared with the "north wind" that merely "blows." Language's connection with speakable meaning ("sense") is at odds with pure sensation ("sense") as it is in "Bouquet of Roses in Sunlight" (see chapter 2). It is resistance to this connection that prevents the "dream," as grammatical subject of the section, from being given any main predicate to attempt logical statement. "A dream, to call it a dream," moreover, is prevented from being what it itself might be, since its very name is a matter of mere convenience and might be replaced by other signifiers.

The poem gropes toward some clarification but with no predestined event as its goal. Just as some kinds of music, modern in particular, induce the experience of "time eventuating," Stevens' by now familiar technique of varying the grammatical place of enjambment contributes to our feeling of moving forward (including "in which / I can believe," "a thing / Of things as they are," "the blue guitar // After long strumming," "they touch / The wind gloss"). In the ongoing movement of the speculation, the poem referentially pauses to mark change over time in "no longer a dream" and "After long strumming," before signing the first unconditional event—the anticipation of "as daylight comes." The extra-ontological exploration of the construction becomes, within its own terms, the primary "thing" of the stanza. Of course the "matter" or reference remains. Stevens' language is English, not the scales of a well-tempered clavier or any other instrument. But the effect of "time eventuating," of "futurity as that toward which the present is directed and always remains directed," in Zuckerkandl's terms, is probably as strong here in section XVIII as in any of Stevens' poems of momentum.

Elsewhere in "The Blue Guitar," in XXVI, a cluster associating the music-language tension with "dreams" defeated sheds light on the primacy though not the exclusiveness of the musical impulse in keeping the poem going. The end of this particular section concentrates the character's conflict over his old illusions, comparing him to a

> . . . giant that fought
> Against the murderous alphabet:
>
> The swarm of thoughts, the swarm of dreams
> Of inaccessible Utopia.
>
> A mountainous music always seemed
> To be falling and to be passing away. (XXVI, 7–12)

According to Stevens' paraphrase, the end refers to things of the imagination "that we have failed to realize." Things having changed, the imagination then "fought against its thoughts and dreams, as if these were an alphabet with which it could not spell out its riddle" (*Letters* #406). Yet Stevens' hallmark colon after "the murderous alphabet" seems to highlight the tension between the discursive and explanatory use of the language's "alphabet" and the positing of inchoate "swarm[s]." In the final couplet, moreover, a "*mountainous* music" sweeps away the "*murderous* alphabet." Music is represented both as having full substance, thus as being perceivable and as enduring in its kinetic flux. Music—the grammatical subject of the section's only complete sentence—is an unavoidable fact of discourse. Despite one's impression that it is "passing away," the dying of music is only what "seemed." And indeed, as we will see later, the next section (XXVII) resuscitates the poem's transforming movement in another metaphor of transformation over time, the shape-shifting of sea-snow-icicles-iceberg that begins as "It is the sea that whitens the roof." In the imagination's desire to be articulate, the music just named at the end of XXVI becomes a promise of the continuity of the sensuous body of language, a perceptible vector of time.[28]

Related to the contest between the senses and referentiality that we noticed in section XVIII, and announcing XXVI, music in XIX also engages the "senses" and enables us to be aware of (and not just "think" of) the ongoingness of meaning but also the ongoingness of time as we read, look, listen. It joins the immediately perceivable thing to the horizontal structure that is developing beyond the present moment. The figure of music in XIX directs us toward the very imbrication of sensibilia in time, something we are rarely aware of, and something allegorical reading tends to overwhelm.

XIX

That I may reduce the monster to
Myself, and then *may be* myself

In face of the monster, *be more* than part
Of it, *more* than the monstrous player of

One of its monstrous lutes, *not be*
Alone, *but* reduce the monster and *be*,

Two things, the two together as one,
And play of the monster and of myself,

Or *better not* of myself at all,
But of that as its intelligence,

Being the lion in the lute
Before the lion locked in stone. (Emphasis added.)

The lute on which the section's enigmatic tune is played is an elegant metonymy for the guitar, a companion to the wind harp, an emblem of lyric poetry in English and French, but one made monstrous here. It is also a homonym in French (*luth*) for *lutte* = "struggle." During the struggle, the persona seems to "reduce" musical tune playing into his own obsessive polar vocabulary by confronting "I" with the world, echoing both XII, "That which momentously declares // Itself not to be I and yet / Must be," and XVIII, "in face of the object" and "a thing / Of Things as they are." But the repetitions of words and sounds (/m/, /b/, /t/ and /l/) in various syntactic combinations push the section toward semiotic noise (as in section III). Throughout the section's progress, there is a tentativeness in its speculation and movement produced by the absence of any main clause (despite the optative "That" expressing volition), the shifting enjambments, the stairlike movement constructed with the verb *to be*, and the negations and comparisons. Such a density of familiar disruptive tactics surely attenuates the success of what Bloom sees here as Stevens' "trope of pathos or Power"[29] or what I would call the player's sparring with the "monster" for total linguistic control.

No copula can fulfill the wish for unity. The playing of "that as its intelligence" ends, as it begins, as a dichotomy: "Being the lion in the lute / Before the lion locked in stone." The final couplet grasps "Being" and puts an end to the ongoingness of random repetitions, but its anaphora imposes a stable stand-off "locked" in space, a confrontation between melody and meaning or sound and thing. And we are reminded that although the struggle is represented in the metaphor of musician, instrument, and object, it is enacted in the sensory medium of the poem's word-sounds. The power struggle, then, can be understood as a struggle within language for dominance by two forces: the content laden expectation inscribed in spatial metaphors, and the musical expectancy of the lute's moving time.

Part of the strangeness of the poem as a whole lies in the variety of tactics it uses to incite an expectation of futurity similar to that we can encounter in music. The music metaphor itself is used inconstantly, but this very inconstancy commends it as a trope for our reading the poem. Playing music on the guitar is the all-inclusive conceit of "The Man with the Blue Guitar" under which other metaphors and discursive themes are subsumed. Thus the unannounced "leaps" of the kind we saw in section XI may be particularly striking when we suddenly leap from a motif centering on musical experience to one that seems to forget music. And this is what happens, for instance, when we move from the stand-off that closes XIX with its "lute" and "stone" to "What is there in life except one's ideas" that begins XX. The switch to *désabusé* abstraction could not be more brutal. Sometimes all we can expect is a future of sound-signs.

Thus we also need to consider the movement of sections that do not allude to music (six in all), attuned as we now are by the music metaphor to the problem of the temporal experience. For indeed, spatial constructions of metaphor and syntax can also be places of speculative moving, as they are in section XV and in many later poems in Stevens' oeuvre.

Sections XXI and XXVII provide a foil that sharpens our sense of how radical the exploration of the musico-temporal dimension is in sections like XVIII and XIX. In section XXI of "The Blue Guitar," Stevens' old dream of creating a new metaphor and even symbol system is represented as a "substitute for all the gods" in the section's first phrase. This would be a desire defined, contained, "locked" perhaps within a word space. The section gropes for this substitute primarily in terms of against-ness and what it wants to do away with: both the high world of Platonic ideas (where the light in the cave deforms "one's shadow") and the defunct theological order (where "Chocorua" is the name by which divine magnification, that of "all the gods," "immenser heaven," and the "most high," is "called"). But the nonreferential and self-referential possibilities of linguistic construction are foregrounded as possibilities that are tended toward rather than representable.

XXI

A substitute for all the gods:
This self, not that gold self aloft,

Alone, one's shadow magnified,
Lord of the body, looking down,

As now and called most high,
The shadow of Chocorua

In an immenser heaven, aloft,
Alone, lord of the land and lord

Of the men that live in the land, high lord.
One's self and the mountains of one's land,

Without shadows, without magnificence,
The flesh, the bone, the dirt, the stone. (Emphasis added.)

The principal structure is binary: The embrace of "This self" and "One's self and the mountains of one's land" is opposed to "all the gods" and "that gold self aloft." Perhaps only "This self" and the last three lines, after the period, belong to the looked-for, purely human, substitute. Yet the structure of logical meaning is far from intelligible, and the punctuating commas in the first four couplets only add to the confusion.

Like section XVIII, this one also seems to be exploring a linguistic field not for a ground or purpose of being, but for a new linguistic definition. Here, however, the exploration is vehicled mainly by a series of assonances and near assonances (italicized above) and alliterative effects like the /l/ in "aloft," "alone," "looking," "lord," "land," but many other phonetic repetitions are also present. Ironically perhaps, "Alone" (ll. 2 and 8) may apply more aptly to the searching persona than to the icon of Chocorua he rejects, as the word provides the rhyme for the final "bone" and "stone" and, punningly, the script of "one" for "One's self" and "one's land."

This phonetic play produces a sense of zigzagging between "aloft" and "down" without knowing where to situate the "substitute." The "murderous alphabet" (XXVI) for the new articulation sharpens only at two moments, with the new consonants of "Chocorua" (although assonance with "lord" resounds within it) and the last line's "The flesh, the bone, the dirt, the stone," pounded out in insistent iambs. These nouns flaunt the physicality of their referents, as opposed to the abstraction of "ideas" that are questioned in the previous section (XX). The living body not only demonstrates its "alone"-ness, but it calls up its death drive, its own mineral mortality of "dirt" and "stone." Linguistically speaking, Stevens' performer is working out various materials for construction, both common nouns and proper nouns. "Chocorua," the name of one of the White Mountains of New Hampshire, later recurs in the title (and voice) of "Chocorua to its Neighbor" (CP 296–302) before becoming generalized as a common noun, a place from which an elderly Stevens looks back on his oeuvre in "The Poem that Took the Place of a Mountain" (CP 512). The phonetic originality of "Chocorua" in XXI of "The Blue Guitar" makes it stand out almost like an invocation, a talismanic word that only heightens the sense that this jumbled catalogue is calling pieces to it, like the "jar in Tennessee" of the "Anecdote of the Jar" (CP 76).

Section XXVII is also "about" physical materials in space and how they change place. Unlike XXI, which employs phonetic permutation to test out its defining terms, it reiterates copular structures with *to be* to emphasize the succession of statements.

XXVII

It is the sea that whitens the roof.
The sea drifts through the winter air.

It is the sea that the north wind makes.
The sea is in the falling snow.

This gloom is the darkness of the sea.
Geographers and philosophers,

Regard. But for that salty cup,
But for the icicles on the eaves—

The sea is a form of ridicule.
The iceberg settings satirize

The demon that cannot be himself,
That tours to shift the shifting scene.

Helen Vendler, before analyzing the rhetoric of the stanza, usefully para-
phrases it as follows:

> Just when geographers (and their interior equivalent, philosophers)
> think they have accurately mapped the world, the multiform sea,
> Stevens says, confounds them in its allotropic forms of encrusting
> snow and ice. New and unexpected contours arise. Geographers and
> philosophers, in Stevens' metaphor, are demons that cannot be them-
> selves, that cannot let the landscape alone, but tour the world trying
> to rearrange it in an orderly way, not realizing that the world, ironi-
> cally enough, is always in the process of arranging itself.[30]

I would add that although this confounding is a "process," temporal mo-
mentum seems strangely ignored by the section. For although the "dark-
ness of the sea" may recall "the belly's dark of time" in XI, and although
the forms "whitens," "falling snow," and "shifting scene" imply process,
the copulas and prepositions create a referential texture of temporary
states rather than temporal movement. The borrowing of "Regard" from
"The Snow Man" even imitates something like an ekphrastic moment in
the second half of the section. Vendler sees this "Regard" as the sign that
the section is "spoken not by the struggling guitarist, but by a preceptor
well versed in ennui."[31] And indeed, in the absence of the musical

metaphor here, there is no expectation of any change beyond the repetition of nature's cyclical transformations. There is no exploratory momentum, no expectation of futurity within this section.

Taken as a whole, on the other hand, "The Man with the Blue Guitar" endows the speculative potentials of the logical, copular and locative constructions of "Thirteen Ways of Looking at a Blackbird" and its like with a time dimension. Its segments are impelled forward by an irregular momentum within certain sections and from section to section. Just as Stevens' persona detaches himself from the world-word dichotomy insisted on by the audience (and by the real-life writer of earlier poems and later lectures), so he develops his potential as musical virtuoso, following a constantly shifting impulse.

Coda to the Whole

Reaching section XXX, the poem comes to signal its own impending temporal end without the benefit of a plot. A plot would, as it does in "The Comedian as the Letter C" (CP 27–46), provide the poem with coherence and intelligibility along a referential timeline. Selecting particular heterogeneous items and fitting them into a represented time scheme is, as Hayden White, Paul Ricœur, and others have pointed out, the way we make sense of both stories and our own lives. Specific parameters that shape the end of the story influence the writer's choice of relevant details and themes so that readers can draw, in Ricœur's words, "a configuration out of a succession."[32] But although some sections of "The Blue Guitar" (XIV, XIX, XXV, XXIX) do contain adumbrations of narrative setting and time, neither the parts nor the whole form any narrative pattern in the sense I mean here. The closing sections resemble the rest in this sense.

As the poem draws to a close, it circles back to the opening setting but with a difference: The contemporary audience is given a new home in "Oxidia, banal suburb," "the seed / Dropped out of this amber-ember pod," "the soot of fire," "Olympia." Into this dirty, hellish environment, which is the everyday counterpart to the fictive audience's desired "green" day (section I) and its rejected poetic inferno-paradise (section V), the performer projects a new character, the "old fantoche," a form of the audience's "other." The guitarist no longer shows off his metaphorical inventiveness but is going to restrict his themes to the interrelations between his own poetic discourse and the workaday discourse of the public's daily life. The guitarist imagines a series of new beginnings that might possibly point to a future connected with the public's modern-day, industrial setting. But the original miniature narrative situation of each section remains of little consequence to the others. Sections XXXI and XXXIII can even be read as possibly ironizing the temptation to reduce the dream of musical time to a narrative situation, and section XXXII can be seen as the guitarist's last, desperate plea to the audience to integrate a freer way of understanding the blue guitar's music into its notion of space.

The opening evocation of the pheasant sleeping in XXXI is a warning that poetry is absent from the workaday world, for as we have seen in chapter 5, the pheasant in Stevens' private universe of his *Adagia* is a metaphor for poetry. The mention of "employer and employee" is accompanied by the grotesque "shriek" and "claw[ing]" of the cock-bird that inhibits the singing of poetry. Poetry is "clutched" rather than played on the guitar. The performer seems resigned to the fact that the audience's demands for social and political relevance inhibit him from singing and playing. He concludes with:

. . . Morning is not sun,
It is this posture of the nerves,

As if a blunted player clutched
The nuances of the blue guitar.

It must be this rhapsody or none,
The rhapsody of things as they are. (XXXI, 11–16)

His "rhapsody," understood as an expressive form or as an ongoing movement, is a mutilated one: as an outpouring of emotions, its very source has been invalidated; as an improvisational romantic form of music, its space and time of development have been severely restricted. "The rhapsody of things as they are" defeats the experiments the guitarist has been working in the rest of the poem with his exploratory combinations and open movements. Thus the music metaphor is squeezed into a metaphor of ironic againstness.

Unexpectedly—but by now we have come to expect the

unexpected—the next section dazzles us with a fully rhapsodic call for
the audience to enter the world of open movement. The music metaphor
itself, however, is delayed until the end.

XXXII

Throw away the lights, the definitions,
And say of what you see in the dark

That it is this or that it is that,
But do not use the rotted names.

How should you walk in that space and know
Nothing of the madness of space,

Nothing of its jocular procreations?
Throw the lights away. Nothing must stand

Between you and the shapes you take
When the crust of shape has been destroyed.

You as you are? You are yourself.
The blue guitar surprises you.

This is what should happen if the audience espoused poetry of the sort
the performer has been performing. The section gives four different ver-
sions of the same process of casting off dead language and discovering
aesthetic pleasure. First an order to annul the very medium by which we
see space organized into shapes—light—is verbalized as a metaphor for
getting rid of the "rotted names." The performer then outfits his exhorta-
tion with the audience's old "space" metaphor in order to clear a space of
"Nothing" for a new freedom. He thus sings or plays of removing the
conditioning factors inscribed in the old language, conceptualized as the
"crust of shape," displacing the material "crusty stacks above machines"
of XXX and denigrating the very notion of spatial boundaries. In this ide-
alized formulation of the performer's desire, the new wholeness projected
in the tautological "You are yourself" can benefit from the "jocular pro-
creations" of the new boundary-free space. The performer envisages the
audience eliminating its own ethos, its volition and its imperious need
for self-completion. The closing "The blue guitar surprises you" induces
expectancy without particular content, expectancy of futurity undefined
except as surprise.

Yet the performer's own use of the imperative mood can be seen as signaling the distance between desire and the possibility of fulfillment. And indeed the final words of the poem retreat both thematically and rhetorically from this vision of an audience transformed.

XXXIII

That generation's dream, aviled
In the mud, in Monday's dirty light,

That's it, the only dream they knew,
Time in its final block, not time

To come, a wrangling of two dreams.
Here is the bread of time to come,

Here is its actual stone. The bread
Will be our bread, the stone will be

Our bed and we shall sleep by night.
We shall forget by day, except

The moments when we choose to play
The imagined pine, the imagined jay.

Like many other sections of "The Man with the Blue Guitar," this final section makes a mid-stanza "leap." At "Here" the text becomes not only a performative presentation of the poet's poetry in the present world but also a wager on its immediate future. Although the meaning of the "imagined" has itself been transformed as a result of the poem— " 'Imagined' here has achieved a transumptive freshness," writes Bloom[33]—I think we feel a letdown that is more than just that of arriving at the term of an exhilarating yet demanding speculation. Although several critics praise this section, some close readers like Bloom, Rehder, and Vendler (but not Cook)[34] seem to run out of energy when they reach it, whether they are taking the sections in order (Bloom and Cook) or not (like Rehder and Vendler). Vendler says Stevens is playing the *faux naïf* here.[35] He does "play" in many senses: the actor is clothing himself for two distinct roles that will allow him to share and be part of the "we"; the juggler is selecting a few exemplary dichotomies; the musician is reserving his guitar for special moments. Some temptation has been overcome, like that of Jesus refusing to change the stones into loaves; some open places have been maintained. But we have a sense of a naïve reduction to a compromise that is too sharply delineated to satisfy us—forgetting or sleeping "except" for certain chosen "moments." Only these "moments" are symmetrically filled with "The imagined pine, the imagined jay." Has Stevens "come home" to the collective place he was seeking, as Cook says?[36] After a radical adventure in which the sound and syntax of English has come into its own as the thing itself, we arrive at a conventional epic or picaresque outcome. After procuring for the reader an experience of "time eventuating," the poem ends by ironically reducing the potential of the music metaphor to a neatly partitioned space.

I think that it is the fixed delimitation of those "moments" that saps our enthusiasm. There is an end here that does not look into a future. Of course the momentum of the poem must be stopped, but the poem seems to point neither toward rereading this particular poem nor toward reading generally. It does not do what Timothy Bahti has discerned in several lyric poems by Stevens, which is to lead us to an ending where we see the language of the poem as concrete, where reading is that "of reading suspended between letter and meaning."[37] Only the possible pun on "jay"-letter j suggests that Stevens' last words may point to the perennity of the poet's alphabet while they directly recognize the pressures of life at the office or factory that vie with the space-time we can devote to poetry.

The return to the topical is thus awkwardly imbricated in the necessity of ending. The performer has assured the ongoing movement of the central sections by listening not to the audience's commands but to his instrument—and to his own inner ear as he sounds out his poem, leading a motif to the briefest statement possible, allowing something rhythmic in a syntactic or phonetic pattern to become just palpable before leaping to the next motif. This is Stevens' most perilous leap into lyric, especially since it borders on abstraction from the signified precisely at a historical moment when demands for specificity of reference and coherent "meaning" were so vociferous. By enacting some of the implications of the music metaphor, it seems to me, this poem makes the transitoriness of all messages one of its own messages. And its own transitoriness becomes a synecdoche of the ever self-erasing, ephemeral conditions of performances, performers, and audiences.

Epilogue

❧

THE TRANSITORINESS OF THE WORD-WORLD

BY CULMINATING THIS METHODOLOGICALLY ORIENTED EXPLORATION OF Stevens' linguistic constructions with "The Man with the Blue Guitar," I have hoped to show that the poem assembles within it in a most radical way what I see as Stevens' chief experiments with the permutational possibilities of English grammar and syntax, and that it is exemplary in this sense.

During the next 27 years of his career, Stevens' work loses some of its verbal rambunctiousness. Topical vocabulary varies as he reads (literature, literary and art journals, art books, books of philosophy, newspapers). Among geographical references, the places of Stevens' travels to southern locales, like Tennessee or Florida, give way to such places as spots in France or Ireland pictured on the postcards he received from Barbara Church and Jack Sweeney. His "occasions" are inflected by observation of his surroundings at home in New Haven, Connecticut. The topoi, fictional characters, and actions inscribed in the poems change. Significantly they no longer partake in the ingenue exuberance of Bonnie and Josie in "Life is Motion" (CP 83), who, "Dressed in calico," cry:

> "Ohoyaho,
> Ohoo" . . .
> Celebrating the marriage
> Of flesh and air. (Ellipsis in original.)

Rather, when Nanzia Nunzio, in "Notes toward a Supreme Fiction" ("It Must Change" VIII [CP 396]), strips herself and demands that Ozymandias speak to her "that, which spoken, will array [her] / In its own only precious ornament," Ozymandias reminds her that "A fictive cover-

ing / Weaves always glistening from the heart and mind": there is no
human state before the fiction we organize of it. There is no state of ab-
solute nakedness but always an increased need to meditate on the work
of constructing versions of "fictive covering" from the artifice of English.

Secondly, and just as obviously, Stevens' poetry builds on his own
life journey interwoven with his exploratory itinerary as a writer. The re-
working of the poet's own poetic past becomes a noticeable feature of the
later poems' allusiveness. Almost any poem from the late forties or fifties
could illustrate this point. The local combinations of "Prologues to What
Is Possible" (CP 515–517), for instance, allude to several poems we have
read here. With different degrees of distinctness we find:

"Thirteen Ways of Looking at a Blackbird" (chapter 4)—in "sparkling in
the one-ness of their motion," and "out of and beyond the familiar";

"The Paltry Nude Starts on a Spring Voyage" (chapter 2)—in "[He d]id
not pass like someone voyaging out of and beyond the familiar. / He belonged to
the far-foreign departure of his vessel and was part of it";

"The Man with the Blue Guitar" XXXII (chapter 6)—in "The this and
that in the enclosures of hypotheses";

"The Motive for Metaphor" (chapter 2)—in "On which men speculated
in summer when they were half asleep";

"Add This to Rhetoric" (chapter 2) and "The Snow Man" (chapter 4)—in
"Creates a fresh universe out of nothingness by adding itself";

"Bouquet of Roses in Sunlight" (chapter 2)—in "The way a look or touch
reveals its unexpected magnitudes."

But this poem is most interesting because it receives its impetus from
Stevens' metaphor of the motion of the boat, thus relating it to the ship
that carries the younger poet north in "Farewell to Florida" (CP
117–118), a poem that Stevens placed as a signpost of a shift to his new,
less sensual mode of poetry at the beginning of Ideas of Order. Indeed,
"Prologues" is also a poem of passage. But now the boat's passenger grap-
ples with the possibility of discovering within himself a "self" "that had
not yet been loosed" before adding it to the nothingness of death. The
enunciation of the words of poetry as part of the "real" seem to be the
only guarantee that the final stage, envisioned in the poem by the fright
caused by a "metaphor," has not yet been reached. On another level, as a
signpost in Stevens' career, the prosodic "possibility" developed here—

the exceptionally long lines along which the waves of the poem's complex syntax is unfurled—ends with this single experience.

As for Stevens' early rhetorical strategies, many remain central to his writing throughout his career, although their prominence may vary. Brogan makes Stevens' increasing adoption of the construction "as if" an important element in her claim that toward the end of his career the poet learned how to overcome the inner contradictions between the unification aimed at by metaphor and the fragmentation implied by metonymy.[1] Miller makes an opposing comment but does not dwell on it. There can be, he says "a figure which functions simultaneously as a metaphor, therefore as mimesis, and as metonymy, therefore as the assertion of a discontinuity or contingency which destroys mimesis. Wallace Stevens' last lyrics can be shown to function this way throughout and therefore to be self-destructive, open to two simultaneous incompatible readings."[2] As concerns syntax (which in my reading contributes to the tendency toward a non-ontological, exploratory language), Vendler notes that the appositional structures used in the late poetry (as in "An Ordinary Evening in New Haven") are integrated in "an inching style" that "must be distinguished from the earlier style it resembles, the piling up of appositional noun phrases to suggest expansiveness and surfeit, as in The Comedian and Owl's Clover."[3] Eleanor Cook, treating the poems chronologically, claims that the kinds of "word-play" she examines in her book remain present even in the late poems of The Rock (CP 501–534) and Opus Posthumous. Her repertory consists of play with grammar (especially prepositions), play with figures (though she says there is less of it in the last poems), etymological play, allusion that she calls "echoing" (though it becomes "very quiet," she says), borrowing, and inventing proper names.[4]

In this Epilogue I would like to look at the rhetorical and syntactical constants of Stevens' poetry that have been the focus of the present work, and see how Stevens experiments with them in two poems written when his actual time for experimentation was coming to an end, and the shadow of death had become one of the "particulars" of his individual life. Although some of Stevens' late poems, like "The Poem that Took the Place of a Mountain" (CP 512) or "The Planet on the Table" (CP 532), look back over the poet's poetic effort and synthesize it, many of the poems in The Rock review the past in order to look forward, in one way or another, toward the approach of death. They rarely make direct reference to the future. They inscribe ongoing time in the texture of the text less noticeably than "The Man with the Blue Guitar" does. They display less densely the verbal virtuosity of *to be* than the earlier poems did, and they unmake less rapidly each successive rapprochement. But these are all questions of degree or frequency.

So we may wonder about the problems that concerned us earlier—what becomes of metaphors of againstness and the ambivalent recognition of metaphor as enabler and inhibitor? Do syntactical and copular relations still direct our attention to the English language as creative artifice, a place of non-ontological speculation, a home the poet creates by defining? And is the "temporality" of the poem salient in its several senses? Do poems inscribe their own perishability within them? How do they point to time not just as a "subject of poetry" (that is, that to which the poetic text refers) but as internal to the chain of language the poet invents? With these questions at the back of our minds, I would like to explore "Metaphor as Degeneration" (*CP* 444), written in 1948, as Stevens was approaching seventy, and "The River of Rivers in Connecticut" (*CP* 533), written in 1953.

It is not fortuitous that both poems are written in neat tercets with a vaguely four-foot line. Stevens experimented very little with variable spatial relations and only in his early poetry, whereas Williams and Pound used spaces in their visual forms almost as "words" and did so throughout their careers. In the Stevens poems we have read, an example of significant spacing can be found in the last line of Stevens' "Add This to Rhetoric" (*CP* 198–199), which performs its own sum visually by isolating "Add this. It is to add" as its own final stanza. "Poem Written at Morning" also plays with spatial form by using indentation literally to "draw" parallels between its three general postulates on the one hand, and the poem's concluding local image of successful poetic transformation on the other in: "Green were the curls upon its head." By *Transport to Summer* (1947), however, Stevens favored the regular repetition of couplets, tercets, or quatrains (often in the tetrameter). Tercets give form to the two late long poems, "The Auroras of Autumn" (1947) and "An Ordinary Evening in New Haven" (1949), as well as to the earlier "Notes toward a Supreme Fiction" (1942); and they become Stevens' major shape-giver for short lyrics, including ten of the 24 poems in *The Rock* (1954).

These numerous poems written in tercets, as we shall see with the two examples below, give an impression of visual orderliness on the printed page. They suggest stability, regularity, predictability. Their spatial regularity places pressure on the syntactic linearity of the poem's language. The printed lines in *The Collected Poems* vary slightly in length, causing a few to spill over the right margin and be printed under their proper line. This variability is more the fruit of the typographer's characters than of the poet's hand, however. In effect, among the rare pencil-written drafts Stevens left is a set of six poems written in tercets that first appeared as a group called "A Half Dozen Small Pieces" in the Autumn 1949 issue of *Botteghe Oscure*.[5] These poems were written on legal-sized paper, lined, with a printed left-hand margin. Each poem is fitted neatly on the page, the tercets forming a series of six rectangles of equal size. Their regularity is surprising, for in the printed text there is a two-inch difference between the shortest and longest lines (in "Study of Images II"). On the draft, the handwriting cramps here and there so as to prevent any line from straggling beyond the imaginary right-hand margin. Stevens was obviously forcing his "Half Dozen Small Pieces" into a visual mold. Since the contours of the lines are already measured, any experimentation with the material words of the text takes place in the opaque laying down of words, phrases, and sentences along the chain of language. If surprises are to take place, they have to happen in phonetic, lexical, and syntactical repetitions and ruptures, and in the relation between syntax and line.

"Metaphor as Degeneration" (CP 444) and "The River of Rivers in Connecticut" (CP 533) deal in similar prosodic form, in eight and six tercets respectively, and with similar metaphors of the "threshold" of death, as Barbara M. Fisher calls it.[6] They look as though they repose in stability, not only in their prosodic shape but also in the conceits they anchor themselves in. Their very titles seem to privilege symbol systems, not only the obvious substitution denoted by "Metaphor" but even the formulation of "The River of Rivers" as a superlative that also replaces one order by another, as in "King of Kings."[7] The poems describe the undescribable by substituting for what cannot be named the description of another river elsewhere: the unnamable is *"not* Swatara" in "Metaphor," *not* the Styx in "The River of Rivers" (emphasis added). The poems both use and resist their conceits, playing with spatial metaphors, gathering within their progress a speculation both of and on the extra-ontological statement of what lies beyond all knowing.

"Metaphor as Degeneration" (CP 444) self-consciously begins by staging metaphorical figures as fictive constructs that it is compelled to transform. Two men-idols are placed in a decor, in spaces of woods and blackness, from which the poem can evolve. The fictional space can be understood as primarily imaginary, logical, or—in my focus—speculative, in the sense of establishing a framework to explore a potentially fluid word-world. It even sets up its stage with a sheer hypothesis and a deduction: "If there is a man," "So there is" a different man. The verbal exploration takes place in the presence of what we have seen as Stevens' favored verb, the verb *to be* (ten instances of *be*, two of *become*).

Infinitesimal metamorphoses begin even before any movement is represented. The first half of the poem has pretensions of representing "death and the imagination" contained in ontological and transcendent being, but they are immediately loaded with artifice.

> If there is a man white as marble
> Sits in a wood, in the greenest part,
> Brooding sounds of the images of death,
>
> So there is a man in black space
> Sits in nothing that we know,
> Brooding sounds of river noises;
>
> And these images, these reverberations,
> And others, make certain how being
> Includes death and the imagination.
>
> The marble man remains himself in space.

The word-world may at first appear to be dual, one image necessarily calling up its opposite, but the symmetry is rapidly disturbed and we are attracted to lexical manipulation within its organizational artifice. For instance, parallels of syntax and image relate the two figures as both "Brooding sounds," making them counterparts of each other and suggesting that in a less complex poem "river noises" might merely be a figure or metaphor for a principle opposing death.[8] But even the comparative descriptions of the men are undone: the "white" of marble describes a man, whereas "black" describes not a man but the space in which he sits. The breakdown of a dual system is made complete in the fourth stanza when the marble man "remains" (contradictorily) in "space" (previously allocated to the second man), and this second man in "black space" "descends" unchanged. There is, as Walker says, an exchange of places,[9] in the sense that "space" is exchanged for "wood" and vice versa in the men's respective decors. But the movement of the men is not chiasmic, since only the second man "descends." This is a moment of tension and even unbalance. Although "The man in the black wood descends unchanged," change has paradoxically taken place and further change is anticipated and provoked here by the contest between symmetrical exchange and exception in the manipulation of the metaphor of the brooding men. Taken allegorically itself, this metaphor is incomplete as a speculative tool. It undoes the metastatement that the poem's "images" "make certain how being / Includes death and the imagination." The inclusion of "Includes" extends the speculative artifice of the previous images that also gravitated around the function word *in* (three times), the neatness of which will be disrupted by the strange changing of represented and linguistic space of the two men in stanza 4.

The speaker moves down to the metaphor of the river, not to sort out the tactical moves of these hieratic icons but to test what the poem can do with the simplicity of the inclusion. The second half of the poem will tell us that this elusive compound is more than any name like Swatara could capture.

> The marble man remains himself in space.
> The man in the black wood descends unchanged.
> It is certain that the river
>
> Is not Swatara. The swarthy water
> That flows around the earth and through the skies,
> Twisting among the universal spaces,
>
> Is not Swatara. It is being.
> That is the flock-flecked river, the water,
> The blown sheen—or is it air?
>
> How, then, is metaphor degeneration,
> When Swatara becomes this undulant river
> And the river becomes the landless, waterless ocean?
>
> Here the black violets grow down to its banks
> And the memorial mosses hang their green
> Upon it, as it flows ahead.

The river becomes the primary working metaphor and primary verbal artefact in the second half of the poem. Strikingly, after the "unchanged" in stanza 4, we find a transition where least expected, in the stanza's third line. Here the speaker leaves the men for the river, exchanges description for defining statements and questions, and initiates many lexical, syntactic, and prosodic changes. With the exception of the last stanza, these changes characterize the attempt to define and then contain the river. The river is the subject of almost all the clauses in stanzas 5 to 7, including the two key copular clauses that leap from stanza 4 to 5 and 5 to 6: "It is certain that the river // Is not Swatara" and "The swarthy water / . . . // Is not Swatara." It creates a fluid center in this poem, despite the blocklike stanza forms. The river is not the equivalent of the river bearing that swarthy, black-sounding name in Pennsylvania, yet Swatara is made its model by the very proposition of denial. Between the two denials, a cosmic image of the river flows beyond its course in the foreign elements of earth and skies, to draw an ancient map, illustrating what is beyond the known, at the periphery of *terra cognita*, where we venture only in our minds. Affirmation—"It is being"—halts this free flow. Yet morphological artifice relates it with the "Brooding" of the men-idols and the "Twisting" of the river, suggesting immobility and movement in search of a direction. The noun complement "being" seems stable and is said to have something "certain" about it. But how can we take the copula of "It is being" to be much more than another speculative statement? Stevens' restless language, so to say, makes this fiction a convenient resting point, an artificial coalescing of what escapes all nominalization and all proposition. The resting point is only temporary. Indeed it is even immediately questioned: "—or is it air?" Even the grammatical subject "that" in "That is the flock-flecked river" has a spurious definiteness about it, pointing to it deictically from afar, as it were, from a safe place after the river's identity has been stated.

We see that the possibility of looking forward to death is inextricably bound to the finite forms of the poet's own language. The poem's ongoing linguistic movement becomes the very metaphorical subject of the last two stanzas. The speaker asks self-referentially, "How, then, is metaphor degeneration"? This question may be both a rhetorical question—meaning that metaphor cannot possibly be degeneration—and a "real" question that will be answered by the last stanza. Swatara and "this" referential and self-referential river are said to become one in the copular "becomes." This seems both to complete the movement of including "death and the imagination" in the levels of "being" the poem speculates in and on, and also to undo the ontological fiction of finding a geographical metaphor to substitute for the unnamable flow. If Swatara "becomes" the river (second line of tercet), it represents the river in language, whereas if the river "becomes" the ocean (third line of tercet), it empties imperceptibly into the boundless. Indeed, what the metaphor becomes has its substance removed in the "land*less*, water*less* ocean" (emphasis added). Metaphor both generates and de-generates the qualities attached to metaphors and thus both affirms and deconstructs the flux of the conceits upon which we build the word-worlds that form the superstrata of our mental lives. The last stanza reconstitutes images of substance, insisting, however, on the place of poetry as a place for doing this, "Here."

This "here" in the speculative itinerary constituted by the poem unfurls images of pomp, a final decor prepared for death. Death has not yet descended but is waiting. There is a tension, an expectancy created by the images which echo the movement of the man who "descends" in stanza 4. A quasi oxymoron joins death's color with nature's vital action in "the black violets grow down"; another one joins nature's vital color with the signs the living make for the dead in "the memorial mosses hang their green." This is not the *point d'orgue* or pedal point of the ending of "Sunday Morning" VIII (CP 70). There, ambiguity is contained in the fullness of a single movement that endures or, as Vendler says, "floats"[10]:

> At evening, casual flocks of pigeons make
> Ambiguous undulations as they sink,
> Downward to darkness, on extended wings.

But in "Metaphor as Degeneration" the speaker has throughout the poem reiterated his terms in unstable equivalences and speculative localities and definitions, attempting to rest in certainty at several points. And in this final decor, the fixity of the "marble man" is troubled by a double reference, a descending, vertical movement and a horizontal movement "ahead." The ambiguity encompasses descent and expansion, mere "memorial" and vitality, a backward and a forward look.

The last, shortened line of the poem must stop and confirm the growing and hanging as a scene rather than as an action while affirming the ongoingness of the river. Yet, in an another important difference with "Sunday Morning" VIII and its catalogue of deer, quail, berries, and pigeons as clear grammatical subjects, the river is reiterated only as the pronoun "it," like the "It" that is "being." In an allegorical reading, the "being" that "Includes death and the imagination" is the river and also this poem. The transformation of the river into "it" may suggest an extension of the signifiers beyond a particular word-space into a word-time, and into future, but unnameable, disappearance.

Whereas the audience in "The Man with the Blue Guitar" harps on containing the song within confining spatial metaphors, this speaker opens his "here" to time and in particular to the past in the future, that time-space of flowing "ahead" that is the representation of unrepresentable death. The direction here is not aleatory as in "The Motive for Metaphor." But the flow of repetitive words and syntactic patterns is interrupted by disruptions in the parallels between images, leaps of enjambment, questions that are ambiguously rhetorical, lexical denials, morphological complications, oxymorons. The direction that develops, then, is a halting, exploratory one, which is given some impression of evenness by the regular succession of tercets. The fundamentally specular stance of the last tercet seems to make a final halt in order to look at the place that is only a decor for what cannot be seen because it lies ahead, where the river is flowing. Yet I would say that Stevens' glance is not averted from the future in this poem; rather, the compositional form transforms itself from a hypothetical fictive landscape to a series of speculative metamorphoses and questions. These hesitate yet move toward that final verge that cannot be written about from the other side.

"The River of Rivers in Connecticut" (CP 533) starts from "this side of Stygia," which is like this side of the resemblance between geographical rivers and mythical, transcendent ones like the Styx. As in "Metaphor as Degeneration," we begin in the country of metaphor. Critical discourse, in its inevitable refractions into complementary categories, has offered various plausible decodings of this river as tenor and vehicle and as oscillating between "reality" and "imagination." Among them, the river has been seen as metaphorizing "being," which can no longer "be discovered anywhere. It flows everywhere, through all space and time and through all the contents of space and time" (Miller).[11] It has been described as "a trope for force as opposed to presence" and for "a saving withdrawal or fresh vision" that provides transcendence (Bloom).[12] The river has been seen as being not exactly a metaphor but "the force in the landscape that mediates between geographical reality and the desire for landscapes of the imagination" without being caught in the tenor-vehicle relationship (Doreski).[13] Or, overstepping the consolations of the "dialectical model for consideration" of Stevens' poetry, Vendler has called the poem's " 'subject' " "the inestimable preciousness of the total stream of life."[14] However we call the river-Styx relation, we will see that the poem shifts to its own potential erasure beyond any possible metaphor.

There is a great river this side of Stygia,
Before one comes to the first black cataracts
And trees that lack the intelligence of trees.

In that river, far this side of Stygia,
The mere flowing of the water is a gayety,
Flashing and flashing in the sun. On its banks,

No shadow walks. The river is fateful,
Like the last one. But there is no ferryman.
He could not bend against its propelling force.

It is not to be seen beneath the appearances
That tell of it. The steeple at Farmington
Stands glistening and Haddam shines and sways.

It is the third commonness with light and air,
A curriculum, a vigor, a local abstraction . . .
Call it, once more, a river, an unnamed flowing,

Space-filled, reflecting the seasons, the folk-lore
Of each of the senses; call it, again and again,
The river that flows nowhere, like a sea.

This poem starts out with that existential locative, "There is" something somewhere, no longer hypothetically as in "Metaphor as Degeneration," but affirmatively. This would shield against the radical estrangement of death's Stygia, where even trees "lack the intelligence" nature gives them. Yet the river claimed as possible compensation in this life is both approached and at first warded off. The deictics of "this side" and "that river" make the river both here and removed. It is also intellectualized by the abstraction of "a gayety." The metaphorical possibilities of the river are as yet open. The copular form, the "flowing . . . is a gayety," is given a temporal and eschatological dimension as its "Flashing and flashing in the sun" is succeeded by "No shadow," but especially by a second copula, "the river is fateful / Like the last one." There is a moment of suspicion in the absolute (not located) existential statement: "But there is no ferryman." Vendler, who is not content with decoding but is moved by the dynamics of the poem, says that this completes the exorcism of death from the poem.[15]

And it is here, in the middle of the poem, that we seem to have not only a departure from the traditional metaphor of the Styx, but the non- or extra-ontological construction of a fiction that revels in the artifice of language—its function words and combinatory possibilities—as our home. The poem divides and expands into a praise of the senses and their pleasures, beginning with the towns on the banks of the river and extending into epithets that join them with natural principles and a "local abstraction" that is no longer distancing.[16]

> It is the third commonness with light and air,
> A curriculum, a vigor, a local abstraction . . .
> Call it, once more, a river, an unnamed flowing

It is by ever so briefly having recourse to Stevens' older habit of piling on appositions, as he did in "The Motive for Metaphor," that the poem overcomes any mere duality or hierarchy. This pleasurable expansion beyond separate orders of things is now detached, without againstness, from all pathos and all superior force. When the river disappears, it is also replaced in the speaker's fiction, as at the end of "Metaphor as Degeneration," by the scene along its banks. The speaker then raises its common noun ("river") from "beneath" the surface of the language by a command, "Call it," and then: "call it, again and again, / The river that flows nowhere, like a sea." Who is "Call it" addressed to? To the speaker himself, searching for a word that can never be found? To the reader, invited to participate in the utterance of the only word that can be found? "Call it" also performs its own signified, calling the river "a river," then "The river," which once again becomes ominous with specificity and uniqueness.

After this series of pronominal and metaphorical or metonymical displacements, "the river" is said ultimately to flow "nowhere," but we need to consider how we reach this stage. The artificer uses the combination "space-filled" to shift from examples designated by the indefinite article to a series of wholes or unique things particularized with the definite article. This seems to signify a temporary shift too from the dominant sense of movement, the "propelling force" of stanza 3, to a global vision of the scene, an almost static unifying of parts, "the seasons," and "each of the senses." While the ongoingness of the river phenomenon is diminished referentially, the grammatical symmetry is jumbled into "Space-filled, reflecting the seasons, the folk-lore / Of each of the senses." The poem then starts itself up again by reiteration, "again and again," calling to itself to repeat in the future that common noun. This call to continue, to go on, encourages the poet. It gives a slight momentum to the line as the poem approaches its end. The provisional nature of all copular, pronominal, metaphorical, and naming relations established by the initial "There is" is about to be confirmed.

The river flows but does not take the speaker with it. As I said earlier, it waits for him to come to it "like a sea." The speaker not only "call[s]" or names it but calls out to it. Its "nowhere" is the place the poet names to replace Stygia, the place where the speaker will go in a future time. It is also the "fateful" future of his work, just as his poem has relegated the Styx to an earlier moment in its own trajectory only to find an avatar of it at the end. Its present name: "The river that flows nowhere." Propulsion or movement directed forward becomes directionless. The word-world cannot stretch beyond its own course except by representing another fictive time. In "Metaphor as Degeneration," the river "flows ahead," bounded and directed by the banks and their funerary decor. At the close of "The River of Rivers in Connecticut," the river's movement is represented not as movement toward the past in the future but as the cessation of ongoingness, what happens when life and writing stop. Taking the poems of *The Rock* as a whole, although each poem deals in its own way with this problem, it can be said that the word-worlds of Stevens' poems of old age envisage within themselves the erasure of their occasion and their origin, the annihilation of their author. The contingency and artifice of language continue to bind human time to the place of speculation.

Such late poems thus bring forth, in the perspective of death, the active forces of Stevens' English: the capacity of metaphor to be taken "beyond" the strain of ontological hierarchy, the possibility of performing speculation despite the distance that exists between the local reference of language and being, and the temporariness of verbal rapprochements along the trajectory of language. This means that metaphor continues as both enabler of invisible visions and inhibitor of final satisfactions. At worst, it leads toward "that distant chamber, a bearded queen, wicked in her dead light" which closes "Madame Fleurie" (CP 507). At best, we have "A Quiet Normal Life" (CP 523). Like "Prologues to What Is Possible" this poem alludes in every stanza to Stevens' life oeuvre. Yet it can define the speaker's perishable "place" outside Stevens' oeuvre, recognize the ephemeral condition of the poem's performance, and end by celebrating the glory of the artifice of language itself in the last line, where the "actual" present becomes the past in the future.

A Quiet Normal Life

His place, as he sat and as he thought, was not
In anything that he constructed, so frail,
So barely lit, so shadowed over and naught,

As, for example, a world in which, like snow,
He became an inhabitant, obedient
To gallant notions on the part of cold.

It was here. This was the setting and the time
Of year. Here in his house and in his room,
In his chair, the most tranquil thought grew peaked

And the oldest and the warmest heart was cut
By gallant notions on the part of nigh—
Both late and alone, above the crickets' chords,

Babbling, each one, the uniqueness of its sound.
There was no fury in transcendent forms.
But his actual candle blazed with artifice.

NOTES

INTRODUCTION

1. J. Hillis Miller, *Poets of Reality: Six Twentieth-Century Writers* (Cambridge, MA: Harvard UP, 1965), pp. 217–284.

2. Melita Schaum's selective commentary on the criticism of the 1965–1985 period focuses on Pearce, Riddel, Miller, Bloom, Bové, Lentricchia, and secondarily Gelpi, Perloff, and Davidson in Melita Schaum, *Wallace Stevens and the Critical Schools* (Tuscaloosa and London: U of Alabama P, 1988), pp. 100–182. Newcomb devotes one chapter to the 1954–1966 period and an Afterword to the historicist tendency current today, in John Timbermann Newcomb, *Wallace Stevens and Literary Canons* (Jackson and London: U of Mississippi P, 1992), pp. 172–235 and 236–244.

3. This unspoken and unquestioned assumption underlies most of the otherwise very diverse articles that appeared in the first collections of essays on Stevens, such as Roy Harvey Pearce and J. Hillis Miller, eds., *The Act of the Mind: Essays on the Poetry of Wallace Stevens* (Baltimore: Johns Hopkins UP, 1965).

4. Miller, *Poets of Reality*, p. 276.

5. Joseph Riddel, *The Clairvoyant Eye: The Poetry and Poetics of Wallace Stevens* (Baton Rouge: Louisiana State UP, 1965), p. vi.

6. Harold Bloom, *Wallace Stevens: The Poems of Our Climate* (Ithaca and London: Cornell UP, 1977).

7. Michel Benamou, *L'Œuvre → Monde de Wallace Stevens* (Paris: Honoré Champion, 1975).

8. Frank Lentricchia, *Ariel and the Police: Michel Foucault, William James, Wallace Stevens* (Madison: U of Wisconsin P, 1988), and B. J. Leggett, *Wallace Stevens and Poetic Theory: Conceiving the Supreme Fiction* (Chapel Hill: U of North Carolina P, 1987).

9. Helen Vendler brings this interpretation to its culmination in *Wallace Stevens: Words Chosen Out of Desire* (Knoxville: U of Tennessee P, 1984).

10. Albert Gelpi, "Stevens and Williams: The Epistemology of Modernism," in Albert Gelpi, ed., *Wallace Stevens: The Poetics of Modernism* (Cambridge:

Cambridge UP, 1985); Marjorie Perloff, "Revolving in Crystal: The Supreme Fiction and the Impasse of the Modernist Lyric" in Gelpi, *Wallace Stevens: The Poetics of Modernism*, pp. 41–64.

11. See Nyquist's feminist reading of "Peter Quince" in Mary Nyquist, "Musing on Susanna's Music," in Chaviva Hosek and Patricia Parker, eds., *Lyric Poetry: Beyond New Criticism* (Ithaca: Cornell UP, 1985), pp. 310–327.

12. Mark Halliday, *Stevens and the Interpersonal* (Princeton: Princeton UP, 1991).

13. Andrew Hollingworth, "Stevens' Rivers and Rocks: Motions to the Center," *Wallace Stevens Journal* 22.1 (Spring 1998): 40.

14. Stanley Fish, *Is There a Text in This Class? The Authority of Interpretive Communities* (Cambridge, MA and London: Harvard UP, 1980), p. 257.

15. Joseph N. Riddel, "Interpreting Stevens: An Essay on Poetry and Thinking," *Boundary 2: A Journal of Postmodern Literature* 1.1 (Fall 1972), 79–80.

16. Miller protests the mixing of Heideggerian and Derridean possibilities in J. Hillis Miller, "Deconstructing the Deconstructers," *Diacritics* (Summer 1975): 24–31.

17. See Jacques Derrida, *Margins of Philosophy*, trans. Alan Bass (Chicago: U of Chicago P, 1982). Few, if any, have noticed that in the same volume Derrida expostulates on undecidability in "White Mythology: Metaphor in the Text of Philosophy," while systematizing intelligible, purely referential meaning in "Le facteur de la vérité," where he analyzes Lacan's reading of Marie Bonaparte reading Poe's "The Purloined Letter." Derrida's philosophical stand is, however, a particularly appropriate response to the nonreferential parameters of Stevens' poetry.

18. It is difficult to avoid thinking in terms of a central reality when writing about Stevens' poetry, since his signifieds constantly bring us back to issues of "self" and "reality" and "completion." Yet it seems to me that it begs the question to say, for instance, of the "rock" in Stevens' later poetry, "Like Mallarmé's 'rock,' Stevens' signifies a point where the word displaces meaning and reality becomes the ground as text, writing, and not meaning." Joseph N. Riddel, "Metaphoric Staging: Stevens' Beginning Again of the 'End of the Book'" in Frank Doggett and Robert Buttel, eds., *Wallace Stevens: A Celebration* (Princeton: Princeton UP, 1980), p. 331.

19. R. P. Blackmur's first discussion of Stevens' poetry dates from 1932, when Stevens' only published volume was *Harmonium* (1923; 1931). This essay, "Examples of Wallace Stevens," has been reprinted many times, most recently in Charles Doyle, ed., *Wallace Stevens: The Critical Heritage* (London, Boston, and Henley: Routledge and Kegan Paul, 1985), pp. 95–125.

20. *Letters* #831 to Sister Bernetta Quinn, dated May 29, 1952, p. 752. Sister Quinn had been particularly interested in systematizing the metaphysical meaning she found in Stevens' poetry.

21. Notice that this is what Vendler also does in adopting the working concept of orders of magnitude in Vendler, "Perfection: 'Washed away by magnitude,' " in *Wallace Stevens: Words Chosen*, pp. 61–79.

22. In particular, Harold Bloom, *Wallace Stevens: The Poems of Our Climate*; Helen Vendler, "The Qualified Assertions of Wallace Stevens" in Pearce and Miller, eds., *The Act of the Mind*, pp. 163–178; Helen Vendler, *On Extended Wings: Wallace Stevens' Longer Poems* (Cambridge, MA: Harvard UP, 1969); Helen Vendler, *Wallace Stevens: Words Chosen*; Eleanor Cook, *Poetry, Word-Play and Word-War in Wallace Stevens* (Princeton: Princeton UP, 1988).

23. Helen Vendler, "The Qualified Assertions of Wallace Stevens," pp. 163–178 and Mac Hammond, "On the Grammar of Wallace Stevens," pp. 179–184, in Pearce and Miller, eds., *The Act of the Mind*.

24. Stevens' use of *as if* is made the centerpiece of Jacqueline Vaught Brogan, *Stevens and Simile: A Theory of Language* (Princeton: Princeton UP, 1986).

25. Respectively Vendler, pp. 164–165, 168, 173–174, and Hammond, p. 180 in Pearce and Miller, eds., *The Act of the Mind*.

26. Anca Rosu, *The Metaphysics of Sound in Wallace Stevens* (Tuscaloosa and London: U of Alabama P, 1995).

CHAPTER 1

1. Frank Doggett is an early representative of this approach. See his *Wallace Stevens' Poetry of Thought* (Baltimore: Johns Hopkins UP, 1966), pp. 143–45.

2. Ralph Waldo Emerson, "Nature," chapter 1, *Ralph Waldo Eme. on: Essays and Lectures*, ed. Joel Porte (New York: The Library of America), 1983, p. 9.

3. See Geoffrey Hartman, *Wordsworth's Poetry 1787–1814* (New Haven: Yale UP, 1971), p. 37.

4. J. Hillis Miller, *Poets of Reality* (New York: Atheneum, 1969), chapter VI, "Wallace Stevens," p. 219. Miller's approach to modernist poets is consonant with Hartman's study of Wordsworth, although it focuses on the poet's vision of the world more than on his struggle with his vocation. Miller has continued to reread Stevens, moving from a phenomenological approach of

reading the text as correlative to the mind, to a deconstructionist approach which emphasizes the impossibility of naming and stating.

5. Miller, *Poets of Reality*, p. 281.

6. This and a number of other ideas expressed in "The Noble Rider" have an affinity with Coleridge as discussed in I. A. Richards, *Coleridge on the Imagination* (London: Kegan Paul, Trench, Trubner Ltd., 1934), p. 149. Coleridge comments that Plato's figure in the *Phaedrus* is "dear, gorgeous nonsense" (*NA* 3). Stevens had pencil-marked this passage in Richards for his own reference (The Huntington Library, 440444).

7. Two notable exceptions in the Anglo-American sphere are Northrop Frye and I. A. Richards. Frye saw the radical form of metaphor as identity (A is B), which can only be ironic and paradoxical if taken literally. I. A. Richards emphasized the principle of holding two ideas simultaneously active. If we do take metaphor as a trope of resemblance, "trope" and "metaphor" cannot be synonymous, for there are tropes that are constructed on a principle of *non*-resemblance and *non*-inclusion. See the distinction first made by Jakobson (1956) between metaphor as a trope of "similarity" (resemblance) and metonymy as a trope of "contiguity" (proximity).

The metaphor-metonymy distinction appeared in the 1970s in Stevens criticism. As we shall see later, Miller applied to Stevens his view that metaphor helps to construct mimesis, while metonymy helps to destroy mimesis by asserting discontinuity. He saw metonymy as a feature of Stevens' late poetry. See J. Hillis Miller, "Deconstructing the Deconstructors," *Diacritics* (Summer 1975): 31. Michel Benamou sketched the dichotomy in his "Displacements of Parental Space: American Poetry and French Symbolism," *Boundary 2: A Journal of Postmodern Literature* 5.2 (Winter 1977): 471–486. Beginning with the evolution of French criticism on Mallarmé (and symbolism), the article cites Derrida as the first to reveal in Mallarmé's poetry "the revolution of metaphor turning it into metonymy, displacement, pure combination," with the effect being that there is no unveiling of a presence behind the signs, no Logos. The nonmimetic here is thus the counterpart of the metonymic (pp. 473–474). Benamou then applies Kristeva's version of Lacanian notions of the symbolic social order and maternal, presymbolic union to Stevens' use of the metaphorical and the metonymic. He finds Stevens still dreaming of overcoming metaphor, logocentrism, and maternal presence at the end of his career.

8. David Cooper questions the philosophical and pragmatic validity of the concept of resemblances in demarcating metaphorical from ordinary language use. To my mind, his approach is limited by the dubious distinction made between literal and metaphorical. See David E. Cooper, *Metaphor*, Aristotelian Society Series (Oxford: Basil Blackwell, 1986).

9. An "eye for resemblances" is proposed in Aristotle, *The Poetics*, trans. W. Hamilton Fyfe, rev. ed. (London: Heinemann, and Cambridge, MA: Harvard UP, 1932), 1459a. An "intuitive perception of the similarity in dissimilars" is given in Aristotle, *Poetics*, trans. I. Bywater, in *The Complete Works of Aristotle*, ed. Jonathan Barnes (Princeton: Princeton UP, 1984), vol. 2, 1459a. The transmitted text of the *Poetics* in Greek says *to nomoion theôrein*, "see the similar."

10. Brogan, in her chapter called "Simile," stresses the dialectical pull of each on the other and Stevens' desire to find a language that will embody "the seeming impossibility of diverging likeness (or converging differences) simultaneously," much like Wordsworth's desire to show " 'similitude in dissimilitude, and dissimilitude in similitude.' " Jacqueline Vaught Brogan, *Stevens and Simile: A Theory of Language* (Princeton: Princeton UP, 1986), p. 142. She quotes from William Wordsworth, "Preface to the Second Edition of the *Lyrical Ballads*" [1800] in *English Romantic Writers*, ed. David Perkins (New York: Harcourt, Brace and World, 1967), p. 328.

11. This key passage of Aristotle was one of a handful marked in pencil in the margin of the book Stevens had in his library at the time of his death: "But the greatest thing by far is to be a master of metaphor. It is the [marginal marking starts here:] one thing that cannot be learnt from others; and it is also a sign of genius, since a good metaphor implies an intuitive perception of the similarity in dissimilars." Aristotle, *Aristotle's Art of Poetry*, intro. and explanation by W. Hamilton Fyfe (Oxford: Clarendon Press, 1940), 1459a, p. 62. Fyfe presents this translation as being that of Ingram Bywater for the most part (University of Massachusetts Library at Amherst, Special Collections and Archives, PN/1040/A5/F9/1940). In the passage on metaphor, Fyfe has indeed used Bywater's original vocabulary. The term Stevens uses in some poems and in his 1941 and 1946 essays, however, is not Bywater's "similarity" but "resemblance," the term used by Fyfe in his own 1932 translation. This suggests that Stevens reread Aristotle when Fyfe's re-edition of Bywater came out in 1940 but retained the earlier vocabulary.

Stevens did not mark the margin of the other famous passage that defines metaphor as a trope of transference or substitution, that of "giving the things a name that belongs to something else" (1457b) (chapter 21, p. 56 of the translation Stevens used), but he did pencil in "Metaphor 56" on the dust jacket.

12. Suzanne Juhasz, *Metaphor and the Poetry of Williams, Pound, and Stevens* (Lewisburg, PA: Bucknell UP, 1974), p. 32.

13. Juhasz, *Metaphor and the Poetry of Williams, Pound, and Stevens*, p. 17. Juhasz' criticism remains determined by the dualism within which Stevens himself worked.

14. This view of association, which Stevens articulates in "The Noble Rider and the Sound of Words," relies on I. A. Richards' citing Coleridge's famous distinction between fancy and creative imagination. See my note 6.

15. This means that resemblance is not the natural manifestation of a relationship between two objects in two realms. It therefore represents a disengagement from relations taken to be natural, like the ones that Foucault identifies as "visible marks for the invisible analogies" or "buried similitudes" typical of seventeenth-century thinking. Michel Foucault, *The Order of Things* (New York: Vintage, 1973), p. 26. For the original see Michel Foucault, *Les mots et les choses: une archéologie des sciences humaines* (Paris: Gallimard, 1966), chap. II "La prose du monde," II "Les signatures," p. 41.

16. Michel de Montaigne, "Essais," *Œuvres complètes* (Paris: Gallimard, Bibliothèque de la Pléiade, 1989), livre III, chap. XII, p. 1028. "Si nous n'avons sçeu vivre, c'est injustice de nous apprendre à mourir, et de difformer la fin de son tout. . . . [I]l m'est advis que [la mort] est bien le bout, non pourtant le but de la vie; c'est sa fin, son extremité, non pourtant son objet." ("Even if we have not known how to live, it is unjust [for doctors] to teach us how to die and to deform the end of the whole. . . . In my opinion [death] is indeed the end, but not the purpose of life; it is its final point, its limit, but not its object.") [My translation.]

17. To my knowledge, no critic has studied or even mentioned "Invective against Swans."

18. The swans secondarily recall Apollo's swan companions. The two sides of this metaphor will be used separately later in the "solar chariot" of "The Pure Good of Theory" (CP 331–332) and the swans and chariots in "Description without Place" (CP 343).

19. Kenneth Burke, *Language as Symbolic Action* (Berkeley: U of California P, 1966), p. 10 as cited by Jacqueline Brogan, *Stevens and Simile*, p. 181.

20. See, for example, *The Odyssey*, Book XI and *The Aeneid*, Book VI. Elysium is described in the latter thus: "Here a more generous air clothed the fields with a generous / Light; they knew their own sun and their own stars."

Vergil, *The Aeneid*, trans., intro., and notes by L. R. Lind (Bloomington: U of Indiana P, 1963), ll. 647–648.

21. Eleanor Cook, *Poetry, Word-Play, and Word-War in Wallace Stevens* (Princeton: Princeton UP, 1988), p. 102.

22. Stevens quotes from the Interpreter in *Pilgrim's Progress*, which he calls "the supreme example of analogy in English," in "The Effects of Analogy" (1948) (NA 107).

23. Although "Sunday Morning" has been frequently summarized, and fragments of it have been quoted and occasionally analyzed, the only full treatments I know of are: Eleanor Cook, *Poetry, Word-Play, and Word-War*, pp. 99–114, where Cook reads sections I, V, and VIII primarily for their "quiet revisions of Milton" and the Bible (p. 107); Robert Rehder, *The Poetry of Wallace Stevens* (New York: St. Martin's Press, 1988), pp. 65–87, where Rehder reads the poem in the light of the task Stevens set for poetry, "the recovery of the first conditions of being" (p. 81); and Harold Bloom, *Wallace Stevens: The Poems of Our Climate* (Ithaca: Cornell UP, 1977), pp. 27–35. See also Joy Pohl, " 'Sunday Morning': Stevens' Equivocal Lyric," *Wallace Stevens Journal* 8.2 (Fall 1984): 83–86. Pohl sees—rightly, I think— an unresolved tension between the woman's and the speaker's perspectives, although I do not see the other "speaker" as one but as multiple or protean.

24. Cook, *Poetry, Word-Play, and Word-War*, p. 100.

25. The metonymical and metaphorical basis of Stevens' stanza distances it from a contemporary poem like Pound's "Albatre" (1914), which presents a descriptive and expository white version of a peignoir-clad woman sitting in a chair:

> This lady in the white bath-robe which she calls a peignoir,
> Is, for the time being, the mistress, of my friend,
> And the delicate white feet of her little white dog
> Are not more delicate than she is,
> Nor would Gautier himself have despised their contrasts in
>   whiteness
> As she sits in the great chair
> Between two indolent candles.

26. Adelaide Kirby Morris, *Wallace Stevens: Imagination and Faith* (Princeton: Princeton UP, 1974), p. 48.

27. Helen Vendler, *On Extended Wings: Wallace Stevens' Longer Poems* (Cambridge, MA: Harvard UP, 1969), p. 55.

28. Milton Bates says of section VII, "The sun resembles a god and in the larger economy of resemblance God may be an idealized likeness of the sun."

Milton J. Bates, *Wallace Stevens: A Mythology of Self* (Berkeley: U of California P, 1985), p. 113.

29. Harold Bloom, *Wallace Stevens: The Poems of Our Climate*, p. 34.

30. Joy Pohl, " 'Sunday Morning': Stevens' Equivocal Lyric," p. 83. Pohl finds "religious forms" in the images of hills, birds, and "the chaos of the sun."

31. Helen Vendler has illustrated the pervasiveness of Wordsworth and particularly Keats in Stevens most thoroughly in *Wallace Stevens: Words Chosen Out of Desire* (Knoxville: U of Tennessee P, 1984), while Harold Bloom has argued for the influence of Coleridge, Wordsworth, Keats, and Shelley, as well as Emerson and Whitman, in *Wallace Stevens: The Poems of Our Climate*. See also George Bornstein, *Transformations of Romanticism in Yeats, Eliot and Stevens* (Chicago: U of Chicago P, 1976).

32. See Geoffrey Hartman, *Wordsworth's Poetry 1787–1814*, which draws out the unconscious paradoxes between Wordsworth's affirmations about the poet's relation to nature and his poetic treatment of it in his *Prelude*.

33. Both Bloom and Fish, though coming at the poem from different angles, would seem to agree that the rhetorical absence of agency is also a sign of indifference. For Fish this is embodied in the grammatical "suppression of agency," which he says "*is* the meaning of the poem." For Bloom it is rhetorically a "death-in-life" that "comes, which is more that of the poem's shaper, speaker, reader than it could have been of the fictive soldier before he fell." See Stanley Fish, *Is There a Text in This Class?* (Cambridge, MA: Harvard UP, 1980), p. 258, and Bloom, *Wallace Stevens: The Poems of Our Climate*, p. 50.

34. Jacqueline Vaught Brogan, *Stevens and Simile*, p. 154. Brogan demonstrates that while simile is relatively rare in *Harmonium*, both it and the related *as if* mark Stevens' late poetry and point to Stevens' growing ability to both recognize the abyss and bridge it.

35. See A. Walton Litz, "Wallace Stevens' Defense of Poetry: *La poésie pure*, the New Romantic and the Pressure of Reality" in George Bornstein, ed., *Romantic and Modern: Revaluations of Literary Tradition* (Pittsburgh, PA: U of Pittsburgh P, 1977), pp. 111–132.

36. A similar resistance inhabits Stevens' search for the motive of poetry itself. He contests, for example, the romantic muse as an incarnation of poetic inspiration. Yet he is caught in the "modernist" quandary of deconstructing the figure by referring to it nonetheless in poems from "To the One of Fictive Music" (1922) and "The Idea of Order at Key West" (1934) to "Final Soliloquy of the Interior Paramour" (1950).

37. See Stevens' letter of July 25, 1915 to his wife in which he tells of a visit to the Botanical Gardens in New York (*Letters* #195). His specific references are frequently triggered by such banal discoveries. Qian also hypothesizes that this poem was inspired by Southern Song painting. See Zhaoming Qian, "Chinese Landscape Painting in Stevens' 'Six Significant Land-scapes,' " *Wallace Stevens Journal* 21.2 (Fall 1997): 123–142.

38. Joan Richardson, *Wallace Stevens: The Later Years, 1923–1955* (New York: William Morrow, 1988), p. 66. This poem was one of nine written in 1929, but Stevens did not include it in the second edition of *Harmonium* in 1931. See Richardson, p. 54.

39. Aristotle, *Poetics*, trans. I. Bywater, in *The Complete Works of Aristotle*, ed. Jonathan Barnes, vol. 2, 1457b.

40. Holly Stevens writes that this line figured in the first documented version of the poem, handwritten on a postcard sent from Florida to Harriet Monroe on January 15, 1919 (*Palm* 401).

41. Harold Bloom, *Wallace Stevens: The Poems of Our Climate*, p. 86.

42. Eleanor Cook, *Poetry, Word-Play and Word-War*, pp. 179–180.

43. Helen Vendler, *On Extended Wings*, p. 149. See also pp. 151–153 and pp. 326–327, n. 5–9, where she also praises Frank Doggett's reading of the poem in his *Wallace Stevens' Poetry of Thought*, pp. 88–90.

44. Vendler, *On Extended Wings*, pp. 152 + 149. Vendler cites, for instance, the use of the suffix *-id* in "metaphorid," a dead suffix that contributes to mak-ing the word sinister.

45. Northrop Frye, "The Realistic Oriole: A Study of Wallace Stevens," *Hudson Review* 10.3 (Autumn 1957): 361.

46. Frank Doggett, *Wallace Stevens' Poetry of Thought*, p. 88.

47. Henry David Thoreau, "Spring," *Walden* in *A Week on the Concord and Merrimack Rivers, Walden: or Life in the Woods, The Maine Woods, Cape Cod*, ed. Robert F. Sayre (New York: The Library of America, 1985), p. 568.

48. Harold Bloom, *Wallace Stevens: The Poems of Our Climate*, p. 282, laconi-cally affirms that the owl represents "central things" in this poem and in "Woman Looking at a Vase of Flowers" (CP 246–247). I am aware of no analysis of the poem by any critic.

49. The groupings created by "And"/"and" can form different, ambiguously overlapping sets.

50. Vidal and Stevens exchanged photographs in 1938, the year this poem was written. It seems likely that Stevens also received the oil portrait of Vidal,

painted by Jean Labasque, not long before writing this poem (a photograph of the oil portrait is on file at the Huntington Library). In his letter dated June 4, 1938, Vidal praises Labasque's art, saying that "l'art de Jean Labasque est par dessus tout moderne et toujours à la recherche de l'idée forte, dominante, de l'individualité,—que cet art ne peut être qualifié de joli, d'aimable, de gracieux" ("Jean Labasque's art is above all modern, and constantly driven by the search for a powerful governing idea of individuality. It cannot be called pretty, pleasant or graceful" [my translation]). (The Huntington Library, WAS 2658). Unfortunately, Stevens' letters to Vidal have not been preserved, and Vidal's letters to Stevens are incomplete. They are missing entirely for a period of more than nine months from July 14, 1938, when Vidal wrote to Stevens that he was going to tell him more about Labasque and two other minor painters (The Huntington Library, WAS 2659). The phrase *qui fait fi des joliesses banales* does not appear in any of the extant letters but is consistent with the ideas Vidal expressed and the language he used in his June 4 letter.

51.   Eleanor Cook, *Poetry, Word-Play, and Word-War*, p. 156. The figure is also taken up in "Les Plus Belles Pages" (CP 245), and the intellectual and scholarly resonances of Aquinas' work are alluded to, only to be laid aside, in the opening to *Transport to Summer* (1947), in "God is Good. It is a Beautiful Night" (CP 285).

52.   Cook, *Poetry, Word-Play, and Word-War*, pp. 155–156. Cook claims that without this reference the poem may seem "bald."

53.   See J. Hillis Miller, "Prosopopoeia in Hardy and Stevens" in *Tropes, Parables, Performatives: Essays on Twentieth-Century Literature* (Hemel Hempstead: Harvester Wheatsheaf, 1990), chapter 15, pp. 245–259. Miller argues in this essay against Kant's claim that prosopopoeia or personification is something added to an idea of first principles. He shows how the personification of the sun in "Not Ideas about the Thing but the Thing Itself" is a necessary trope of the absent, the hidden, that which it is impossible to name.

54.   Foucault calls this "perfidiously mixing (and by a ruse that seems to indicate just the opposite of what it means) the painting and what it represents." Michel Foucault, *This is Not a Pipe*, trans. and ed. James Harkness (Berkeley: U of California P, 1983), p. 50. In his essay on modernist art, Foucault makes an interesting distinction between "resemblance," which implies referential model and imitation or copy, and "similarity," which dispenses with the anchor of reference. A Magritte painting is no more a copy than the

natural landscape is a model. They are both examples of similar scenes in a theoretically infinite series.

55. Jacques Derrida, "La mythologie blanche: La métaphore dans le texte philosophique" in *Marges de la philosophie* (Paris: Ed. de minuit, 1972). Derrida maintains that in seeking etymology, we seek a diachronic sequence and thus privilege a symbolical conception at the expense of an apprehension of the system. This is because it pushes us to see in the link between the signifier and the signified a bond of natural necessity (*"de nécessité naturelle"*) consisting of analogy or resemblance, and thus emphasizes semantic depth (*"profondeur"*). See the English translation, "White Mythology: Metaphor in the Text of Philosophy" in *Margins of Philosophy*, trans. Alan Bass (Chicago: U of Chicago P, 1982).

56. Eleanor Cook, *Poetry, Word-Play, and Word-War*, p. 156.

57. As Joseph Kronick points out, the examples Stevens himself gives of the resemblances existing among objects in a natural scene in "Three Academic Pieces" (*NA* 71) are in fact examples of synecdoche, where part substitutes for whole on the basis of "semantic contiguity." Kronick sketches Stevens' theory on the basis of the first of the "Three Academic Pieces." He sees Stevens as adopting the terms of Romanticism (mind/nature) while suggesting what Derrida expounds in his celebrated "White Mythology" essay, that resemblance is impossible because the desired object must always be absent. Kronick's reference is to the earlier translation, Jacques Derrida, "White Mythology: Metaphor in the Text of Philosophy," trans. F. C. T. Moore, *New Literary History* 6.1 (1974): 37. Joseph Kronick, "The Metamorphic Stevens," *The Wallace Stevens Journal* 6.1/2 (Spring 1982): 3–10.

CHAPTER 2

1. Altieri is almost alone in avoiding this defect. See his analysis of some poems by Stevens read in the light of "The Effects of Analogy" and of theories of metaphor propounded by Donald Davidson, Wayne Booth, Paul Ricœur, and Jacques Derrida, in Charles Altieri, "Wallace Stevens' Metaphors of Metaphor: Poetry as Theory," *American Poetry* 1.1 (1983): 27–48.

2. It should be said that Stevens left ample and often quotable, if rambling, material on the subject. Altieri and Parker are among those who have

remarked that someone could and should examine the very vagaries of Stevens' position. See Charles Altieri, "Wallace Stevens' Metaphors of Metaphor," 27–48, and Patricia Parker, "The Motive for Metaphor: Stevens and Derrida," *The Wallace Stevens Journal* 7.3/4 (Fall 1983): 76–88.

3. Aristotle, *Poetics*, trans. I. Bywater, in *The Complete Works of Aristotle*, ed. Jonathan Barnes (Princeton: Princeton UP, 1984), vol. 2, 1457b.

4. In *Poetics* 1457b, 1458a, 1458b he uses terms derived from *metapherein* = "to carry across, transfer," *metatitein* = "to place across, replace, supplant, substitute," and *epipherein* = "to carry onto or towards, to add" (*epiphora* translated by Bywater as "transference").

5. The notion of the proper and improper use of words contributed in French structuralist criticism to the concept of literary language as a deviation or *écart* from a norm. For an early example see Jean Cohen, *Structure du langage poétique* (Paris: Flammarion, 1966).

6. Bloom, whose reading centers on the genealogy of the poem and on criticism concerning it, writes: "A. Walton Litz usefully relates *The Paltry Nude* to the first stanza of *Le Monocle de Mon Oncle*, written the year before, where the speaker has an ironic vision of the beloved as the Botticelli 'Birth of Venus': 'The sea of spuming thought foists up again / The radiant bubble that she was.' Robert Buttel demonstrates the parodistic relation of Stevens' *Paltry Nude* to imagistic poems on the same subject by Amy Lowell and H. D. They may indeed have been Stevens' starting point, but his fierce lyric confronts a true precursor in Pater's great prose poem *Sandro Botticelli* in *The Renaissance*. I suspect that Pater's account of the painting 'The Birth of Venus' is one of the hidden sources of Stevens' notion of the First Idea, called by Pater 'the first impression.' " Harold Bloom, *Wallace Stevens: The Poems of Our Climate* (Ithaca: Cornell UP, 1977), p. 25.

7. William Wordsworth, *The Prelude: 1799, 1805, 1850*, ed. Jonathan Wordsworth et al., Norton Critical Edition (New York and London: W. W. Norton, 1979), 1805, IV, ll. 111–114; 1850, IV, ll. 111–114.

8. Tautology is the only possible statement that is not metaphorical. This is also noted in Susan Weston, *Wallace Stevens: An Introduction* (New York: Columbia UP, 1977), p. 31. Thus, ironically, "Metaphors of a Magnifico" consists of non-metaphors of a non-magnificent "magnifico." Weston sees the magnifico's naïveté about metaphors as pointing to the implicit metaphoricity of all language: all language is an act of analogy performed by the mind when confronted with rival sense experience ("reality"). Vendler's more complete account emphasizes the difference between sense experience and "speculation." Helen Vendler, *Wallace Stevens: Words Cho-*

sen Out of Desire (Knoxville: U of Tennessee P, 1984), p. 22. Both writers see sense perception as vanquishing speculation in the poem. See also Anca Rosu, *The Metaphysics of Sound in Wallace Stevens* (Tuscaloosa and London: U of Alabama P, 1995), pp. 50–51.

9. Linda Welshimer Wagner, *Interviews with William Carlos Williams: "Speaking Straight Ahead"* (New York: New Directions, 1966), pp. 23–24.

10. Albert Gelpi, "Stevens and Williams: The Epistemology of Modernism," in Albert Gelpi, ed., *The Poetics of Modernism* (Cambridge: Cambridge UP, 1985), p. 16. Gelpi's purpose in this essay is to contrast Williams the Imagist with Stevens the practitioner of "Symboliste aestheticism," the empiricist with the skeptical Platonist.

11. Susan Weston, *Wallace Stevens: An Introduction*, p. 31.

12. Anca Rosu, *The Metaphysics of Sound in Wallace Stevens*, pp. 114–116.

13. David Walker, *The Transparent Lyric: Reading and Meaning in the Poetry of Stevens and Williams* (Princeton: Princeton UP, 1984), is not quite accurate about this. He says about stanza 6: "For a moment the poem becomes a demonstration of the way in which feeling is evoked not by discourse but by the experience of the imagination" (pp. 71–72). He does not see that the word "real" is also linked to "senses." He is the only critic I know of to have paid the slightest attention to this poem.

14. The restrictive sense of the word *syllogism* would apply only to a series of three predicate nominative sentences (subject + copula + noun) like those we shall encounter in the analysis of "Thirteen Ways of Looking at a Blackbird" in chapter 4.

15. I. A. Richards, *Coleridge on the Imagination* (London: Kegan Paul, Trench, Trubner, 1934), p. 108. Stevens used this book in writing his 1942 lecture, "The Noble Rider and the Sound of Words" (*NA* 1–36), and had pencilmarked this sentence in his personal copy (The Huntington Library, 440444).

16. Chinese color words, for example, often cover different ranges of the spectrum from Western words. *Qing*, which is the "first" color, is the color of natural scenery, including the sea and distant mountains. It is applied to what we would describe as sky blue, navy blue, and aquamarine but also light green and even black.

17. Bloom, *Wallace Stevens: The Poems of Our Climate*, p. 143.

18. Suzanne Juhasz, *Metaphor and the Poetry of Williams, Pound and Stevens* (Lewisburg, PA: Bucknell UP, 1974), pp. 138–189.

19. "Poem Written at Morning" has attracted little critical attention. David Walker, *The Transparent Lyric*, pp. 67–69, concentrates on what happens

to readers as we read the poem, and comes to the conclusion that its "play-ful metamorphosis" (p. 68) is what allows us to experience the pineapple at all, because the poem's metaphors allow "imaginative comparison to other things we know" (p. 69). He is replying to the didactic reading of Helen Regueiro, *The Limits of Imagination: Wordsworth, Yeats, and Stevens* (Ithaca: Cornell UP, 1976), p. 183, who sees the poem as saying that metaphor does not allow valid experience. Juhasz, *Metaphor and the Poetry of Williams, Pound, and Stevens*, pp. 138–139, tracing the abstraction-metaphor pattern in the poem, sees the "act of metaphor" as "the embodi-ment of abstractions, which is why the eye is 'buxom,' " but she reads the end of the poem as going further in making the giant "a being in his own right—in his own story" (p. 139). These readings focus on the general the-ses of their authors rather than on the actual linguistic procedures Stevens uses.

20. This possibility is reallegorized in "Gigantomachia" (CP 289), written the following year (1943). Here the giant metaphor signifies soldiers at war stripping off "the complacent trifles" and being imbued with the giant's spirit that gives them a truly tragic, enlarged courage.

21. This is not to consider that all "natural" languages, as opposed to mathe-matical and logical languages, escape to some degree from the coherence the word *system* implies.

22. Vendler, *Wallace Stevens: Words Chosen*, pp. 23–24; Bloom, *Wallace Stevens: Poems of Our Climate*, pp. 221–222; Walker, *The Transparent Lyric*, pp. 78–80; Parker, "The Motive For Metaphor: Stevens and Derrida," pp. 76–88. Parker avoids reading the poem solely as an allegory of the self's self-scrutiny. Taking a cue from Derrida, she focuses on the difficulties of the reading process.

23. David Walker, *The Transparent Lyric*, pp. 79–80.

24. Patricia Parker, "The Motive for Metaphor: Stevens and Derrida," p. 85. But Parker still considers the basic relationship of opposition within the cognitive categories Stevens himself thought in, primarily fact/fiction, sub-ject/object (p. 87).

25. See Bloom's and Vendler's opposing interpretations of this type in Bloom, *Wallace Stevens: The Poems of Our Climate*, pp. 221–222, and Vendler, *Wallace Stevens: Words Chosen*, pp. 23–24.

26. Stevens had reviewed Marianne Moore's *Selected Poems* in 1935 for *Life and Letters*. He copied the last sentence of "The Past Is the Present" on the in-side of the back cover of his copy of the book (The Huntington Library,

440488): "Ecstasy affords / The occasion and expediency determines the form." The poem's speaker also mentions being "goaded" "by XY, who was speaking of unrhymed verse." Parker's slightly different repertory of echoes includes Pound's "ABC of Reading" and Spenser's figure of Vulcan-Mammon. See Patricia Parker, "The Motive for Metaphor: Stevens and Derrida," p. 86.

27. It has been suggested that the forge metaphor refers to the manufacture of war machinery. This is a relevant covert allusion since the poem was written in 1943.

28. Bloom defines this *stance* (in italics in his book) in this way: "Shelley, rising and seeing the dawn, sighs for night: 'When light rode high, and the dew was gone, / And noon lay heavy on flower and tree.' This is 'the weight of primary noon' from which Stevens shrinks in *The Motive for Metaphor*, still 'desiring the exhilarations of changes.' Stevens' love for that moment in the day when light has come but the sun has not yet risen above the horizon is a thoroughly Shelleyan passion . . ." Bloom, *Wallace Stevens: The Poems of Our Climate*, p. 221.

29. The X also suggests the Christian cross, the x of algebra, the x of checking in a box, the Greek letter *xi*, chiasmus, etc.

30. The relation between metaphorical and other linguistic movement and death is the subject of the Epilogue.

31. Percy Bysshe Shelley, *A Defence of Poetry* in *Shelley's Poetry and Prose*, ed. Donald H. Reiman and Sharon B. Powers, Norton Critical Edition (New York: W. W. Norton, 1977), pp. 483–485.

CHAPTER 3

1. Nonetheless, Stevens' "meanings" do not seem to me to have so clear a trajectory or so patent a result as Litz would have it. See A. Walton Litz, "Wallace Stevens' Defense of Poetry: *La poésie pure*, the New Romantic and the Pressure of Reality" in George Bornstein, ed., *Romantic and Modern: Revaluations of Literary Tradition* (Pittsburgh: U of Pittsburgh P, 1977), pp. 111–132.

2. William Wordsworth, "Preface to Lyrical Ballads" (1850) in *The Prose Works of William Wordsworth*, ed. W. J. B. Owen and Jane Worthington Smyser (Oxford: Oxford UP, 1974), pp. 119–143.

3. In his late essay, "The Imagination as Value" (1948), Stevens develops his idea that with "the man of strong powers, accustomed to thought, accustomed to the essays of the imagination . . . the whole imaginative substance changes" as compared to the mind of a shepherd boy, for instance (*NA* 151). Similarly, Stevens asks rhetorically in "About One of Marianne Moore's Poems" (1948) whether one of Moore's poems "make[s] us so aware of the reality with which it is concerned, because of the poignancy and penetration of the poet, that it forces something upon our consciousness" (*NA* 175).

4. William Wordsworth, *The Prelude 1799, 1805, 1850*, ed. Jonathan Wordsworth et al., Norton Critical Edition (New York and London: W. W. Norton, 1979), *1850*, III, ll. 176–179, p. 101.

5. Stevens' conscious conceptualization of grammatical categories is exceedingly rare, however. His poems contain slightly more numerous explicit references to sounds generally and to the sounds of words, as in "The Comedian as the Letter C," which Stevens described as a poem that puts into play the sound of the letter *c* found in different letter combinations (*Letters* #329, 397, and 862). There are also allusions to what used to be known as the "numbers" of poetry, as in Stevens' recourse to the word *syllable* in his poems, used over thirty times according to Thomas F. Walsh, *Concordance to the Poetry of Wallace Stevens* (University Park: Pennsylvania State UP, 1963).

6. Percy Bysshe Shelley, *A Defence of Poetry* in *Shelley's Poetry and Prose*, ed. Donald H. Reiman and Sharon B. Powers, Norton Critical Edition (New York: W. W. Norton, 1977), p. 481.

7. Brogan centers her argument about unity and fragmentation in Stevens' poetry on the distinction between metaphor and simile. Jacqueline Vaught Brogan, *Stevens and Simile: A Theory of Language* (Princeton: Princeton UP, 1986).

8. Aristotle, in *The Categories*, chapter IV, defines ten categories of the predication of being and shows that the distinctions among these categories correspond to (Benveniste would say *derive from*) grammatical distinctions in Greek such as the difference between media tantum and the perfective mode, the difference between active and passive modes, or the classification of adjectives (for example, categories of substance, quantity, position). Although Emile Benveniste was not the first to highlight the interdependency of expression and existential situation (or *logos* and *physis*) in Aristotle's conception, his commentary on it is very clear. See his "Categories of Thought

and Language" in *Problems in General Linguistics*, trans. Mary Elizabeth Meed (Coral Gables: U of Miami P, 1966), pp. 55–64.

9. Emile Benveniste, "The Nominal Sentence" in *Problems in General Linguistics*, p. 131. Benveniste cites A. Meillet as providing the groundbreaking study defining the situation of the nominal sentence in Indo-European (M.S.L. [*Mémoires de la Société de linguistique de Paris*] XIV [1906]: 1–26). Meillet's argument is contested by Charles H. Kahn, *The Verb 'Be' in Ancient Greek*, chap. 4, pp. 85–184 in John W. M. Verhaar, ed., *The Verb 'Be' and its synonyms* (Part 6), (Dordrecht and Boston: D. Reidel, 1973).

10. Kahn avoids the term *nominal sentence* because, he says, it "tends to confuse two quite distinct contrasts: (1) between a sentence with an ordinary verb and a copulative sentence with *be*, and (2) between a sentence with any finite verb (including *be*) and a sentence with none." Kahn, *The Verb 'Be' in Ancient Greek*, p. 85. I will avoid technical discussions that are the terrain of specialists.

   As for the term *copula*, Benveniste designates as "copula" only statements of equivalence formed with the verb *to be*, while some other linguists extend the notion of the copula to embrace other means of attaching the attribute to the subject (see my discussion of Ernst Locker below), or even all joining words such as the conjunction *and*.

11. Benveniste, "The Nominal Sentence," pp. 137–138, 143–144.

12. Benveniste, "The Nominal Sentence," p. 131.

13. Ernst Locker, " 'Etre' et 'avoir': Leurs expressions dans les langues," *Anthropos* 49 (1954): 481–510. He includes references to Benveniste's Greek, Latin, and Spanish examples from the original of "The Nominal Sentence" ("La phrase nominale," 1950).

14. A striking example of the nonverbal copula used in an Indo-European language that neither Benveniste nor Locker mentions is to be found in modern Russian, in which two parts of a qualifying (adjectival) statement are simply juxtaposed when the statement is assumed to be in the present tense.

15. Benveniste, "The Nominal Sentence," pp. 137–138. The original reads: "[i]l a dû avoir un sens lexical défini, avant de tomber—au terme d'un long développement historique—au rang de «copule»." "La phrase nominale," repr. in *Problèmes de linguistique générale* (Paris: Gallimard, 1966), pp. 159–160.

16. Locker, " 'Etre' et 'avoir' ", p. 496.

17. Locker, " 'Etre' et 'avoir' ", p. 482.

18. "It is undoubtedly not by accident that the distinctly verbal conception of the copula's syntactic function, which inserts "being" into the dominant notion of acting, is found precisely in [the languages of] those nations which, however small originally, have managed to play a dominant role in world history and impose their political power and thoughts on most of the world" (Locker, " 'Être' et 'avoir' ", p. 500; my translation). Locker forgets that Indo-European speakers have not had the monopoly of durable imperial influence entailing both political power and the transmission of philosophical and linguistic culture. The historical growth of China, as well as the borrowing by other Asian countries of Chinese script and Confucian values, provides a counterexample.

19. Immanuel Kant, *Immanuel Kant's Critique of Pure Reason*, trans. Norman Kemp Smith (London: Macmillan, [1929 + 1933] 1983), pp. 504–505. Kant's section heading for this excerpt is "Of the Impossibility of the Ontological Proof of the Existence of God," Part 2, Div. 2, Book 2, ch. 3, sec. 4.

20. Jacques Derrida, "The Supplement of Copula: Philosophy before Linguistics" in Josué V. Harari, ed., *Textual Strategies: Perspectives in Post-Structuralist Criticism* (Ithaca and London: Cornell UP, 1979), pp. 82–120. *Textual Strategies* makes a few corrections and improvements to the English translation that first appeared in *Georgia Review* 30.2 (1976): 527–564.

21. Derrida is harsh with Benveniste's structuralist approach, seemingly because it ignores the one-way "history" that Derrida claims for the (to me, problematic) relationship between philosophy (or ideas) and linguistics (which Derrida implicitly equates with languages). Although Benveniste might be qualified as Whorfian and Derrida as anti-Whorfian, we do not have to categorize them this way. Their explanations are best seen not as being mutually exclusive but as asking different questions—and getting different answers—about the semantic manifestations of "being" in language.

22. Derrida, "The Supplement of Copula," p. 117.

23. A. C. Graham notes that when a Chinese translator tried to render this passage from English into Chinese, "Kant's argument disappears; successful translation is impossible because Chinese does not allow of the mistake Kant is exposing." A. C. Graham, " 'Being' in Classical Chinese" in John W. M. Verhaar, ed., *The Verb 'Be' and its Synonyms*, Part 1, *Classical Chinese. Athapaskan. Mundari* (Dordrecht and Boston: D. Reidel, 1967), p. 34. I will discuss some implications of the absence of *to be* in Chinese in chapter 4.

24. Here we see another limitation of Locker's generalizations when they reach beyond descriptive linguistics. The intellectuality of English and French, compared to Amerindian languages and Chinese, for instance, is clear. However, the English speaker's attitude toward language is much more dependent on coordinating language with the "empirical" world than is the French speaker's.

25. See Ludwig Wittgenstein, *Philosophical Investigations,* trans. G. E. M. Anscombe (Oxford: Basil Blackwell, 1976). §1–86 concern the language-game analogy generally. Wittgenstein develops the difference between the ostensive (pointing, naming) function of words and the various ways in which we make meaning with those words or names. Richard Rorty develops the proposition in "Is There a Problem About Fictional Discourse?" in chapter 7 of *Consequences of Pragmatism* (Minneapolis: U of Minnesota P, 1982), pp. 110–138.

26. Shelley, *A Defence of Poetry*, p. 481.

27. Vendler, one of the poem's rare commentators, assumes that Vincentine preexists. She interprets the poet's initial act as one of trying to "deprive" the creature of her humanity and interiority. For her, there is no question of the poet-painter trying to constitute a creature. See Helen Vendler, *Wallace Stevens: Words Chosen Out of Desire* (Knoxville: U of Tennessee P, 1984), pp. 15–16. The parallel with Mallarmé's "Hérodiade," seen by Benamou, also makes the poem unequivocally begin with an act of stripping away but, in his view, with the purpose of unveiling. See Mallarmé: "De mes robes, arôme aux farouches délices, / Sortirait le frisson blanc de ma nudité." See Michel Benamou, *L'Œuvre → Monde de Wallace Stevens* (Paris: Honoré Champion, 1975), p. 113.

28. Locker uses Zulu to counter the idea that the subject + predicate order is somehow more "natural" for making statements. Zulu expressions for "The man is big" and "a big man" are respectively *omuntu mkhulu* and *omuntu omkhulu.* The nominal subject comes second in both cases, the predicate or epithet first. Locker, " 'Etre' et 'avoir'," p. 489.

29. Semantically, the words of the poem give the impression of being chosen rather traditionally out of a given set of predominantly bipolar signifieds: small versus large, lean versus fat, animal versus human, nameless versus named, green among the colors of the rainbow versus green as one of the painter's palette of oil tubes (including perhaps burnt sienna and cobalt), earth versus sky, earth-sky versus heaven. The last canto of the final poem of "Notes Toward a Supreme Fiction" dialectically responds to the

categories of "The Apostrophe" in "fat girl, terrestrial, my summer, my night" and a future act in which "I call you by name, my green, my fluent mundo" (CP 406, 407).

30. Shelley, *A Defence of Poetry*, p. 483. The examples he mentions are "the choruses of Aeschylus, and the book of Job, and Dante's Paradise."

31. Richard Rorty, "Is There a Problem about Fictional Discourse?" in *Consequences of Pragmatism*, p. 136. Rorty gives only the Greek characters for *nomos, physis, episteme* and *poiesis.*

32. Rorty, "Is There a Problem about Fictional Discourse?" p. 136.

CHAPTER 4

1. An example is the summary of Schopenhauer quoted in "A Collect of Philosophy" (OP 273–274). Stevens' distance from philosophy as a "discipline" might be seen in the publishing history of this article: it was written for a professional philosophy journal in 1951 "but was judged by the editor to be better suited for a literary review" (*Wallace Stevens: Opus Posthumous*, ed. Samuel French Morse [New York: Knopf, 1957, 1982], p. xxxvi). It appears that no literary review ever did publish it during the poet's lifetime, but Stevens read the paper as a lecture at at least two American universities or colleges (OP, ed. Bates, p. 330). See also Peter A. Brazeau, " 'A Collect of Philosophy': The Difficulty of Finding What Would Suffice" in Frank Doggett and Robert Buttel, eds., *Wallace Stevens: A Celebration* (Princeton: Princeton UP, 1980), pp. 46–49.

2. *Letters* #729 to Barbara Church, February 27, 1950, p. 670.

3. Stevens was very conscious of the "shape" of his volumes, arranging them not chronologically or in a way that would show his own "progress," but alternating pieces of a mosaic within a frame while moving from beginning themes to new horizons at the end.

4. Eleanor Cook, *Poetry, Word-Play, and Word-War in Wallace Stevens* (Princeton: Princeton UP, 1988), p. 27.

5. I suspect a typographical error here. There needs to be a comma after "then."

6. Helen Vendler, *Wallace Stevens: Words Chosen Out of Desire* (Knoxville: U of Tennessee P, 1985), p. 49.

7. Among the critics who have taken "The Snow Man" seriously have been Blackmur, Winters, and more recently Vendler, Keyser, Fish, Bloom, Cook, and Bahti. See also Lakritz and Haft.

8. Marjorie Allen Seiffert, from "The Intellectual Tropics" (originally appeared in *Poetry* 23.3 [December 1923]: 156–60), repr. in Charles Doyle, ed., *Wallace Stevens: The Critical Heritage* (London, Boston, and Henley: Routledge and Kegan Paul, 1985), p. 45.

9. Harold Bloom, *Wallace Stevens: The Poems of Our Climate* (Ithaca: Cornell UP, 1977), pp. 53–63.

10. Timothy Bahti, "End and Ending: On the Lyric Techniques of Some Wallace Stevens Poems," *Modern Language Notes* 105. 5 (December 1990): 1052.

11. Richard A. Macksey, "The Climates of Wallace Stevens" in Roy Harvey Pearce and J. Hillis Miller, eds., *The Act of the Mind: Essays on the Poetry of Wallace Stevens* (Baltimore: Johns Hopkins UP, 1965), p. 195. Macksey gives no reference for the quotation from Santayana.

12. Bahti uses the phonetic pattern as a link in his argument that makes the antepenultimate "the" a key term; it looks back to the "the" of the title and beckons the reader towards the very language of the poem. See his *MLN* article, "End and Ending: On the Lyric Techniques of Some Wallace Stevens Poems."

13. Ralph Waldo Emerson, "Nature," chapt. 1, *Essays and Lectures*, ed. Joel Porte (New York: Library of America, 1988), p. 10. See the exegesis in Bloom, *Wallace Stevens: Poems of Our Climate*, p. 61.

14. Cook, *Poetry, Word-Play, and Word-War*, p. 50.

15. Cook, *Poetry, Word-Play, and Word-War*, p. 49.

16. For several noninclusive definitions of *tautologie*, however, see André Lalande, *Vocabulaire technique et critique de la philosophie* (Paris: Presses universitaires de France, 1983), pp. 1103–1104.

17. Ludwig Wittgenstein, *Tractatus Logico-Philosophicus*, trans. D. F. Pears and B. F. McGuinness (London: Routledge and Kegan Paul, [1922] 1961), p. 35, article 4.462. This translation is much more readable than the earlier English rendition by C. K. Ogden (London: Routledge and Kegan Paul, [1922], 1955) which reads "presenting" (p. 99) for Pears' and McGuinness' "representational," for instance.

18. Wittgenstein, trans. Pears and McGuinness, p. 34, article 4.4611.

19. Not only is there no lyrical "I," as Vendler stresses (*Words Chosen Out of Desire*, p. 48), but literally even the "one" may or may not be associated with the "snow man" of the title; similarly, it may or may not be excluded from the "listener" (the most reduced human representative) who experiences the not-feeling of misery.

20. In his *Poésies*, for example, Mallarmé's language techniques are the opposite of Stevens'. I am thinking of the disarticulation of his grammar (see "Toast

funèbre"), his dependence on juxtaposition or *éloignement* rather than grammatical function (see "Le Vitrier"), his progressive elimination of the verb *être* (noted by Derrida), his emphasis on visual page-space. Derrida, basing his analysis on other texts and other concepts than mine, notes that in Mallarmé the word *jeu* ("game") comes into play as the verb *être* ("to be") disappears. He cites Jacques Scherer, *L'Expression littéraire dans l'Œuvre de Mallarmé*, pp. 142 ff., as noting the progressive ellipsis of *être* in Mallarmé's work. See Jacques Derrida, *Dissemination* (Chicago: U of Chicago P, 1981), p. 216. See also de Man's reflection on Blanchot's analysis of Mallarmé's supposedly impersonal (and alienated) language in de Man, "Impersonality in the Criticism of Maurice Blanchot," chap. V of *Blindness and Insight: Essays in Contemporary Criticism* (New York: Oxford UP, 1971), pp. 60–78.

21.   A. C. Graham, *Disputers of the Tao: Philosophical Argument in Ancient China* (LaSalle, IL: Open Court, 1989), p. 389.

22.   A. C. Graham, *Disputers of the Tao*, p. 414. See pp. 412–414 for his demonstration and examples.

23.   A. C. Graham, " 'Being' in Classical Chinese" in W. M. Verhaar, ed., *The Verb 'Be' and Its Synonyms: Philosophical and Grammatical Studies*, Part 1 (Dordrecht, Holland: D. Reidel, 1967), p. 8. Although Graham attends only to classical Chinese in his examples, this part of his analysis applies to modern Chinese as well. See also Graham, " 'Being' in Western Philosophy Compared With 'Shih/Fei' and 'Yu/Wu' in Chinese Philosophy," as reprinted in his *Studies in Chinese Philosophy and Philosophical Literature* (Singapore: Institute of East Asian Philosophies, 1986), pp. 322–359.

24.   Jacques Gernet, *China and the Christian Impact: A Conflict of Cultures*, trans. Janet Lloyd (Cambridge: Cambridge UP, 1985), p. 242.

25.   The poem's main commentators have been Susan Weston, *Wallace Stevens: An Introduction to the Poetry* (New York: Columbia UP, 1977), pp. 20–24; Helen Vendler, *On Extended Wings: Wallace Stevens' Longer Poems* (Cambridge, MA: Harvard UP, 1969), pp. 75–78; Hugh Kenner, *A Homemade World* (London: M. Boyars, 1977), pp. 78–81; Beverly Coyle, *A Thought to be Rehearsed: Aphorism in Wallace Stevens' Poetry* (Ann Arbor: UMI Research Press, 1983), pp. 45–54. Taking a clue from the poem's title and from the Imagist cultural context of 1917, these critics have read the poem in terms of the relation between perception or sensation and thought or idea. My 1987 article takes the first steps in breaking away from this. See Beverly

Maeder, "Resemblance among Wallace Stevens' Blackbirds," *Etudes de lettres* (oct.-déc. 1987): 93–104.

26. See Coyle, *A Thought to be Rehearsed,* pp. 46, 54.

27. I place "rhymes" in quotation marks because the word *rhyme* is conventionally applied only to stressed syllables.

28. Benamou links it to the terrifying "birds of black" of "The Palace of the Babies" (*CP* 77) in Michel Benamou, "Wallace Stevens and the Symbolist Imagination," in Roy Harvey Pearce and J. Hillis Miller, eds. *The Act of the Mind: Essays on the Poetry of Wallace Stevens* (Baltimore: Johns Hopkins UP, 1965), p. 101.

29. We should remember that in the decade before Stevens started writing *Harmonium,* not only Freud but the home-grown William James were taking innovative views on the subjective and unconscious factors that go into constituting the object.

30. The syllogism would parallel that of the Philosopher in Ionesco's *Rhinoceros* who says, "Socrates was mortal; cats are mortal; therefore Socrates was a cat."

Where S = subject, P = predicate, and M = the middle term (or medium), the four basic formulae for valid syllogisms are:

1) M – P
$\underline{S – M}$
S – P

2) P – M
$\underline{S – M}$
S – P

3) M – P
$\underline{M – S}$
S – P

4) P – M
$\underline{M – S}$
S – P

Source: Anthony Flew, ed. consultant, *A Dictionary of Philosophy* (London: Pan Books, 1984).

31. William Wordsworth, *The Prelude, 1799, 1805, 1850,* ed. Jonathan Wordsworth et al., Norton Critical Edition (New York: Norton, 1979), *1850,* XII, ll. 83–87, p. 421.

32. Ralph Waldo Emerson, "Circles," *Essays and Lectures,* ed. Joel Porte (New York: Library of America, 1983), p. 403. All further references are from this opening page.

33. *After* ← O. E. *æfter* (adverb and preposition) = "behind in place or time." *Prefer* ← Latin prefix plus verbal form: L. *præ* (adverb and preposition) = "before, in front, in advance" + *ferre* = "to bear."

CHAPTER 5

1. Helen Vendler, *On Extended Wings: Wallace Stevens' Longer Poems* (Cambridge, MA: Harvard UP, 1969), p. 124. Vendler is the critic who has been the most sensitive to the play of Stevens' vocabulary and syntax in the poem.

2. Harold Bloom in *Wallace Stevens: The Poems of Our Climate* (Ithaca and London: Cornell UP, 1977), p. 119. Bloom also calls Vendler "Stevens' most astute rhetorical critic," while finding in "The Blue Guitar" the pattern of the "post-Enlightenment crisis poem," and not, as Vendler has said, a poem whose internal order is indifferent. Helen Vendler, *On Extended Wings*, pp. 119–120.

3. A. Walton Litz, *Introspective Voyager: The Poetic Development of Wallace Stevens* (New York: Oxford UP, 1972), p. 233 "The Man with the Blue Guitar," like "The Snow Man" and "Sunday Morning," is one of the most copiously analyzed and consistently mentioned poems of the pre–World War II period. Among the authors cited in my bibliography several stand out. Vendler, Bloom, and Rehder read the poem from beginning to end and provide the deepest and most detailed insight into the poem. A recent unpublished doctoral dissertation by Vejdovsky also probes the whole poem, notably for its subtle play of voice. Cook's interesting reading is very selective. Bates gives a good picture of the context of writing. Newcomb and Longenbach have treated its reception and publishing history, especially Newcomb's chapter 4. Articles by Brogan, MacLeod, and Weston have explored the allusion to Picasso, and MacLeod's book details Stevens' relation to modern art. More recently, Alan Filreis has documented the politico-literary right-left debate that is the occasion of the poem and has explicated parts of the poem in terms of Stevens' positioning within this debate. See also Stevens' own retrospective commentary on specific sections in letters written to Hi Simon (*Letters*, to Hi Simon, 1940, pp. 359–364) and to the translator of "The Blue Guitar" into Italian, Renato Poggioli (*Letters*, to Renato Poggioli, 1953, pp. 783–793).

4. Bloom, *Wallace Stevens: The Poems of our Climate*, p. 122.

5. William Wordsworth, "Essay Supplementary to the Preface" in *The Prose Works of William Wordsworth*, ed. W. J. B. Owen and Jane Worthington Smyser (Oxford: Oxford UP, 1974), p. 63.

6. Alan Filreis, *Modernism from Right to Left: Wallace Stevens, the Thirties and Literary Radicalism* (Cambridge and London: Cambridge UP, 1994), pp. 262–263.

7. Quoted in Charles Doyle, ed., *Wallace Stevens: The Critical Heritage* (London, Henley, and Boston: Routledge and Kegan Paul, 1985), p. 140.

8. Robert Emmett Monroe, "Figuration and Society in 'Owl's Clover,'" *Wallace Stevens Journal* 13.2, Special Issue: *Stevens and Politics* (Fall 1989): 127–149.

9. Filreis additionally attributes section III to the audience. For him it is a section in which "the detractors subject the guitarist's polemical language to a sort of historicist analysis." Filreis, *Modernism from Right to Left*, p. 265.

10. Bloom, *Wallace Stevens: The Poems of Our Climate*, p. 119. But neither Bloom nor any other critic examines why or how the audience's requirements are "wrong."

11. Bloom, *Wallace Stevens: The Poems of Our Climate*, p. 124 and Eleanor Cook, *Poetry, Word-Play, and Word-War in Wallace Stevens* (Princeton: Princeton UP, 1988), p. 143. I will suggest another—entirely contemporary or "contemporaneous"—association later.

12. T. S. Eliot, "Burnt Norton" (1936). Cook also sees the allusion to "Burnt Norton" in *Poetry, Word-Play, and Word-War*, p. 138.

13. Jacques Lacan, *Ecrits: A Selection*, trans. Alan Sheridan (New York: Norton, 1977). To go back to the original discussion of the "mirror stage" see Jacques Lacan, "Le stade du miroir comme formateur de la fonction du Je" in *Ecrits I* (Paris: Seuil, Points, 1970), pp. 89–97. I do not mean to consider Stevens' poem as a demonstration of the psychic distress Lacan attributed to this stage of development.

14. Joseph Carroll, *Wallace Stevens' Supreme Fiction: A New Romanticism* (Baton Rouge: Louisiana State UP, 1987), p. 177.

15. Quoted from an article on American poetry by Dorothy Van Ghent, a Marxist sympathizer, in the January 11, 1938 issue of *New Masses*. Doyle, ed., *Wallace Stevens: The Critical Heritage*, p. 180.

16. Filreis, *Modernism from Right to Left*, p. 280.

17. He cites three stages of events: "News incomparably more pretentious than any description of it, news, at first, of the collapse of our system, or, call it, of life"; then "news of a new world," uncertain from the start and still unknown; and "finally," as he says of the First World War, "news of a war, which was a renewal of what, if it was not the greatest war, became such by this continuation" (*NA* 20). In a contrasting tone, see his joking formulation of new year's greetings for 1937 in "[O]r as they say on the radio, a healthy prosperous and safe New Year" (*Letters* #356).

18. It may therefore seem remarkable that most academic criticism since Stevens' death in 1955 has focused on Stevens' way of distilling memories

of Dante, Keats, Whitman, Nietzsche, and Kant, and the *Book of Revelation* and other works into highly literate subtexts. This critical bias is consonant, as Alan Filreis has remarked, with Stevens' own exclusion of the polemically political "Owl's Clover" from his *Collected Poems* in 1954, after years during which he had also clearly recentered his attention on the private lyric. His literary canonization by (American) humanist critics of the sixties and seventies continued a critical practice that eschewed explicit confrontation with political issues. It was thus convenient for (American) Cold War critics to condone the noncommunist Stevens while ignoring leftist artists. See Filreis, *Modernism from Right to Left*, pp. 23–24. Melita Schaum has used lessons learned from the feminist reflection on image-making to attempt to break down the often reductive view of the relation between "art" and "politics." See Melita Schaum, "Lyrical Resistance: View of the Political in the Poetics of Wallace Stevens and H. D.," *Wallace Stevens Journal* 13.2, Special Issue: *Stevens and Politics:* (Fall 1989): 190–205.

Just as some of Stevens' contemporaries in the late thirties were measuring *Ideas of Order* and "Owl's Clover" against the demand for ideological engagement in the right-left debate, readers at the end of the twentieth century, with Milton Bates as vanguard, have started to reexamine the interaction between Stevens and his contemporary critics in the same light and to extend their query to Stevens' integration of the disaster of World War II into his slightly later poetry, most notably into "Notes toward a Supreme Fiction." See Milton Bates, *Wallace Stevens: A Mythology of Self* (Berkeley: U of California P, 1985). The special issue of the *Wallace Stevens Journal* 13.2 (Fall 1989) called *Stevens and Politics* demonstrates two centers of critical interest, the national right-left debate at the time of "Owl's Clover" (Monroe) and the question of Stevens' poetic reaction to war, World War I (Longenbach), but primarily World War II (Perloff and Schaum).

19. Cook, in *Poetry, Word-Play, and Word-War*, p. 149, mentions the importance of "bread" in the 1930s in the United States.

20. Burnshaw describes Stevens as a representative of what he called "a class menaced by the clashes between capital and labor." Doyle, ed., *Wallace Stevens: The Critical Heritage*, p. 140.

21. Filreis, *Modernism from Right to Left*, p. 284–288. Filreis also mentions that Stevens anachronistically wrote that he had been thinking of Truman here (*Letters* #789).

22. During the mid-thirties Stevens ordered books from booksellers in London and Paris and had access to French and English journals. By 1935 at the lat-

est he had started his correspondence with the Parisian bookseller, Anatole Vidal, whose portrait he mentions in "The Latest Freed Man." From Vidal he ordered mainly bibliophile books and contemporary French paintings but also the works of contemporary French writers such as the philosopher Alain.

23. Almost twenty years later, in 1953, Stevens would reply to a query by one of his correspondents that he "did have the Spanish Republicans in mind when [he] wrote *The Men that are Falling*" (*Letters* #881). Although this claim can be hardly be said to reflect a precise memory and may even seem self-serving, it seems obvious enough that in 1936 the Spanish Civil War was the narrow occasion for, or what Stevens would call the "nominal subject" of, "The Men That Are Falling." Another of its "subjects" is the World War I poem, "The Death of a Soldier" (1918, *CP* 97), which it revises by substituting "The Men That Are Falling" for "The soldier falls," while still presenting a single, exemplary case.

24. Capa's photographic reports on the war in Spain appeared regularly in *Vu*, *Regards*, *Ce Soir*, *Weekly Illustrated* (London), and *Life*. See Jean Lacoutre, William Manchester, and Fred Ritchin, *Magnum. 50 Ans de photographie* (Paris: Nathan, 1989), p. 446. Richard Whelan, in *Robert Capa: A Biography* (New York: Knopf, 1985, pp. 98–99), reproduces the two-page spread that appeared in the September 23, 1936 issue of *Vu*, bearing the title "La Guerre civile en Espagne." On the left-hand page, the subtitle, "Comment ils sont tombés" ("How They Fell") heads two photographs of a single soldier falling. On the right-hand page, five pictures illustrate "Comment ils ont fui" ("How They Fled") (*Vu* [1936]: 1106–1107).

25. O. W. Riegel, *Mobilizing for Chaos: The Story of the New Propaganda* (New Haven: Yale UP, 1934), p. 87. See also the U.S. Congress investigations into communist, Nazi, and other propaganda activities starting in 1930, and a wave of books from university and commercial presses on various aspects of propaganda, with such titles as *The Propaganda Menace* (1933), *Pressure Groups and Propaganda* (1935), *Propaganda and the News: or what makes you think so?* (1936), *Propaganda and Dictatorship* (1936), and *Propaganda in the Next War* (1938).

26. Frederick Lewis Schuman, *The Nazi Dictatorship: A Study in Social Pathology and the Politics of Fascism* (New York: Knopf, 1935), pp. 78, 83.

27. Filreis, *Modernism from Right to Left*, p. 285.

28. Photographs of the 1936 Nuremberg Nazi Party Congress show the stadium of the Zepplinwiese encircled by a dense alignment of columns of light, variously called vaults, columns, or stripes by the press, projected from tall

electric poles. This extravaganza brought together over 140,000 Nazi leaders. I should note in passing that the term "final solution," which appears as "A few final solutions" in section XXIII of "The Blue Guitar," was not yet used by the Nazi regime. It seems to have appeared first (as *Endlösung*) in an internal document written by Goering at the end of 1939 where it meant enclosing the Jews in camps. It came to denote extermination in 1941. See Hélène Coulonjou, "Hitler et la «solution finale»: le jour et l'heure" in François Bédarida, ed., *L'Allemagne de Hitler, 1933–1945* (Paris: Seuil, Points, 1991), pp. 262–270.

29. See Bloom, *Wallace Stevens: The Poems of Our Climate*, p. 126.

30. After several years of casting around, large-scale road tests of the Volkswagen finally began in 1937 with thirty prototypes of the "VW 30." Fabien Sabatès and Jacky Morel, *Cox en stock* (Paris: Massin, n.d.), pp. 12–16.

31. See John Hollander, "The Sound of the Music of Music and Sound" in Frank Doggett and Robert Buttel, eds., *Wallace Stevens: A Celebration* (Princeton: Princeton UP, 1980), pp. 235–255.

32. See again, "Add This to Rhetoric," discussed earlier in chapter 2, for the burden of expansion beyond reference that can be borne by the word "compose."

33. Frank Lentricchia, *Ariel and the Police: Michel Foucault, William James, Wallace Stevens* (Madison: U of Wisconsin P, 1988), p. 4.

34. Lentricchia, *Ariel and the Police*, p. 18. See also pp. 4–19 passim.

35. Bloom reads Stevens' echoes as an acknowledgment of the Shelleyan ideal of a poetry that has its sights set on broadening rather than reducing our world as Marxist criticism does. Bloom, *Wallace Stevens: The Poems of Our Climate*, pp. 120–122.

36. For an analysis of the implications of the audience for the lyric genre, see Beverly Maeder, "Performance, Lyric, and the Audience's Demands in Wallace Stevens' 'The Man with the Blue Guitar' " in Peter Halter, ed., *Performance*, Swiss Papers on English Language and Literature 11 (Tuebingen: Gunter Narr, 1999), pp. 129–144.

CHAPTER 6

1. Helen Vendler, " 'Notes toward a Supreme Fiction': Allegorical Personae," *Wallace Stevens Journal* 17.2 (Fall 1993): 161.

2. Robert Rehder, *The Poetry of Wallace Stevens* (New York: St. Martin's P, 1988), p. 155–156.

3. Julia Kristeva, *La révolution du langage poétique, L'avant-garde à la fin du xixe siècle: Lautréamont et Mallarmé* (Paris: Seuil, Points, 1985), especially the theoretical introduction, "Sémiotique et symbolique," pp. 17–100. For the gist of her argument, see selections from the parts of Margaret Waller's translation reproduced in Toril Moi, ed., *The Kristeva Reader* (Oxford and Cambridge, MA: Blackwell, 1986), "Revolution in Poetic Language," pp. 89–136.

4. The "tock" (L. *toccare*, of onomatopoetic origin) realizes one of its wish-fulfilling potentials in the " 'touch that topples men and rock' " of X. In an opposing move, "the touch of the senses" in XVIII fulfills the need for fusion between the intimate self and guitar-playing.

5. "Man in a Room" (1919), in William Carlos Williams, *The Collected Poems of William Carlos Williams*, eds. A. Walton Litz and Christopher MacGowan (New York: New Directions, 1986), vol. 1, p. 123. Stevens' "Blue buds or pitchy blooms" also recall Williams' "Nor ditch-pool nor green thing" in the same poem.

6. Marie Borroff, "Sound Symbolism as Drama in Wallace Stevens," *ELH* 48 (1981): 931.

7. Milton J. Bates, *Wallace Stevens: A Mythology of Self* (Berkeley and London: U of California P, 1985), p. 287.

8. J. Hillis Miller, *Poets of Reality* (Cambridge, MA: Harvard UP, 1965), p. 260.

9. Miller, *Poets of Reality*, p. 261.

10. Holmes cites Riddel, Miller, Vendler, Frye, Hollander, Perloff, Pladott, and Turner in Barbara Holmes, *The Decomposer's Art: Ideas of Music in the Poetry of Wallace Stevens* (New York, Bern, Frankfurt and Paris: Peter Lang, 1991), p. 116. Her attempt to draw a tighter circle around the terms by using music history and definitions from musicology is only slightly more convincing. See especially chapter 4, "A New Resemblance" (pp. 102–137), in which she treats questions of structure, drawing on literature describing "variations" from the days of Haydn and Mozart, up through Brahms (with whom Holmes sees Stevens as having an affinity), and the early moderns. Most of her examples correspond to the works Willi Apel mentions in *The Harvard Dictionary of Music*, 2nd ed. (Cambridge, MA: Belknap Press of Harvard UP, 1969).

11. For Holmes, "Thirteen Ways" are close to the classical form of variations with their "highly structured, programmatic formats." She helpfully sees this poem and "Six Significant Landscapes" as having a "structural unity [that] is episodic rather than developmental; a sense of closure or full ca-

dence occurs at the end of each variation." Holmes, *The Decomposer's Art*, p. 121.

12. Willi Apel, *The Harvard Dictionary of Music*, 2nd ed., "Improvisation," p. 404.

13. Holmes, *The Decomposer's Art*, p. 120.

14. Holmes, *The Decomposer's Art*, p. 127.

15. Holmes, *The Decomposer's Art*, p. 127. She gives no examples.'

16. Holmes, *The Decomposer's Art*, p. 9. She quotes the beginning of this passage but gives the impression that Stevens is formulating a general rule and not simply describing the ruling paradigm of this section of "The Man with the Blue Guitar."

17. Anca Rosu, *The Metaphysics of Sound in Wallace Stevens* (Tuscaloosa: U of Alabama P, 1994), p. 113.

18. Several writers have tried to establish empirical relationships—relationships of influence, for instance—between Stevens' works and specific composers or musicians. Linebarger mentions some of these in David M. Linebarger, "On Hearing Modern American Music in Stevens' Poetry," *Wallace Stevens Journal* 22.1 (Spring 1998): 57–71, and interprets sections III and IV of "The Man with the Blue Guitar" as alluding to the pianist Henry Cowell.

19. Rudolf Arnheim, "A Stricture on Space and Time," *Critical Inquiry* 4 (1977–1978): 652.

20. Arnheim, "A Stricture on Space and Time," pp. 653–654. It should be noted that most of the examples he gives concern experiences in which the discrepancy is not entirely within either the musical or the visual sphere but between them.

21. Theodor Adorno, "Zemlinsky," *Quasi una Fantasia* (London and New York: Verso, 1992), p. 123. For the original German edition, see Theodor W. Adorno, "Zemlinsky," *Quasi una Fantasia, Musikalische Schriften* III, in *Gesammelte Schriften*, Band 16 (Frankfurt am Main: Suhrkamp, 1978), p. 362.

22. Victor Zuckerkandl, *Sound and Symbol: Music and the External World*, Bollingen Series XLIV, trans. Willard R. Trask (Princeton: Princeton UP, 1969), p. 233.

23. The section's Picasso and his "hoard of destructions" has been read as a reference to the artist's celebrated painting *Guernica*, memorializing the horrors of the bombing of this Spanish town. But Ronald Sukenick indicated Stevens' actual source in 1967 in his *Musing the Obscure*: the source is Christian Zervos' interview with Picasso, which appeared as "Conversation

avec Picasso" in *Cahiers d'Art* 10 (1935). See A. Walton Litz, *Introspective Voyager: The Poetic Development of Wallace Stevens* (New York: Oxford UP, 1972), p. 298, n. 69. Weston discusses Stevens' debt to *Cahiers d'Art* in Susan Brown Weston, "The Artist as Guitarist: Stevens and Picasso," *Criticism* 17 (1975): 111–120, and MacLeod sets the record straight with ample, chronologically detailed documentation in Glen MacLeod, "Stevens and Surrealism: The Genesis of 'The Man with the Blue Guitar,' " *American Literature* 59 (October 1987): 359–377 (reproduced with additions in his *Wallace Stevens and Modern Art*, Chapter 3). Finally, Robert Rehder provides a lengthy and well-informed note in his book, *The Poetry of Wallace Stevens*, pp. 311–312, n. 10.

In his interview with Zervos, "Conversation avec Picasso," Picasso calls his work a *"somme de destructions"* (*Cahiers d'Art* 10 [1935]: 173)—that is, an accumulation of destructions. He describes painters up to his time as having painted by adding each day to their pictures, whereas he claims to paint by a process of "destroying" his pictures, but losing nothing because what he removes from one part of the painting reappears somewhere else. Picasso seems to be describing his process of reworking the very composition of his canvases as he goes along.

24. Walter Pater, "The School of Giorgione," *The Renaissance: Studies in Art and Poetry* in *Walter Pater: Three Major Texts*, ed. William E. Buckler (New York and London: New York UP, 1986), p. 158. See the comment by James Anderson Winn, *Unsuspected Eloquence: A History of the Relations between Poetry and Music* (New Haven: Yale UP, 1981), p. 290.

25. Walter Pater, "Style," *Appreciations* in *Walter Pater: Three Major Texts*, p. 413.

26. Stevens gives a gloss of his Latin *ex* in terms of his imagination-reality dichotomy, first in its spatial dimension: "The imagination takes us out of (Ex) reality into a pure irreality;" then in its temporal dimension (of having already changed): "One has this sense of irreality often in the presence of morning light on cliffs which then rise from a sea that has ceased to be real and is therefore a sea of Ex." *Letters* #404.

27. Some contemporary musicologists and linguists, freeing themselves from the sensation-thought dichotomy, have tried to define the purely cognitive function of music.

28. Litz, working within another conceptual scheme, describes XXVI (and VI) as expressing a longing for living in space, free of time. For him the sections show that it is an impossible but necessary longing that reveals the limits of Wallace Stevens' romanticism. Litz, *Introspective Voyager*, p. 249.

29. Bloom, *Wallace Stevens: The Poems of Our Climate* (Ithaca: Cornell UP, 1977), p. 130: "[T]he trope of *pathos* or Power, 'the lion in the lute,' attempts to outface the *ethos* of nature and Fate, 'the lion locked in stone.'"

30. Vendler, *On Extended Wings: Wallace Stevens' Longer Poems* (Cambridge, MA: Harvard UP, 1969), p. 129.

31. Vendler, *On Extended Wings*, p. 130. Vendler interprets this section as a mockery of man vehicled by a rhetorical form that is monotonous and primitive and full of artifice.

32. Paul Ricœur, "Life in Quest of Narrative" in David Wood, ed., *On Paul Ricœur: Narrative and Interpretation* (London: Routledge, Warwick Studies in Philosophy and Literature, 1991), pp. 20–33. See also Hayden White, *The Content of the Form: Narrative Discourse and the Representation of Reality* (Baltimore: Johns Hopkins UP, 1987), especially chap. 1, "The Value of Narrativity in the Representation of Reality," pp. 1–25.

33. Bloom, *Wallace Stevens: The Poems of Our Climate*, p. 135.

34. Bloom, *Wallace Stevens: The Poems of Our Climate*, p. 135; Rehder, *The Poetry of Wallace Stevens*, p. 173; Vendler, *On Extended Wings*, pp. 123–24; Eleanor Cook, *Poetry, Word-Play, and Word-War in Wallace Stevens* (Princeton: Princeton UP, 1988), pp. 148–51.

35. Vendler, *On Extended Wings*, p. 124. She judges the poem generally as "incapable of the vastnesses explored by the later long poems" because of the presence of "the controlling figure with his reductive guitar." I hope to have shown that the figure is not necessarily reductive but suggests an area of exploration almost inaccessible to words.

36. Cook, *Poetry, Word-Play, and Word-War*, p. 150.

37. Timothy Bahti, "End and Ending: On the Lyric Technique of Some Wallace Stevens Poems," *Modern Language Notes* 105.5 (Dec. 1990): 1058, 1061.

EPILOGUE

1. Jacqueline Vaught Brogan, *Stevens and Simile: A Theory of Language* (Princeton: Princeton UP, 1986). See her comment on "Prologues to What is Possible," concentrated solely on the issue of the trope of metaphor as threatening unity, pp. 15–18, 111–112.

2. J. Hillis Miller, "Deconstructing the Deconstructors," *Diacritics* (Summer 1975): 31.

3. Helen Vendler, *On Extended Wings: Wallace Stevens' Longer Poems* (Cambridge, MA: Harvard UP, 1969), p. 307.

4. Eleanor Cook, *Poetry, Word-Play, and Word-War in Wallace Stevens* (Princeton: Princeton UP, 1988), pp. 297–301.

5. The Huntington Library, WAS 4154. The six poems are "What We See Is What We Think," "A Golden Woman in a Silver Mirror," "Old Lutheran Bells at Home," "Questions Are Remarks," "Study of Images I," and "Study of Images II" (*CP* 459–465).

6. Barbara M. Fisher, *Wallace Stevens: The Intensest Rendezvous* (Charlottesville and London: UP of Virginia, 1990), p. 148.

7. Vendler gives this expression as an example of "the order of transcendence of kind" in Helen Vendler, *Wallace Stevens: Words Chosen Out of Desire* (Knoxville: U of Tennessee P, 1984), p. 74. Fisher sees it as "a superlative abstraction, a unique universal commanding all the particulars of its class." See Fisher, *Wallace Stevens: The Intensest Rendezvous*, p. 151.

8. The poem is mentioned in this tenor-vehicle way, for instance, in B. J. Leggett, *Wallace Stevens and Poetic Theory: Conceiving the Supreme Fiction* (Chapel Hill and London: U of North Carolina P, 1987), p. 193.

9. David Walker, *The Transparent Lyric: Reading and Meaning in the Poetry of Stevens and Williams* (Princeton: Princeton UP, 1984), p. 81. If "Metaphor as Degeneration" is mentioned by many only in passing, Walker is the only one to analyze it, if summarily (pp. 81–83).

10. Vendler, *On Extended Wings*, p. 58.

11. J. Hillis Miller, *Poets of Reality: Six Twentieth-Century Writers* (Cambridge, MA: Harvard UP, 1965), p. 281. Miller describes in these terms both this river and the one in "Metaphor as Degeneration."

12. Harold Bloom, *Wallace Stevens: The Poems of Our Climate* (Ithaca and London: Cornell UP, 1977), pp. 365–366.

13. William Doreski, *The Modern Voice in American Poetry* (Gainesville: UP of Florida, 1995), p. 33.

14. Vendler, *Wallace Stevens: Words Chosen*, pp. 62, 74. Vendler's reading seems to have been the most fertile for critics, along with the older work, Frank Doggett, *Stevens' Poetry of Thought* (Baltimore: Johns Hopkins UP, 1966), pp. 68–74. Fisher gives a detailed reading of the metaphorical itinerary of the poem around her concepts of threshold and temple and relates the river with the sacred river in Psalm 46. Fisher, *Wallace Stevens: The Intensest Rendezvous*, pp. 147–155.

15. Vendler, *Wallace Stevens: Words Chosen*, p. 75.

16. The "third commonness," articulating the metamorphoses into the senses, also connotes sense pleasure. It recalls, as Vendler accurately reminds us, the epigraph to "Evening Without Angels" (CP 136): "the great interests of man: air and light, the joy of having a body, the voluptuousness of looking," attributed to Mario Rossi. Vendler, *Wallace Stevens: Words Chosen*, p. 76.

SELECTED BIBLIOGRAPHY

1. WORKS AND OTHER COLLECTED MATERIALS BY WALLACE STEVENS

Stevens, Wallace. *The Collected Poems of Wallace Stevens*. New York: Knopf, 1954.

———. *Letters of Wallace Stevens*. Edited by Holly Stevens. New York: Knopf, 1966.

———. *The Necessary Angel: Essays on Reality and the Imagination*. New York: Knopf, 1951.

———. *Opus Posthumous*. Edited by Samuel French Morse. New York: Knopf, 1957.

———. *Opus Posthumous*. Revised, enlarged, and corrected ed. Edited by Milton J. Bates. New York: Knopf, 1989.

———. *The Palm at the End of the Mind: Selected Poems and a Play*. Edited by Holly Stevens. New York: Knopf, 1972.

———. *"Sur Plusieurs Beaux Sujects": Wallace Stevens' Commonplace Book*. Edited by Milton J. Bates. Stanford: Stanford University Press, 1989.

2. WORKS ENTIRELY OR PARTIALLY ABOUT WALLACE STEVENS

Altieri, Charles. "Wallace Stevens' Metaphors of Metaphor: Poetry as Theory." *American Poetry* 1.1 (1983): 27–48.

Bahti, Timothy. "End and 'Ending': On the Lyric Techniques of Some Wallace Stevens Poems." *MLN* 105.5 (December 1990): 1046–1062.

Bates, Milton J. *Wallace Stevens: A Mythology of Self*. Berkeley and Los Angeles: University of California Press, 1985.

Benamou, Michel. "Displacements of Parental Space: American Poetry and French Symbolism." *Boundary 2: A Journal of Postmodern Literature* 5.2 (Winter 1977): 471–486.

———. *L'Œuvre → Monde de Wallace Stevens*. Paris: Librairie Honoré Champion, 1975.

———. "Wallace Stevens and the Symbolist Imagination." In *The Act of the Mind: Essays on the Poetry of Wallace Stevens*, edited by Roy Harvey Pearce and J. Hillis Miller, pp. 92–119. Baltimore: Johns Hopkins University Press, 1965.

Blackmur, R. P. "Examples of Wallace Stevens." *Hound and Horn* 2 (1932): 223–255. Reprinted in *Wallace Stevens: The Critical Heritage*, edited by Charles Doyle, pp. 95–125. London, Boston and Henley: Routledge & Kegan Paul, 1985.

———. *Language as Gesture*. New York: 1952; repr. London: Allen & Unwin, 1961.

Bloom, Harold. *Wallace Stevens: The Poems of Our Climate*. Ithaca and London: Cornell University Press, 1977.

Bornstein, George. *Transformations of Romanticism in Yeats, Eliot and Stevens*. Chicago: University of Chicago Press, 1976.

Borroff, Marie. "Sound Symbolism as Drama in the Poetry of Wallace Stevens." *ELH* 48 (1981): 914–934.

———. "Wallace Stevens' World of Words, Parts 1 & 2." *Modern Philology* 74.1 (August 1976): 42–66; and 74.3 (November 1976): 171–193.

Brazeau, Peter. *Parts of a World: Wallace Stevens Remembered*. New York: Random House, 1983.

Brogan, Jacqueline Vaught. *Stevens and Simile: A Theory of Language*. Princeton: Princeton University Press, 1986.

———. "Stevens and Stevenson: The Guitarist's Guitarist." *American Literature* 59 (October 1987): 228–241.

Buttel, Robert. *Wallace Stevens: The Making of 'Harmonium.'* Princeton: Princeton University Press, 1967.

Carroll, Joseph. *Wallace Stevens' Supreme Fiction: A New Romanticism*. Baton Rouge: Louisiana State University Press, 1987.

Cook, Eleanor. "Directions in Reading Wallace Stevens: Up, Down, Across." In *Lyric Poetry: Beyond New Criticism*, edited by Chaviva Hosek and Patricia Parker, pp. 298–309. Ithaca: Cornell University Press, 1985.

———. *Poetry, Word-Play, and Word-War in Wallace Stevens*. Princeton: Princeton University Press, 1988.

Costello, Bonnie. "Effects of an Analogy: Wallace Stevens and Painting." In *Wallace Stevens: The Poetics of Modernism*, edited by Albert Gelpi, pp. 65–85. Cambridge: Cambridge University Press, 1985.

Coyle, Beverly. *A Thought to Be Rehearsed: Aphorism in Wallace Stevens' Poetry*. Ann Arbor: UMI Research Press, 1983.

Doggett, Frank. *Wallace Stevens' Poetry of Thought*. Baltimore: Johns Hopkins University Press, 1966.

————. *Wallace Stevens: The Making of the Poem*. Baltimore: Johns Hopkins University Press, 1980.

————, and Robert Buttel, eds. *Wallace Stevens: A Celebration*. Princeton: Princeton University Press, 1980.

Doreski, William. "Fictive Music: The Iridescent Notes of Wallace Stevens." *The Wallace Stevens Journal* 20.1 (Spring 1996): 55–75.

————. *The Modern Voice in American Poetry*. Gainesville: University Press of Florida, 1995.

Doyle, Charles, ed. *Wallace Stevens: The Critical Heritage*. London, Boston, and Henley: Routledge & Kegan Paul, 1985.

Filreis, Alan. *Modernism from Right to Left: Wallace Stevens, the Thirties and Literary Radicalism*. Cambridge: Cambridge University Press, 1994.

————. "Stevens, 'J. Ronald Lane Latimer,' and the Alcestis Press." *The Wallace Stevens Journal* 17.2 (Fall 1993): 180–202.

————. *Wallace Stevens and the Actual World*. Princeton: Princeton University Press, 1991.

Fish, Stanley. *Is There a Text in This Class?* Cambridge, MA: Harvard University Press, 1980.

Fisher, Barbara M. *Wallace Stevens: The Intensest Rendezvous*. Charlottesville: University of Virginia Press, 1990.

Frye, Northrop. "The Realistic Oriole: A Study of Wallace Stevens." In *Wallace Stevens: A Collection of Critical Essays*, edited by Marie Borroff, pp. 161–176. Englewood Cliffs, NJ: Prentice-Hall, 1963.

Gelpi, Albert. "Stevens and Williams: The Epistemology of Modernism." In *Wallace Stevens: The Poetics of Modernism*, edited by Albert Gelpi, pp. 3–23. Cambridge: Cambridge University Press, 1985.

————, ed. *Wallace Stevens: The Poetics of Modernism*. Cambridge: Cambridge University Press, 1985.

Halliday, Mark. *Stevens and the Interpersonal*. Princeton: Princeton University Press, 1991.

Hammond, Mac. "On the Grammar of Wallace Stevens." In *The Act of the Mind: Essays on the Poetry of Wallace Stevens*, edited by Roy Harvey Pearce and J. Hillis Miller, pp. 179–184. Baltimore: Johns Hopkins University Press, 1965.

Hollander, John. "The Sound of the Music of Music and Sound." In *Wallace Stevens: A Celebration*, edited by Frank Doggett and Robert Buttel, pp. 235–255. Princeton: Princeton University Press, 1980.

Holmes, Barbara. *The Decomposer's Art: Ideas of Music in the Poetry of Wallace Stevens*. New York and Bern: Peter Lang, 1990.

Juhasz, Suzanne. *Metaphor and the Poetry of Williams, Pound and Stevens*. Lewisburg, PA: Bucknell University Press, 1974.

Kenner, Hugh. *A Homemade World*. London: M. Boyars, 1977.

Kermode, Frank. *Wallace Stevens*. Edinburgh and London: Oliver & Boyd Ltd., 1960.

———. "Wallace Stevens, Dwelling Poetically in Connecticut." In *An Appetite for Poetry: Essays in Literary Interpretation*. London: Collins, 1989, pp. 79–96.

King, Terrance. "The Semiotic Poetry of Wallace Stevens." *Semiotica* 23 (1978): 77–98.

Kronick, Joseph. "The Metamorphic Stevens." *The Wallace Stevens Journal* 6.1/2 (Spring 1982): 3–10.

Lakirtz, Andrew M. *Modernism and the Other in Stevens, Frost, and Moore*. Gainesville: University Press of Florida, 1996.

Leggett, B. J. "Apollonian and Dionysian in 'Peter Quince at the Clavier.'" *The Wallace Stevens Journal* 14.1 (Spring 1990): 39–61.

———. *Wallace Stevens and Poetic Theory: Conceiving the Supreme Fiction*. Chapel Hill: University of North Carolina Press, 1987.

Lensing, George. *Wallace Stevens: A Poet's Growth*. Baton Rouge: Louisiana State University Press, 1986.

Lentricchia, Frank. *Ariel and the Police: Michel Foucault, William James, Wallace Stevens*. Madison: University of Wisconsin Press, 1988.

Litz, A. Walton. *Introspective Voyager: The Poetic Development of Wallace Stevens*. New York: Oxford University Press, 1972.

———. "Space and Time in 'Notes toward a Supreme Fiction.'" *The Wallace Stevens Journal* 17.2 (Fall 1993): 162–167.

———. "Wallace Stevens' Defense of Poetry: 'La Poésie Pure,' the New Romantic, and the Pressure of Reality." In *Romantic and Modern: Revaluations of Literary Tradition*, edited by George Bornstein, pp. 111–132. Pittsburgh: University of Pittsburgh Press, 1977.

Longenbach, James. *Wallace Stevens: The Plain Sense of Things*. Oxford: Oxford University Press, 1991.

Macksey, Richard A. "The Climates of Wallace Stevens." In *The Act of the Mind: Essays on the Poetry of Wallace Stevens*, edited by. Roy Harvey Pearce and J. Hillis Miller, pp. 185–223. Baltimore: Johns Hopkins University Press, 1965.

MacLeod, Glen. "Stevens and Surrealism: The Genesis of 'The Man with the Blue Guitar.'" *American Literature* 59 (October 1987): 359–377.

————. *Wallace Stevens and Modern Art: From the Armory Show to Abstract Expressionism*. New Haven: Yale University Press, 1993.

Maeder, Beverly. "Performance, Lyric, and the Audience's Demands in Wallace Stevens' 'The Man with the Blue Guitar.' " In *Performance*, edited by Peter Halter, pp. 129–144. Swiss Papers in English Language and Literature, No. 11. Tuebingen: Gunter Narr, 1999.

————. "Resemblance among Wallace Stevens' Blackbirds." *Etudes de lettres* (oct.-déc. 1987): 93–104.

Marsh, Alec. "Stevens and Williams: The Economics of Metaphor." *The Williams Carlos Williams Review* 18.2 (Fall 1992): 37–49.

Miller, J. Hillis. "Deconstructing the Deconstructors" (Review of Joseph N. Riddel, *The Inverted Bell: Modernism and the Counterpoetics of William Carlos Williams*). *Diacritics* (Summer 1975): 24–31.

————. "Impossible Metaphor." In *Tropes, Parables, Performatives*. Hemel Hempstead: Harvester Wheatsheaf, 1990, pp. 213–226.

————. *Poets of Reality: Six Twentieth-Century Writers*. Cambridge, MA: Harvard University Press, 1965.

————. *Tropes, Parables, Performatives*. Hemel Hempstead: Harvester Wheatsheaf, 1990 .

————. *The Linguistic Moment*. Princeton: Princeton University Press, 1985.

————. "Theoretical and Atheoretical in Stevens." In *Wallace Stevens: A Celebration*, edited by Frank Doggett and Robert Buttel, pp. 274–285. Princeton: Princeton University Press, 1980.

Morris, Adelaide Kirby. *Wallace Stevens: Imagination and Faith*. Princeton: Princeton University Press, 1974.

Newcomb, John Timberman. *Wallace Stevens and Literary Canons*. Jackson: University of Missouri Press, 1992.

Nyquist, Mary. "Musing on Susanna's Music." In *Lyric Poetry: Beyond New Criticism*, edited by Chaviva Hosek and Patricia Parker. Ithaca: Cornell University Press, 1985, pp. 310–327.

Parker, Patricia. "The Motive for Metaphor: Stevens and Derrida." *The Wallace Stevens Journal* 7.3/4 (Fall 1983): 76–88.

Pearce, Roy Harvey and J. Hillis Miller, eds. *The Act of the Mind: Essays on the Poetry of Wallace Stevens*. Baltimore: Johns Hopkins University Press, 1963.

Perloff, Marjorie. "Pound/Stevens: Whose Era?" In *The Dance of the Intellect: Studies in the Poetry of the Pound Tradition*. Cambridge: Cambridge University Press, 1985, pp. 1–32.

————. "The Supreme Fiction and the Impasse of the Modernist Lyric." In *Wallace Stevens: The Poetics of Modernism*, edited by Albert Gelpi, pp. 41–64. Cambridge: Cambridge University Press, 1985.

Quinn, Sister Bernetta. "Metamorphosis in Wallace Stevens." *Sewanee Review* 60 (Spring 1952): 230–252.

Rehder, Robert. *The Poetry of Wallace Stevens*. New York: St. Martin's Press, 1988.

Richardson, Joan. *Wallace Stevens: The Early Years, 1879–1923*. New York: William Morrow, 1986.

————. *Wallace Stevens: The Later Years, 1923–1955*. New York: William Morrow, 1988.

Riddel, Joseph N. "Bloom—A Commentary—Stevens." *The Wallace Stevens Journal* 1.3/4 (Fall/Winter 1977): 111–119.

————. "The Climate of Our Poems." *The Wallace Stevens Journal* 7.3/4 (Fall 1983): 59–75.

————. "The Contours of Stevens Criticism." In *The Act of the Mind: Essays on the Poetry of Wallace Stevens*, edited by Roy Harvey Pearce and J. Hillis Miller, pp. 243–276. Baltimore: Johns Hopkins University Press, 1965.

————. "Interpreting Stevens: An Essay on Poetry and Thinking" (Review of Helen Vendler, *On Extended Wings: Wallace Stevens' Longer Poems*). *Boundary 2: A Journal of Postmodern Literature* 1.1 (Fall 1972): 79–97.

————. "Metaphoric Staging: Stevens' Beginning Again of the 'End of the Book'." In *Wallace Stevens: A Celebration*, edited by Frank Doggett and Robert Buttel, pp. 308–38. Princeton: Princeton University Press, 1980.

Rosu, Anca. *The Metaphysics of Sound in Wallace Stevens*. Tuscaloosa: University of Alabama Press, 1995.

Salusinszky, Imre. *Criticism in Society: Interviews With Jacques Derrida, Northrop Frye, Harold Bloom et al.* London: Methuen, 1987.

Schaum, Melita. "Lyric Resistance: Views of the Political in the Poetics of Stevens and H. D." *The Wallace Stevens Journal* 13.2 (Fall 1989): 191–205.

————.*Wallace Stevens and the Critical Schools*. Tuscaloosa: University of Alabama Press, 1989.

Simons, Hi. "Wallace Stevens and Mallarmé." *Modern Philology* 43 (1946): 235–259.

Steinman, Lisa. "Figure and Figuration in Stevens' Long Poems." *The Wallace Stevens Journal* 1.1 (Spring 1977): 10–16.

Stevens, Holly. *Souvenirs and Prophecies*. New York: Knopf, 1978.

Vendler, Helen. " 'Notes toward a Supreme Fiction': Allegorical Personae." *The Wallace Stevens Journal* 17.2 (Fall 1993): 147–161.

———. *On Extended Wings: Wallace Stevens' Longer Poems*. Cambridge, MA: Harvard University Press, 1969.

———. "Stevens and Keats' 'To Autumn'." In *Wallace Stevens: A Celebration*, edited by Frank Doggett and Robert Buttel, pp. 171–195. Princeton: Princeton University Press, 1980.

———. "The Qualified Assertions of Wallace Stevens." In *The Act of the Mind: Essays on the Poetry of Wallace Stevens*, edited by Roy Harvey Pearce and J. Hillis Miller, pp. 163–178. Baltimore: Johns Hopkins University Press, 1965.

———. *Wallace Stevens: Words Chosen Out of Desire*. Knoxville: University of Tennessee Press, 1984.

Vejdovsky, Boris. "Ideas of Order: Ethics and Topos in American Literature." Ph.D. diss., University of Lausanne, 1997.

Walker, David. *The Transparent Lyric: Reading and Meaning in the Poetry of Stevens and Williams*. Princeton: Princeton University Press, 1984.

Walsh, Thomas F. *Concordance to the Poetry of Wallace Stevens*. University Park: Pennsylvania State University Press, 1963.

Weston, Susan Brown. "The Artist as Guitarist: Stevens and Picasso." *Criticism* 17 (Spring 1975): 111–120.

———. *Wallace Stevens: An Introduction*. New York: Columbia University Press, 1977.

3. WORKS ON LINGUISTICS, PHILOSOPHY, LITERATURE, ART, MUSIC, AND HISTORY

Abrams, M. H. *The Mirror and the Lamp: Romantic Theory and the Critical Tradition*. New York: Oxford University Press, 1953.

Adorno, Theodor W. *Quasi una fantasia. Essays in Modern Music*. Translated by Rodney Livingstone. London: Verso, 1994; originally published as *Gesammelte Schriften*, Band 16: *Quasi Una Fantasia. Musikalische Schriften II*. Frankfurt-am-Main: Suhrkamp, 1978.

Apel, Willi. *Harvard Dictionary of Music*. 2nd rev. ed. Cambridge, MA: Harvard University Press, 1969.

Aristotle. *Aristotle's Art of Poetry*. Translated by Ingram Bywater. Introduction by W. Hamilton Fyfe. Oxford: Clarendon Press, 1940.

———. *The Poetics*. Translated by W. Hamilton Fyfe. Rev. ed. London: Heinemann, and Cambridge, MA: Harvard University Press, 1932.

———. *Poetics*. Translated by Ingram Bywater. *The Complete Works of Aristotle*. The Revised Oxford Translation, vol. 2. Edited by Jonathan Barnes. Princeton: Princeton University Press, 1984, pp. 2316–2340.

Arnheim, Rudolph. "A Stricture on Space and Time." *Critical Inquiry* 4 (1977–1978): 645–655.

Barzun, Jacques. *Critical Questions: On Music and Letters, Culture and Biography 1940–1980*. Chicago: University of Chicago Press, 1982.

Bédarida, François, ed. *L'Allemagne de Hitler, 1933–1945*. Paris: Seuil, 1991.

Benveniste, Emile. "Categories of Thought and Language." In *Problems in General Linguistics*. Translated by Mary Elizabeth Meek. Coral Gables: University of Miami Press, pp. 55–64.

———. "The Nominal Sentence." In *Problems in General Linguistics*. Translated by Mary Elizabeth Meek. Coral Gables: University of Miami Press, pp.131–144.

———. "The Linguistic Functions of 'To Be' and 'To Have.'" In *Problems in General Linguistics*. Translated by Mary Elizabeth Meek. Coral Gables: University of Miami Press, pp.163–180.

Cohen, Jean. *Structure du langage poétique*. Paris: Flammarion, 1966.

Coleridge, Samuel Taylor. *Biographia Literaria, or Biographical Sketches of My Literary Life and Opinions. The Collected Works of Samuel Taylor Coleridge*. vol. 7, part 1. Edited by James Engell and W. Jackson Bate. Princeton: Princeton University Press, and London: Routledge & Kegan Paul, 1983.

Cooper, David. *Metaphor*. Aristotelian Society Series. Oxford: Basil Blackwell, 1986.

De Man, Paul. *Allegories of Reading: Figural Language in Rousseau, Nietzsche, Rilke, and Proust*. New Haven and London: Yale University Press, 1979.

———. "Impersonality in the Criticism of Blanchot." In *Blindness and Insight*. New York: Oxford University Press, 1971, pp. 60–78.

Derrida, Jacques. *Dissemination*. Translated and with an Introduction by Barbara Johnson. Chicago: University of Chicago Press, 1981.

———. "White Mythology: Metaphor in the Text of Philosophy." In *Margins of Philosophy*. Translated by Alan Bass. Chicago: University of Chicago Press, 1982.

———. "The Supplement of Copula: Philosophy Before Linguistics." Translated by Josué Harari and James Creech. In *Textual Strategies: Perspectives in Post-Structuralist Criticism*, edited by Josué V. Harari, pp. 82–120. Ithaca and London: Cornell University Press, 1979.

Eliot, T. S. "The Music of Poetry." In *Selected Prose*. Harmondsworth: Penguin, 1953, pp. 53–64.

———. "The Perfect Critic." In *The Sacred Wood: Essays on Poetry and Criticism*. 6th ed. London: Methuen, 1948, pp. 1–16.

Foucault, Michel. *The Order of Things: An Archaeology of the Human Sciences*. A translation of *Les Mots et les choses*. New York: Random House, Vintage, 1973.

———. *This Is Not a Pipe*. Translated by James Harkness. Berkeley and Los Angeles: University of California Press, 1983.

Frye, Northrop. *Anatomy of Criticism: Four Essays*. Princeton: Princeton University Press, 1957, 1971.

Gelpi, Albert. *A Coherent Splendor: The American Poetic Renaissance, 1910–1950*. Cambridge: Cambridge University Press, 1988.

Gernet, Jacques. *China and the Christian Impact*. Translated by Janet Lloyd. Cambridge: Cambridge University Press, 1985.

Goodman, Nelson. *The Languages of Art*. Indianapolis: Hackett Publishing Co., 1976.

———. *Ways of Worldmaking*. Indianapolis: Hackett Publishing Co., 1978.

Graham, A. C. " 'Being' in Linguistics and Philosophy: A Preliminary Inquiry." In *Urdu, Turkish, Bengali, Amhavic, Indonesian, Telugu, Estonian*, part 5 of *The Verb 'Be' and Its Synonyms: Philosophical and Grammatical Studies*, edited by John W. M. Verhaar, pp. 225–231. Dordrecht, Holland: D. Reidel, 1972. Reprinted in A. C. Graham, *Unreason within Reason: Essays on the Outskirts of Rationality*. LaSalle, IL: Open Court, 1992, pp. 85–96.

———. " 'Being' in Classical Chinese." In *Classical Chinese, Athapaskan, Mundari*, part 1 of *The Verb 'Be' and Its Synonyms: Philosophical and Grammatical Studies*, edited by John W. M. Verhaar, pp. 1–39. Dordrecht, Holland: D. Reidel, 1967.

———. " 'Being' in Western Philosophy Compared With 'Shih/Fei' and 'Yu/Wu' in Chinese Philosophy." In *Studies in Chinese Philosophy and Philosophical Literature*. Singapore: Institute of East Asian Philosophies, 1986, pp. 322–359.

———. *Disputers of the Tao: Philosophical Argument in Ancient China*. LaSalle, IL: Open Court, 1989.

Hartman, Geoffrey. *Wordsworth's Poetry, 1787 - 1814*. New Haven and London: Yale University Press, 1964.

Hollander, John. *Vision and Resonance: Two Senses of Poetic Form*. New York: Oxford University Press, 1975.

Jakobson, Roman. "Two Aspects of Language and Two Types of Aphasic Disturbances." In *On Language*. Edited by Linda R. Waugh and Monique Monville-Burston. Cambridge, MA: Harvard University Press, 1990, pp. 116–133.

Kahn, Charles H. *The Verb 'Be' in Ancient Greek*, part 6 of *The Verb 'Be' and Its Synonyms: Philosophical and Grammatical Studies*, edited by John W. M. Verhaar. Dordrecht, Holland: D. Reidel, 1973.

Keilar, Allan. "Bernstein's 'The Unanswered Question' and the Problem of Musical Competence." *Musical Quarterly* 64.2 (April 1978): 195–222.

Kramer, Jonathan D. *The Time of Music: New Meanings, New Temporalities, New Listening Strategies*. New York and London: Schirmer Books, 1988.

Kristeva, Julia. *La Révolution du langage poétique. L'avant-garde à la fin du XIXe siècle: Lautréamont et Mallarmé*. Paris: Seuil, 1974.

———. "Revolution in Poetic Language." In *The Kristeva Reader*. Edited by Toril Moi. Oxford, UK and Cambridge, MA: Blackwell, 1986, pp. 89–136.

Lacan, Jacques. "Le Stade du miroir comme formateur de la fonction du 'Je.' " In *Ecrits I*. Paris: Seuil, 1970, pp. 89–97.

———. *Ecrits: A Selection*. Translated by Alan Sheridan. New York: W. W. Norton, 1977.

Lecoutre, Jean, William Manchester, and Fred Ritchin. *Magnum. 50 ans de photographie*. Paris: Nathan, 1989.

Locker, Ernst. "Etre et avoir. Leurs expressions dans les langues." *Anthropos* 49 (1954): 481–510.

McAdams, Stephen, and Irène Deliège, eds. *La Musique et les sciences cognitives*. Liège and Bruxelles: Pierre Mardaga, 1989.

Meyer, Leonard B. *Style and Music: Theory, History and Ideology*. Philadelphia: University of Pennsylvania Press, 1989.

Mitchell, W. J. T. "Spatial Form in Literature." *Critical Inquiry* 6 (Spring 1960): 539–567.

Moi, Toril. *Sexual/Textual Politics: Feminist Literary Theory*. London: Methuen, 1985.

Owen, Stephen. *Traditional Chinese Poetry and Poetics: Omen of the World*. Madison: University of Wisconsin Press, 1985.

Pater, Walter. "Style." In *Appreciations. Walter Pater: Three Major Texts (The Renaissance, Appreciations, and Imaginary Portraits)*, edited by William E. Buckler, pp. 393–413. New York: New York University Press, 1986.

———. "The School of Gorgione." In *The Renaissance: Studies in Art and History. Walter Pater: Three Major Texts (The Renaissance, Appreciations, and Imaginary Portraits)*, edited by William E. Buckler, pp. 153–168. New York: New York University Press, 1986.

Richards, I. A. *Coleridge on the Imagination*. London: Kegan Paul, Trench, Trubner and Co Ltd., 1934.

Ricœur, Paul. "Life in Quest of Narrative." In *On Paul Ricœur: Narrative and Interpretation*, edited by David Wood, pp. 20–33. London: Routledge, 1991.

———. "Metaphor and the Main Problem of Hermeneutics." *New Literary History* 6 (Autumn 1974): 95–110.

———. "The Metaphorical Process As Cognition, Imagination, and Feeling." In *On Metaphor*, edited by Sheldon Sacks, pp. 141–158. Chicago: University of Chicago Press, 1979.

Rorty, Richard. "Is There a Problem About Fictional Discourse?" In *Consequences of Pragmatism*. Minneapolis: University of Minnesota Press, 1982, pp. 110–138.

———. "Professionalized Philosophy and Transcendentalist Culture." In *Consequences of Pragmatism*. Minneapolis: University of Minnesota Press, 1982, pp. 60–71.

Shelley, Percy Bysshe. "A Defense of Poetry." In *Shelley's Poetry and Prose*. Edited by Donald H. Reiman and Sharon B. Powers. New York: W. W. Norton, 1977, pp. 480–508.

Scher, Steven Paul. "Literature and Music." In *Interrelations of Literature*, edited by Jean-Pierre Barricelli and Joseph Gibaldi, pp. 225–250. New York: Modern Language Association of America, 1982.

Shopen, Timothy, ed. *Language Typology and Syntactic Description*. Cambridge: Cambridge University Press, 1985.

Stravinsky, Igor. *Poetics of Music*. Cambridge, MA: Harvard University Press, 1970.

Vergil. *The Aeneid*. Translated by L. R. Lind. Bloomington and London: University of Indiana Press, 1963.

Wagner, Linda Welshimer. *Interviews with William Carlos Williams: "Speaking Straight Ahead."* New York: New Directions, 1966.

Whelan, Richard. *Robert Capa: A Biography*. New York: Knopf, 1985.

White, Hayden. *The Content of the Form: Narrative Discourse and the Representation of Reality*. Baltimore: Johns Hopkins University Press, 1987.

Winn, James Anderson. *Unsuspected Eloquence: A History of the Relations Between Poetry and Music*. New Haven: Yale University Press, 1981.

Wittgenstein, Ludwig. *Tractatus Logico-philosophicus*. Translated by D. F. Pears and B. F. McGuinness. London and Henley: Routledge & Kegan Paul, 1974.

Wordsworth, William. "Essay, Supplementary to the Preface." In *The Prose Works of William Wordsworth*, vol. 3. Edited by W. J. B. Owen and Jane Worthington Smyser. Oxford: Oxford University Press, 1977, pp. 62–84.

————. "Preface to 'Lyrical Ballads'" (1850). In *The Prose Works of William Wordsworth*, vol. 1. Edited by W. J. B. Owen and Jane Worthington Smyser. Oxford: Oxford University Press, 1974, pp. 115–159.

Yu, Pauline. *The Reading of Imagery in the Chinese Poetic Tradition*. Princeton: Princeton University Press, 1987.

Zervos, Christian. "Conversation avec Picasso." *Cahiers d'Art* 10 (1935): 173–178.

Zuckerkandl, Victor. *Sound and Symbol: Music and the External World*. Princeton: Princeton University Press, 1956.

INDEX